Praise for *Cryptography*

"Keith Martin has a knack for explaining one of today's toughest inter-disciplinary problems in an accessible and accurate way. There's no math required, just a willingness to engage your brain. You will finish this book both entertained and better informed."

—Kenny Paterson, professor of computer science, ETH Zürich

"In his typical low-key style, Keith Martin explains how digital security is necessarily based on cryptosystems, secret keys, and public keys. A must-read for anyone who wants to participate competently in discussions on the role of cryptography in our society."

—Vincent Rijmen, codesigner of the
Advanced Encryption Standard

"[Martin] shows a knack for communicating demanding ideas.... This timely book will leave digital neophytes significantly better informed about a vital area in computer science."

—*Publishers Weekly*

"Highly informative. . . . Tech-savvy readers will come away with a greater appreciation for the science involved in keeping secrets from prying eyes."

—*Kirkus Reviews*

ALSO BY KEITH MARTIN

Everyday Cryptography:
Fundamental Principles and Applications

CRYPTOGRAPHY

The Key to
Digital Security,
How It Works, and
Why It Matters

KEITH MARTIN

W. W. NORTON & COMPANY
Independent Publishers Since 1923

For information about permission to reproduce selections from this book, write to
Permissions, W. W. Norton & Company, Inc., 500 Fifth Avenue, New York, NY 10110

For information about special discounts for bulk purchases, please contact
W. W. Norton Special Sales at specialsales@wwnorton.com or 800-233-4830

Manufacturing by LSC Communications, Harrisonburg
Book design by Chris Welch
Production manager: Beth Steidle

Library of Congress Cataloging-in-Publication Data

Names: Martin, Keith, author.
Title: Cryptography : the key to digital security, how it works, and why it matters / Keith Martin.
Description: First edition. | New York, NY : W. W. Norton & Company, Inc., [2020] |
Includes bibliographical references and index.
Identifiers: LCCN 2019058806 | ISBN 9781324004295 (hardcover) |
ISBN 9781324004301 (epub)
Subjects: LCSH: Data encryption (Computer science) | Cryptography.
Classification: LCC QA76.9.A25 M3735 2020 | DDC 005.8/24—dc23
LC record available at https://lccn.loc.gov/2019058806

ISBN 978-0-393-86745-9 pbk.

W. W. Norton & Company, Inc., 500 Fifth Avenue, New York, N.Y. 10110
www.wwnorton.com

W. W. Norton & Company Ltd., 15 Carlisle Street, London W1D 3BS

1 2 3 4 5 6 7 8 9 0

To Fred: cryptographer, visionary, mentor

Contents

CRYPTOGRAPHY

Introduction

J ulius Caesar used it. Mary, Queen of Scots, also used it, but lost her head as a result. Napoleon misused it, costing himself an empire. During the Second World War, all sides relied on it, with Allied superiority in mastering it widely credited for shortening the duration of the conflict. Spies deployed it throughout the Cold War, and still do. Yet there is someone who uses it more often, for a far greater diversity of purposes. Someone who completely depends on it for much, if not most, of their daily activity. That person is you. And this vital tool is cryptography.

You use cryptography to secure a host of everyday tasks. You use it when you make a mobile phone call, withdraw cash from an ATM, connect to a Wi-Fi network, log in to a computing device, search for information on Google, and watch movies using a service such as Netflix. Cryptography helps to secure more than a billion Apple devices,[1] over 7 billion bank cards,[2] and 55 billion daily WhatsApp messages.[3] The Bitcoin digital-currency scheme and its associated blockchain are built entirely from cryptography.

Cryptography also protects over three-quarters of all global connections made to the World Wide Web.[4] Did you know that when your web browser connects to a secure website, you are using cryptographic tools that helped to drive a computing revolution that led to the development of the internet we know today? Did you know that each time you open your car door, your car key fob is doing something beyond the capabilities of an attacker with access to the world's most powerful supercomputer? Were you aware that messages sent from your phone are often protected by cryptography so strong that it worries some governments and intelligence agencies?

Cryptography is, essentially, an application of mathematics. However, few applications of mathematics have achieved the profile, social importance—even notoriety—of cryptography. Most of the time, mathematics does not provide a focus for blockbuster movies—but in the case of cryptography, it has inspired such films as *Enigma*, *Skyfall*, and *Sneakers*;[5] such television series as *CSI: Cyber* and *Spooks*;[6] and such bestselling novels as Dan Brown's *Digital Fortress*.[7] Nor does mathematics normally end wars or disturb world leaders.

What cryptography does is to provide a set of tools that can be used to protect information. Although it can be applied to information represented in physical space, such as words written on a page, it is our increasing reliance on digital information that has made cryptography so essential to our everyday lives. Cryptography enables us to keep sensitive information secret. It can detect when information has been accidentally, or deliberately, modified. It allows us to determine who we are communicating with. In fact, to establish the basic elements of digital security, cryptography is pretty much the only game in town.

Cryptography is like antibiotics. You can get through your life by taking antibiotics without any real understanding of them. Yet there are two important reasons for knowing what they do and how they work. First, the knowledge improves your understanding of human health, as well as helps you decide when to take antibiotics, for the good of both yourself and others. Second, our individual use of antibiotics raises important issues for the wider society, including concerns about overuse and the rise of superbugs.

Similarly, you can breeze through your life using cryptography without even being aware of it. However, I am convinced that a little bit of knowledge about cryptography can make a big difference to your life. First and foremost, I want to open your eyes to the critical role that cryptography plays in supporting your everyday life. By learning what cryptography does and how it works, I believe, you will acquire greater confidence in reasoning about your own personal digital security. Use of cryptography also raises wider social questions about how society should balance personal freedom with control of information, which I will also explore in this book.

Cyberspace

I will not make any significant attempt to define what *cyberspace* is[8] other than to observe that anything you currently regard as being in cyberspace, for our purposes, almost certainly is. Cyberspace is "electronic stuff."[9]

Cyberspace consists of computers communicating with other computers across networks. These computers include things clearly recognizable as computers, such as laptops. They also include gadgets such as mobile phones, gaming consoles, and voice assistants, which we mostly recognize as devices capable of accessing the internet yet do not always regard as computers.

Cyberspace also consists of millions of computers we directly interact with, such as sales terminals, automatic teller machines, and passport control gates, and many we don't, such as computers that support business, defense, and industrial control systems. Perhaps most importantly, and to an extent alarmingly, many everyday devices that traditionally we don't think of as having a digital element, let alone as being computers, are rapidly becoming devices in cyberspace. These include cars, homes, and domestic appliances. The networks connecting all these devices in cyberspace can be wired or wireless, short- or long-range, open to all or dedicated to specific purposes such as telecommunications. By far the most significant of these networks is the internet.

Of course, cyberspace and the physical world are not entirely different concepts. Aspects of the physical world increasingly interact with cyberspace. It is generally becoming hard to find people who do not use the internet,[10] businesses without an online presence, or technologies not interacting with cyberspace in some way. And most things that happen in cyberspace occur because human beings press buttons on physical devices that execute instructions on machines in physical places.

Your Security in Cyberspace

Just for a moment, reflect on how much you depend on cyberspace. Consider how you communicate with your friends, where you get your news, and how you research your next vacation. Think about how you manage your money and how you pay for things. Don't forget how you access music, movies, and personal photographs. Did you remember to include your car? It opens its doors at the click of a button, always knows exactly where it is, reports its problems to the manufacturer, and in the future it will undoubtedly drive itself. And this is just the tip of the iceberg. There's all the invisible stuff you rely on every day that just seems to happen. Planes fly, electricity powers, and traffic lights change. These days, almost everything relies on cyberspace.

Because we increasingly live our lives in cyberspace, so, too, do criminals. Cyberspace is a wonderful place to commit crime. Freed from the tyranny of distance, cyberspace enables criminals from anywhere in the world to raid your home. It's a place of smoke and mirrors, where a teenager in a bedroom can pretend to be your bank or build a website resembling that of a major department store. Hence the endless stories in the media about security incidents involving computers—and these are just the ones we hear about.

Exact figures are notoriously hard to establish, but cybersecurity firm Norton claims there were 978 million global victims of cybercrime in 2017 (altogether losing $172 billion),[11] the professional services firm PwC reported that 31 percent of organizations victimized by fraud were affected by cybercrime in 2016 and 2017,[12] and the research firm Cybersecurity Ventures reckons that cybercrime will cost the global economy $6 trillion by 2021.[13] Cyberspace is invisible, out of sight, and, too often, out of mind. Just ask the Iranian scientists at the Natanz uranium enrichment facility whose centrifuges mysteriously started failing in 2010,[14] or the executives at Sony Pictures who unwittingly became the stars of their own horror movie in 2014 when their internal emails, salaries, and unreleased movies were exposed to the world.[15]

We are physical beings who have evolved in a physical world in which we have a reasonable understanding of what security means (locked doors, passport controls, signed documents, etc.). However, we appear to lack the equivalent common sense to operate safely in cyberspace. The invisibility of cyberspace doesn't help, but I suspect our main lack of intuition comes from a failure to understand even the basics of what security in cyberspace might mean. As a result, we're all capable of doing daft things in cyberspace. We leave our front doors wide open, we hand over our bank account details to strangers, and we etch highly personal messages into tablets of digital stone that will remain legible forever. I will show you how cryptography attempts to address the heart of the problem of securing cyberspace and, as a result, will equip you with an ability to make much better judgments about your own cybersecurity.

Understanding the basics of cryptography will help you recognize the significance of some of the security technologies you rely on every day. Passwords are commonly used but have many flaws. Did you know, however, that your online banking is often protected by a "perfect" cryptographic password? Cryptography ultimately relies on secrets, known as keys. I hope to increase your awareness of how vital these keys are to your digital security, and to encourage you to look after them just as carefully as your physical keys—ideally more so, because for many of the things you do in cyberspace your key is the only thing that separates you from the 4.5 billion other users of the internet, so it is crucial to be aware of these keys and where they reside.

An appreciation of cryptography will also help you to respond appropriately to cybersecurity issues you encounter. What are the implications of connecting to an unprotected Wi-Fi network? Is it really so important to have different passwords for different accounts? If you are told a website does not have a valid certificate, should you click and proceed anyway? And what about all these news stories about cybersecurity that just keep coming? In 2017 it was widely reported that Wi-Fi networks running a particular cryptographic protocol were insecure[16] and that Infineon cryptographic hardware was crackable.[17] And 2018 began with a report that many Apple devices had a chip flaw.[18] Should we panic? Do we need to take personal action, or is it someone else's problem to solve? Should you be excited about blockchains? Or worried about quantum computers?

A rudimentary knowledge of cryptography will also aid you in making decisions about whether and how to engage with technologies, now and into the future. Is it safe to submit sensitive personal information to a given app? Could you lose all your money if you convert it to bitcoin? Which security issues should you consider when investing in a new mobile phone?

But it's not just about you; we're all in this together. When you leave your front door open and a thief grabs your diamonds, it's your loss, not mine. The same cannot be said about cybersecurity.

If you are inadvertently too trusting when opening an unsolicited link to an amusing video of a dancing sheep, then your computer could easily be inducted into a global network of machines conducting criminal activities. Your computer might end up attacking mine, so we all have a stake in your ability to defend yourself in cyberspace. Every reader who equips themselves with a basic knowledge of cryptography will, with luck, also make the rest of us a little bit safer.

A Social Dilemma

Cryptography is vital to our daily lives, something we can no longer live without. Yet there is a case for regarding cryptography as troublesome, even dangerous. Because it works so well, cryptography presents society with a social dilemma.

In May 2017, the network administrators of forty UK hospitals found themselves in a state of crisis. The computer systems that support their day-to-day operations were out of action because of cryptography. Attackers had hijacked these systems using cryptography within the WannaCry software to make the systems' data inaccessible, and they were now demanding a ransom to restore the systems to normal. The cryptography that makes us so secure in cyberspace was, in this case, the cause of a serious problem.[19]

Even more problematically, while cryptography protects you in cyberspace, it can also be deployed to protect the communications of organized crime, terrorist cells, and child pornographers. For this reason, some national security agencies around the world have expressed concern about its widespread use. Former FBI director James Comey was particularly outspoken about this issue, repeatedly expressing his worries about the way cryptography hampers intelligence gathering.[20] In 2013, former US National Security Agency (NSA) contractor Edward Snowden gave up his career and personal freedom to reveal a raft of techniques that the agency had been using in attempts to overcome everyday use of cryptography in order to support its surveillance activities.[21]

Some politicians partially blame cryptography for serious security incidents. Following the November 2015 terrorist attacks in Paris, UK prime minister David Cameron asked: "In our country, do we want to allow a means of communication between people that we cannot read?"[22] In June 2017, Australian attorney general George Brandis announced that Australia would lead international discussions on the involvement of industry in "thwarting the encryption of terrorist messaging."[23] Around the same time, German interior minister Thomas de Maizière announced that his government was preparing a law to enable state authorities to access private encrypted messages, arguing that the state "can't allow there to be areas that are practically outside the law."[24] And in May 2018, US attorney general Jeff Sessions claimed that it is "critical that we deal with the growing encryption or the 'going dark' problem."[25]

All these political interventions are essentially suggestions that cryptography should be made less effective. However, the UN high commissioner for human rights, Zeid Ra'ad Al Hussein, proclaimed that without cryptography, "lives might be endangered."[26] Can these different viewpoints be reconciled?

Today's political debates about the use of cryptography are, in fact, modern takes on a much older conversation about the tensions between freedom and control of information in civilized society. The invention of the printing press in the mid-fifteenth century heralded an era of political conflict over the control of book printing. Restricting who could print books, and for whom, allowed the governing authorities of church and state to manage wider society's access to information.[27] Today, cryptography protects the flow of digital information in a way that worries some governments.

There are no simple compromises between freedom and control here. Many politicians and journalists seem to struggle with this issue because they don't appear to understand what cryptography does or how it works.[28] By providing information about how cryptography benefits our lives, as well as the challenges it creates, I will help you to develop an informed opinion about its use. This knowledge will be useful both now and in the future, because we are only going to increase our dependence on cryptography in the years ahead. In all likelihood, the social tensions arising from its use will expand rather than be resolved.

My Approach

Even though cryptography is an application of mathematics, appreciating the fundamentals does not require readers to become armchair algebraists. The mathematics behind cryptography is not a primary concern of this book—just as it is possible to learn how to drive a car without understanding the mechanics of fuel injection.

In addition, although cryptography has an intriguing past, particularly its wartime use, this is not a history book. Past use of cryptography is excellently covered in other literature.[29] Instead, I concentrate on today's use of cryptography, reflecting on selected historical examples only when relevant.

Nor is this a book about puzzles.[30] Some aspects of cryptography are about creating "challenges" that must be "solved." Indeed, during the Second World War the UK government recruited trainee cryptographers by seeking people who were adept at solving crosswords. Unlike some authors, however, I will not present cryptography purely as a source of entertainment (cryptography, after all, is a very RDQHNTR ATRHMDRR*).

In Chapter 2 I explore what security means in cyberspace and how cryptography helps to provide it. In Chapter 3 I explain the

---

* If this ciphertext has defeated you, then try shifting the letters forward one position in the alphabet!

different cryptographic roles of keys and algorithms. I then devote a separate chapter to each of the main functions of cryptography— namely keeping secrets, exchanging keys, detecting changes to data, and establishing who is out there. With the intention of understanding how to get things right, in Chapter 7 I look at the different ways that cryptography can go wrong. In Chapter 8 I then examine societal challenges arising from the use of cryptography, as well as political responses. Finally, in Chapter 9 I consider what the future might hold for cryptography and how we use it.

This book is about why cryptography matters to the whole of society and how knowledge about cryptography can keep us secure. I want to show you that cryptography, quite literally, provides the keys to cyberspace.

1

Security in Cyberspace

What does it mean to be secure in cyberspace? To begin to understand the idea of cybersecurity, it's worth reflecting on the fundamental elements of security in the physical world. Doing so will reveal how several important aspects of physical security are lost in cyberspace. While cryptography alone cannot replace them, the essential role of cryptography is to provide tools from which security can be constructed in cyberspace.

A Typical Day

You get up in the morning and find a bill in the mailbox from your energy supplier, which you promptly arrange to pay. You're not feeling well (especially after paying the bill), so after breakfast you go out, lock the door behind you, and catch a scheduled bus into town. At the local pharmacy you discuss your symptoms with a pharmacist, who recommends some medication. You pay cash and return home. By the afternoon, you're on the road to recovery.

That's just a snapshot of one part of a normal day in the *physical world* we live in. This world consists of tangible objects and physical interactions, many of which require us to be in specific geographical locations. Let's begin by considering how *secure* this world is. In other words, how well protected is this world from threats that could cause us harm?

For those of us fortunate enough to live in relative peace and prosperity, most days in the physical world are quite uneventful in terms of "bad things" happening directly to us. We hear about alarming incidents every day in the media, but most of these are exceptional, which is what makes them "news." Since we seem to do a good job of staying secure in the physical world, it's worth identifying some of the features of this physical world that provide protection.

Let's consider what bad things *could* have happened during your typical day. Although engaging in this exercise may require worst-case thinking bordering on the paranoid, it is precisely through contemplation of what might go wrong that security processes are established. Hopefully, after doing so, you'll still be willing to get out of bed in the morning!

An Atypical Day

You get up in the morning and find a bill in the mailbox, which appears to be from your energy supplier but is, in fact, from a fraudster who is attempting to trick you into sending money, which you promptly do. You're not feeling well (you'd be feeling much worse if you knew what you had just done), so after breakfast you go out, locking the door behind you. As soon as you're gone, a burglar picks the lock and breaks into your home. Meanwhile, you catch a bus into town. Unfortunately, you discover, the bus has been hijacked. By some miracle, you manage to escape from the bus in town. At the local pharmacy you discuss your symptoms with someone in a white coat who resembles a pharmacist but is, in reality, a psychopath on the run, who prescribes some poison. The fake pharmacist later relates your medical problem to the town gossip, and within hours the whole town knows you are unwell. You pay cash but, to add insult to injury, your change contains a fake coin and a forged banknote. You return to your freshly burgled home with your toxic medicine. The end.

This is an utterly ridiculous story. Interestingly, however, each paranoid segment of this fable must have at least been contemplated by somebody, sometime, since we have security processes in the physical world that are designed to prevent most of these unfortunate events from happening. The first day is "typical" and the second "atypical" because of three different aspects of security— security mechanisms, security context, and threat likelihood— each of which is worth some consideration.

The Physical Things That Make Us Secure

We use various tools and techniques to establish security, which I will call *security mechanisms*. Let's review some of the security mechanisms that might have been used during your typical day.

Mailboxes come in a variety of forms. Some mailboxes simply provide protection against the weather, while others feature a physical lock that requires a key to open. Some homes have letter boxes (mail slots) on the front door, rather than mailboxes. Letters delivered through such a slot are protected from external threats by the physical lock on the front door itself, although not against internal threats (such as the family dog).

Your mailbox contained a letter, which arrived in an envelope. An envelope offers a degree of physical protection to the contents from threats such as rough handling during the delivery journey. An envelope also protects the contents from being seen by anyone other than the intended recipient. This protection is relatively weak, since envelopes are flimsy and easily opened. However, perhaps the most significant security provided by an envelope is that anyone opening it during its journey normally needs to break a seal. Unless this is done with great care, the recipient will notice the intrusion.

The letter you received allegedly came from a large organization. The familiar logo of this organization was emblazoned on the envelope and its contents. The letter had a familiar look and feel in terms of general layout, fonts, and use of language. All of these features are, to varying degrees, security mechanisms.

Your front door had a physical lock. Although some modern homes have electronic access control systems, most door locks are still mechanical. While some locks require the insertion of a key, others activate as soon as the door is shut. You will later see, from a cryptographic perspective, that the difference between these two types of locks caused a revolution.

The bus you rode was a familiar-looking vehicle, sporting expected company branding and route number. The driver displayed a badge, including a name and photograph alongside an official logo. The driver possibly wore a company uniform and possessed the key to the bus.

The pharmacist also displayed an official name badge. Or, more likely, you recognized the pharmacist because you had been to the pharmacy before. Both the pharmacist's face and voice are security mechanisms. The conversation with the pharmacist took place aside from other customers, with quiet voices used to prevent others overhearing. The medicine the pharmacist prescribed was in a sealed container. The packaging was branded, had an informative label, and perhaps bore a stamp from the pharmacy itself.

Finally, there was the cash. Coins have lettering and other embossing to make them hard to counterfeit. Banknotes feature many different security mechanisms designed to make them difficult to forge, including watermarks and holograms. More fundamentally, the look and feel of cash are perhaps the security mechanism most readily verified.[1]

The physical world is full of security mechanisms, and each one is designed to counter a variety of specific threats that could imperil the objects they are designed to protect.

The Importance of Security Context

Perhaps more subtle is the importance of *security context* in the physical world. By this, I mean the setting in which events take place, and against which we interpret and make sense of their security. Context is something we tend not to focus our minds on, yet it plays an important background role in our assessment of security in the physical world. Once you start to focus on context, you will notice how informative it is.

Returning to your typical day, the letter in the mailbox was from an organization you expected to receive payment notices from. Indeed, it was from an organization that regularly sends you such requests, at relatively predictable times. Had the energy bill arrived one week after you paid the previous bill, you might have been suspicious. The size of the requested payment is also informative, since it can be interpreted within the wider context of your typical energy use. The precise value might well have caused surprise, but it most likely fell within an expected range.

The bus runs on an advertised timetable, so when an apparently normal bus arrived at approximately the correct time, there was no reason to doubt it was a genuine bus. Had the bus been extremely late, had it been driven erratically, or had the driver looked lost, you would probably have had some concerns.

Behind the pharmacy counter was someone who not only looked like a pharmacist but, more importantly, behaved like a pharmacist. They reacted to your conversation professionally and discussed your medication in a knowledgeable way. You would surely have become concerned if the pharmacist had smirked during your conversation or seemed confused while preparing your medication.[2]

Even cash involves some context. If you had tried to pay for your medication with a note of much higher denomination than the cost of the medicine, the pharmacist might have hesitated and checked the validity of the cash you were offering.

In the physical world, security context is really important. We are often advised: "If you see anything suspicious, please report it to a member of the staff." What this really means is: "If you see anything out of context, please raise the alarm."

What Are the Odds?

We also assess security by forming an opinion of how likely it is that a perceived danger could materialize. The likelihood of an unpleasant event occurring is not normally possible to calculate in any precise way, but during our lives we develop a gut feeling as to how realistic many threats are.[3]

Our instincts suggest the atypical day is absurd. Why?

Do fraudsters exist who attempt to cheat you for financial gain? Yes, they absolutely do, and there are plenty of them around.[4] They have many potential targets, however, so the chance of your being singled out is relatively low. Would they deploy a fake energy bill as a means of conducting fraud? To do so, they would need to produce a letter that looked like a genuine payment notice. They would also have to overcome the context concerns raised previously, about the scheduling and amount of the deceptive bill. Such a fraud would take effort and would need to be highly personalized. These requirements don't make the fraud impossible, but there are many easier scams with greater chances of criminal success.

Similarly, while burglary is always a risk, on most days a specific house, even one in a less-than-desirable neighborhood, is not broken into. Buses are rarely hijacked, and pharmacists are not normally serial killers. These bad things could happen, but we know, largely through our inherent understanding of the physical world, that they probably won't.

The Security of the Physical World

Your atypical day in the physical world is a nightmarish fantasy consisting of a series of improbable events, which a combination of security mechanisms and security context render even more unlikely. Three features of the physical world contribute to this unlikelihood.

The first is, literally, the *materiality* of the physical world. Most of the previously described security mechanisms rely on the use of core physical senses. The letter in the post *looked* correct, you *recognized* the pharmacist, the cash *felt* right, and so on. We use these senses in all aspects of our lives and are accustomed to deploying them to help us make security decisions. Indeed, we are born with an understanding of some types of physical threat. For example, research suggests that babies have an innate fear of spiders and snakes.[5] We learn about other threats in the physical world as we grow. Through a combination of nature and nurture, we equip ourselves with an ability to apply our senses to form a notion of security in the physical world.

The second important feature of the physical world is *familiarity*, since we have considerable experience of living in the physical world. This doesn't mean we comprehend all aspects of it, but we're used to making sense of the physical situations we find ourselves in. We may not know exactly how a bus works from a mechanical perspective, but we do understand what a bus looks like, how to catch one, and what it feels like to be on a normal bus ride. Many of the security mechanisms, and some of the security context relied upon during your typical day, relate to familiarity. The letter in the mail looked right because you had seen many such letters before. The bus seemed to be a normal bus, and it showed up at a familiar bus stop at an expected time. In the physical world we tend to feel vulnerable in new situations precisely because they are unfamiliar. We are cautious around strangers. If the payment demand had arrived in a handwritten envelope, with an international stamp, and had requested payment to a foreign bank account, then you would have been highly unlikely to pay it.

Finally, there is the *situational* aspect of the physical world. People and objects are physically located in both space and time in ways we are able to reason about when making security decisions. Had the bill been fraudulent, it would still have needed to arrive in your mailbox at the appropriate time in your payment cycle. Had the bus been hijacked, the hijacker would have needed to physically board the scheduled bus and take command of driving it. A psychopathic pharmacist would have had to turn up at the pharmacy on a day when the regular pharmacist was not working. None of these breaches of physical security are impossible, but the situational aspects make them challenging. The terrorists who hijacked and then crashed aircraft in the US on September 11, 2001, not only had to train as pilots, but then had to get themselves onto different aircraft that were flying to nearby locations at about the same time.[6] Their actions were horrific, but the situational security challenges they overcame in order to conduct this attack were extraordinary. So remarkable, in fact, that nobody had previously even imagined a threat of this nature could occur in the physical world.

We are material people, used to securing a material world. The problem is that cyberspace is somewhere else entirely.

A Cyber Day

It's time to consider a different type of day: a *cyber day*.

You get up in the morning and check your email. Amid a flurry of spam is a payment notice from your energy supplier, which you promptly arrange to pay. You're not feeling well but, thanks to the joys of cyberspace, there's no need to leave home in order to seek a remedy. Instead, you type your symptoms into a search engine, which directs you to an online pharmacy. You order some medication, pay online using your bank card, and await delivery of the goods.

Or what about this?

You get up in the morning and check your email. Amid a flurry of spam is a payment notice that appears to be from your energy supplier but is, in fact, from a fraudster who is attempting to trick you into sending money, which you promptly do. You're not feeling well, so you type your symptoms into a search engine, which directs you to a website advertising medication at a remarkably reasonable price. The search engine shares your symptoms with several partner organizations, one of which is your life insurance company, which decides to increase your premium as a result. You order some medication and pay online using your bank card. Unfortunately for you, the "pharmacy" website is hosted in the spare bedroom of a small house in Ruritania[7] and dispatches products of questionable safety. It also has several side "businesses," one of which consists of quickly making a series of online purchases using your bank card details. Another involves remotely installing some software onto your computer, giving the Ruritanians control of your machine and allowing them to trawl through your files for anything of interest, including passwords and financial data. You might not have left your home, but you've certainly just been burgled. It's been a bad cyber day.

Which of these two cyber days is "typical"? It is natural to hope that the second version is less likely. While this is probably true, my description of the second day is certainly not the flight of imagination of your preposterous atypical day in the physical world. The bad cyber day is plausible. Indeed, elements of it are common. How so?

Online fraud of the type first described, the fake bill, is much easier to conduct in cyberspace than in the physical world. For one thing, it's substantially cheaper and easier to send out millions of fake electronic demands for payment into cyberspace. While most will be ignored, it only takes one or two successful responses to make such a fraud worth conducting. The fake digital payment demand is also harder for a customer to detect, since much of our digital communication lacks the variety of form and style we obtain from physical equivalents.[8]

When we type information into a search engine, we have very little idea what happens to the search data. It vanishes into cyberspace and is, at least in theory, available for the company behind the search engine to process in any way it desires. Once the search results put us in contact with an online merchant, all we potentially have to gauge the honesty and quality of this merchant is the text and images on the website, as well as the language used and prices offered. If we are unfamiliar with the merchant, then, to an extent, conducting business with them involves a leap of faith. Most people fail to appreciate how easy it is to set up an online business in cyberspace and present a seemingly genuine merchant website from a bedroom in Ruritania.

Using the details of someone else's bank card to make purchases online is likely to be a successful crime until a fraud engine at the bank questions the resulting purchase patterns, by which point it may be too late. For this reason, the stealing and selling of bank card details is one of the major criminal industries in cyberspace. Remotely installing harmful software on a computer is also straightforward, typically just requiring an unsuspecting user to click on a link or download an attached file. Such malicious software can, for example, easily scan a computer for potential passwords and bank details. Worse, it can remain on the computer and act as a digital "spy" in perpetuity.[9]

A bad cyber day is much, much more likely to occur than your atypical day in the physical world.

The Insecurity of Cyberspace

Cyberspace, whatever and wherever it might be, is undoubtedly a very different kind of place from the physical world. This distinction has significant consequences for security in cyberspace. To see why providing security in cyberspace is particularly challenging, it is worth reflecting on what is different with regard to the three features of the physical world discussed previously.

First, cyberspace is inherently not *physical*. Of course, elements of cyberspace such as data centers, computers, routers, and wires are part of the physical world. However, the information relating to, and being produced and processed by, these components is not physical. Information in cyberspace is represented by digital data. You can't pick digital data up, feel it, or stuff it into an envelope. Indeed, it's the nonmateriality of digital data that allows us to do such amazing things with it. We can copy it, transform it, and transfer it at lightning speed around the planet. Being able to represent and utilize information digitally has been truly revolutionary.

Because digital data is not physical, very few of the security mechanisms we use in the physical world are appropriate for protecting digital information. It's true that we can securely store a USB memory stick by locking it in a drawer, but the moment we want to use the information on this device, we have to connect it in some way to cyberspace, and then the physical protection is no longer effective. We need very different kinds of security mechanisms in order to secure cyberspace.

Nor is cyberspace particularly *familiar*. That's not to say we aren't used to going about our daily lives in cyberspace. We have, after all, come to depend on looking for information on the web, many of us buy and sell goods over the internet, and we use social media platforms to keep in touch. We are thus increasingly comfortable with using cyberspace. But are we familiar with cyberspace itself? How many of us have even the vaguest understanding of how all this is possible? Few people know how a computer works, let alone how computers are programmed, how they connect with one another, and how they exchange information. And few people understand the workings of systems that process information in cyberspace. Where does data we submit to cyberspace really go? Who can see it? What do they do with it? To most of us, cyberspace is magic. We press the button and—abracadabra—stuff happens.[10]

This lack of familiarity with cyberspace brings dangers, since, without even a basic intuition of what cyberspace is and how it works, we conduct ourselves in cyberspace somewhat blindly, relying on systems to do the "right things" on our behalf. The security implications are significant, for this lack of familiarity with cyberspace renders us naive and exposed. We don't identify when things are going wrong, or indeed what could go wrong, because we don't understand how things work when they're going right. *If you see anything suspicious, please report it to a member of the staff.* That's not going to happen if you have no inkling of what suspicious might even look like.

Most fundamentally, we lack the basic commonsense principles that govern our security decision-making in the physical world. In cyberspace people do amazingly risky things they would never contemplate in the physical world, such as sending postcards to burglars when they go on holiday (sending out-of-office messages and posting live holiday photos online),[11] emblazoning their bank account details on a T-shirt (buying goods from an untrustworthy website), and installing surveillance cameras all over their home and publicly broadcasting the feed on live television (overzealously using social media). On the savannahs of Africa our ancestors instinctively knew, when approached by a lion, that they should sprint for the nearest tree, and so do we. We don't need a second thought to lock the front door of a house in the middle of a big city when we're not at home. In cyberspace, however, we have very little established "cyber common sense" to call upon. We don't see open electronic doors, let alone know how to lock them shut. We fail to spot digital lions, even when they are pacing back and forth across our screens.

Finally, cyberspace is liberated from the constraints of physical *situation*. This is arguably the greatest advantage of cyberspace. We can sit in our own home and buy from stores, chat with friends, view photographs, do business, and plan outings anywhere in the world. It's incredible that we can do this, and even more amazing that we've come to expect it.

However, we're not the only people who can do things from far away. So, too, can those who wish to act against our interests. A fraudster intent on making illegal money can seek targets anywhere in the world. As can a government or corporation intent on extracting information about our daily lives. In the physical world, most threats come from the things around us. In cyberspace, threats come from anywhere.

The Nub of the Problem

The three aspects of security identified at the start of this discussion are worth returning to in order to reflect on the potential for insecurity in cyberspace. Let's consider these in reverse order.

First, for many potential types of danger, the threat likelihood is much higher in cyberspace than in the physical world. Ordinary folk going about their daily business in the physical world tend not to be the target of fraud by Ruritanian criminals. They are much more likely to be such a target in cyberspace.[12] Only a totalitarian state would go to the lengths of monitoring the daily lives of all its citizens using purely physical techniques, such as deploying a pervasive network of informants.[13] It's becoming increasingly easy to do this in cyberspace, without people even realizing it's happening.[14]

Second, our ability to utilize context in making decisions about security is weaker in cyberspace. Should we trust this website? It's often hard to answer such a question. This is a difficulty we rarely encounter in the physical world, where the look and atmosphere of a shop's premises provide a rich source of contextual intuition. If someone knocks at your door and asks personal questions about your bank account, you are unlikely to cooperate. But for many people, a fraudulent email alleging to be from their bank and asking such questions may not raise the same level of concern. Freed from the security provided by physical context, we are less equipped to reason about security threats.

Finally, the basic security mechanisms around which we build security in the physical world are not appropriate for cyberspace. We can't whisper an email, place a wax seal on a digital document, or easily recognize the shopkeeper behind the counter of an online store.

Cyberspace has shrunk the world, bringing many potential dangers much closer to home. Cyberspace is a place most of us don't really understand. Worse still, our traditional security tools cannot be used there. It seems we have a problem.

Cryptography to the Rescue

I've painted a dark picture about the potential for security in cyberspace. It's true that the dangers are real and the challenges to providing security are significant. But most of us use the internet daily without too much nastiness coming our way. Is this merely good fortune?

It would be wrong to suggest there is no notion of security in cyberspace. Many of the perils of cyberspace are understood by experts, and much of our technology has been built with a degree of security in mind. Things may not be perfect, but "perfect" security does not exist, neither in cyberspace nor in the physical world.

Most fundamentally, any notion of security in cyberspace needs to be built around core security mechanisms suitable for protecting digital information. If we can construct effective digital security mechanisms to replace the likes of locks, seals, and face recognition, we can then embed those tools into wider systems and processes for protecting our activities in cyberspace. Ideally, we can use these tools to emulate the level of security we experience in the physical world. If we're lucky, we might occasionally even get more security in cyberspace.

This, in a nutshell, is the crucial role that cryptography plays. Cryptography provides a suite—a tool kit, if you like—of security mechanisms that can be deployed in cyberspace. These cryptographic tools are each, on their own, quite simple security mechanisms that can be used to perform essential tasks such as hiding digital information from unauthorized eyes, detecting changes made to an electronic document, or identifying a computer. However, these mechanisms, when combined in clever ways, can be used to build extremely complex security systems, such as those required to support secure financial transactions, protect electronic power distribution networks, or conduct secure online elections.

Cryptography on its own does not, cannot, make cyberspace secure. Establishing a notion of security involves many different aspects, not simply the provision of security mechanisms. However, although home security is not just about locks on doors, it's hard to imagine how to secure a home without the use of locks. Likewise, cryptography alone does not secure banking networks, but the global financial system would certainly collapse without cryptography.[15]

2

Keys and Algorithms

C ryptography provides the mechanisms we need to operate securely in cyberspace. Before we explore these, it's necessary to understand the basic anatomy of a cryptographic security mechanism. Two critical components—*keys* and *algorithms*—form the entire basis for cryptography.

The Critical Role of a Key

Let's revisit, once again, your typical day in the physical world and reconsider the purpose of some of the featured security mechanisms.

The purpose of the envelope containing the bill was to make sure *only* you and the energy company knew the details of the bill. The front-door lock and key made sure *only* you could enter your house. The pharmacist behaved in a way *only* a genuine pharmacist should be able to do. The private conversation ensured that *only* you and the pharmacist could hear the details. The cash had physical features *only* found on genuine currency.

Only, only . . . the essence of any security mechanism is to allow something to happen *only* in certain circumstances. A security mechanism can be used to keep out the rabble or distinguish a particular item from a crowd. A security mechanism enables some *special* capability. The front-door lock and key of your house provide you with the special capability to enter the house. A whispered conversation grants those in earshot the special capability of being able to hear the details. A banknote's security features provide it with the special capability to serve as legal tender.

In the physical world, special security capabilities are facilitated in various ways. The most obvious means is *something you have*, such as a door key, a badge, a ticket, or a letter of introduction.[1] It can be *somewhere you are*, such as being close enough to hear a private conversation, or being inside a concert hall for an event you purchased a ticket to. It can be *something you are*, such as a fingerprint or an iris scan. It can also be *something you know*, such as a friend's voice or the fact that you have to say "Open sesame" to enter a cave of treasure.[2] A special capability can also be facilitated through a mixture of different approaches. Your pharmacist potentially had something special (a badge), was standing somewhere special (behind the counter of the pharmacy), was something special (maybe someone you recognized), and knew special things (how to talk pharmacology to you).

The method of providing a special security capability that translates most readily to cyberspace is the last one: something you know. In cryptography, this special information is referred to as a *key*. The terminology is no coincidence, since a cryptographic key plays a role similar to that of a front-door key. Only someone knowing a cryptographic key will be able to do some particular thing, just as only the holder of a front-door key can unlock the door and enter a particular house. In most cases, a key is a secret piece of information, knowledge of which is used to separate one person from another in cyberspace. Notice that I used the phrase "in most cases." Let's assume for now that keys are secrets, but this is not always true.

Here I have to confess that I've been a little lax in my use of language. In most situations in cyberspace it is *computers*, not people, who are communicating. It's not even always true that a person is actively operating these computers. It might thus be more accurate to regard the function of a cryptographic key as not ensuring that "knowledge" of the key distinguishes one "person" from another, but ensuring that only an *entity* (could be a human, could be a computer) who has *access* to the key will be able to perform certain tasks in cyberspace.

The most important thing to realize about keys is this: you don't have the special capability to enter your own home; this capability belongs to whoever has a copy of your front-door key. It's the same for cryptographic keys. Access to the appropriate cryptographic key is all that's required to charge mobile calls to your account, make bank card payments, download movies, open your car door, and so on.

Bits and Bytes

We use cryptography every day, and on most such occasions we use keys. Although we often use cryptography unconsciously and never see our keys, it's worth considering what cryptographic keys look like.

First let's consider how computers represent information. Just as our brains convert information into things such as language, computers convert information into numbers. All the information we store, send, and process in cyberspace is represented in computers as numbers. When we type text into a computer, it first translates this text into numbers before doing whatever it has been tasked to do. When we want information back, the computer converts these numbers back into text so that we can make sense of them. A similar process takes place when we upload images. These are made up of tiny pixels, each of which is translated by a computer into a number that specifies the precise pixel color.

The numbers that computers use are not the decimal numbers that we are most familiar with. Computers operate on *binary* numbers, which consist only of the digits 0 and 1. Binary is simply a different way of writing numbers. Every decimal number has a binary representation, and vice versa. For example, the decimal number 17 is written as 10001 ("one zero zero zero one," not "ten thousand and one") in binary, and the binary number 1101 is written as 13 in decimal. Each digit of a binary number is referred to as a *bit*. These bits form the atomic units of digital information. Four bits are referred to as a *nibble*, and two nibbles form a *byte*. (Don't ever think computer scientists lack a sense of humor!)

The information we want computers to process does not normally consist only of decimal numbers. Suppose you type the characters "K9!" into a computer. In order to do anything with this data, the computer first needs to represent "K9!" as a binary number. Keyboard symbols are converted into bits (in fact, bytes) by a system called ASCII (American Standard Code for Information Interchange), which defines the rules for switching between keyboard characters and bits. In our example, the ASCII code for the character "K" is the byte 01001011, character "9" is 00111001,[3] and character "!" is 00100001. A computer faced with the ASCII code 01001011 00111001 00100001 knows to reconvert the code, for our benefit, back into the character string "K9!".

Sometimes it's useful to talk about the size of data. Since data consists of binary numbers, the simplest measure of its size is the number of bits. The size could also be measured in bytes. For example, 1011001100001111 is 16 bits long, which is the same as saying it is 2 bytes long. When data is large, all sorts of grander terms are used, such as *kilobytes* (1,000 bytes), *megabytes* (1,000 kilobytes), *gigabytes* (1,000 megabytes), and *terabytes* (1,000 gigabytes).

Cryptographic keys are just special items of data, so a computer needs to represent a key as a binary number. Since the size of a cryptographic key is an important security measure, you will often encounter references to the *key length*[4] of a cryptographic algorithm. A common key length for much of the cryptography we use today is 128 bits.

Where's My Key?

If you use cryptographic keys all the time, then where are they? Let's consider a specific example. You use cryptography every time you make a call on your mobile phone. The security of this process is based on the ability of your mobile-network operator to distinguish you from the other 5 billion phone users on the planet.[5] The operator does so by giving you a secret cryptographic key, a secret number, that *only* you and your mobile operator "know." Use of this number tells the operator it's you trying to make the mobile phone call. This is only *almost* correct, as I will now explain.

What is the special secret number used when you make a mobile call? It's certainly not your mobile phone number; that's not a secret, is it? You almost certainly don't know the cryptographic key you use on your mobile phone. There are two good reasons why, neither of which is that you're not allowed to know it.

The first, and probably most important, reason is that cryptographic keys are *big* numbers. Asked to remember a number between 0 and 10, you will, in all likelihood, succeed. You are probably even capable of remembering numbers up to 10,000, even 1 million, since numbers of this length are often used as PINs, which is something I'll return to shortly. On the cryptographic scale of things, 1 million is *not* a big number. Cryptographic keys are not even *very* big numbers. Keys are typically numbers of a size almost beyond our comprehension.

As an example, try to imagine what 40,000 times the number of stars in our universe looks like.[6] Even if you can wrap your head around this number, you will still be operating at the wrong level of magnitude. While we once used cryptographic keys of this approximate size, such keys are no longer regarded as anywhere close to large enough to provide security for most modern applications of cryptography. Instead, we use keys that are 1 trillion times this number in size. If you're now suffering from numerical vertigo, then you understand the point. No average human being can readily remember a contemporary secret cryptographic key.

The second reason you don't know the key used by your mobile phone is that you, the person currently using the phone, are not necessarily the one who matters. What your mobile operator really cares about is not who is using your mobile phone, or even which mobile phone is being used to make the call. The operator really cares only about where to send the bill. What it needs, then, is something uniquely linked to a particular mobile phone account that is capable of "knowing" and using a spectacularly large secret number. You were given precisely such a thing when you first opened your account. It's a very small plastic card with a tiny embedded microchip called a *subscriber identity module* (*SIM*), which is inserted into your phone. The main purpose of this SIM is to store a secret cryptographic key. Since this key is what distinguishes your account from all others on the planet, if you let someone else borrow your phone, or stick your SIM into a different phone, you will still receive the bill.

Most cryptographic keys are gigantic numbers that are directly used by computers, not people. Hence, most keys are either to be found on computers themselves, or stored on devices that connect to computers. For example, the keys that protect transactions made using your bank card are stored on the chip embedded in your card. The keys to your Wi-Fi network are stored on your router. The keys used to protect data you exchange while shopping online are in your web browser software. The cryptographic key that enables the computer in your car to release the door lock when you approach the vehicle is stored in the fob of your car key ("keyless" entry is quite the misnomer, since this process, in fact, involves two keys—

one physical and one cryptographic). You, personally, don't know what number any of these keys represent, but you have access to the places where they reside.

When a Secret Is Not a Key

Cryptographic keys, then, are secrets, knowledge of which can be used to distinguish one entity from another in cyberspace. What about secrets such as passwords and PINs?[7] Are these crypto-graphic keys?

No, not quite, but sometimes they sort of are. Confused? Well, the distinction between these concepts is subtle.

Thinking of cryptographic keys as being a bit like passwords and PINs is the right idea, but it's not strictly accurate. It's certainly true that passwords and PINs are secrets used to support security in cyberspace. Whether they are actually cryptographic keys depends on how they are used.

A common use of passwords and PINs is to verify an identity. For example, a computer you are logging in to asks for your password, which you supply, and the computer then checks whether the offered password is the expected one. If it is, the computer smiles "Welcome." This is not particularly exciting from a cryptographic perspective, because the heart of this process does not involve cryptography.[8] All that's happening during this login process is that you're offering your password to the computer so that it can be checked.

However, the critical issue here is that, during a computer login, you submit your password to the computer. Your password is a secret that you have been trusted to guard, but during the login process you "give it away." In a sense, you have lost control of the secret password, since you are now required to trust that the device you submitted it to, and indeed any subsequent networks and devices to which your password is forwarded, will not misuse it.

You probably don't regard typing a password into your computer at home as a particularly reckless act, and of course it isn't. Sometimes, however, we log in to computers that are far away—for example, when you enter a password in order to access some resources on a web page. In this case, the password might pass unprotected over computer networks on its journey from your web browser to the remote computer hosting the website (a well-designed website will use cryptography to protect it, but some websites don't). Anyone with access to the network in between could then observe your password, and later use it to pretend to be you. Similarly, when we withdraw cash from an ATM, we "give away" our PIN to the cash machine. Once again, an important personal secret is submitted to another device.[9]

Cryptographic keys should never be exposed in such a way. Instead, cryptographic keys are *used* to demonstrate knowledge of the key without revealing the key itself. In this way, the key remains secret throughout the process, both before and after the key is used. This level of secrecy of a key is a much stronger requirement than we apply to passwords and PINs.

Sometimes, however, cryptographic keys are directly linked to passwords in order to make keys easier to use. Recall that cryptographic keys are enormous numbers that we cannot reasonably be expected to memorize. For this reason, we normally store keys on devices, but this is not always feasible. Suppose you decide to use cryptography to hide the contents of a particularly sensitive file on your computer. Let's assume this is not something you regularly do, so you haven't set up your computer to automatically use cryptography for file protection (you can do this, by the way). This is thus a "casual" use of cryptography, and you'll need to create a key specifically for this occasion. Having done so, you'll then need to have a means of remembering this key in the future.

One common technique for making an enormous cryptographic key something we can remember is to compute the key *from* a password. In other words, we first choose a password. This password is converted by the computer into a number (there are standard ways of doing this). This number is then put through a process that expands it into a much bigger number (there are also standard ways of doing this), which can then be used as a cryptographic key. Whenever we need this cryptographic key, we need only recall the password, from which the key can be recomputed. The password itself is not the key, but rather a "seed" from which the key is "grown."[10]

Passwords and PINs are secrets we are capable of remembering. This is their greatest strength, but also their most fundamental weakness. Many people select dictionary words as passwords. The twenty volumes of the *Oxford English Dictionary* contain fewer than 300,000 words.[11] As secrets, passwords and PINs offer relatively weak security because they do not have sufficiently many different possibilities. This limitation highlights one distinction between secrets such as passwords and PINs, and cryptographic keys: if you can remember a secret, it's unlikely to be sufficiently large to be a good cryptographic key.

Recipes for Cooking Up Security

Cryptographic keys are secrets that are never "given away" but are, instead, "used." So, how are they used?

It's worth revisiting physical-world security mechanisms. The most natural to consider is the front-door lock, since this also involves a physical key. Let's assume you have a traditional physical lock on your door, with no computer wizardry involved. (If you have a digital lock, then you will almost certainly be using cryptography to open your door.) You don't simply show your key to the door in order to open it. Rather, you insert your key into the physical lock, rotate it around, and with luck, you can push the door open. Precisely what goes on here depends on the type of lock you have.

The exact process is largely invisible to you but is very precise. You might, for example, rotate the key in a clockwise direction while the key pushes down a sequence of metal "tumblers" inside the lock, which turn a crank and, if correctly configured, ultimately free the bolt that physically secures the door. Importantly, this chain of events involves the key. If the correct key is included in this process, then the lock will open. If the wrong key is inserted into the lock, then it will fail to release the bolt, and the door will remain locked.

Mere possession of a physical key is not sufficient to open a lock. The key needs to be incorporated into a process, which ultimately results in the lock being released. This process consists of a series of separate, but precise, actions that collectively free the bolt. To unlock the door, these actions must *all* be executed. If the key is not inserted fully into the lock, or the key is turned in the wrong direction, or one of the metal tumblers inside the lock is not pressed down, then the process will fail. These actions must also be conducted *in the correct order*. The tumblers will not free the bolt unless the key has first been turned, which itself cannot happen unless the key has been inserted into the lock.

The important point to note here is the separate roles of the door key and the unlocking process in securing your front door. The unlocking process is somewhat generic. All locks of the same model are unlocked by the same process. The door key, on the other hand, is unique. All locks of a particular model should have different keys.

Since cryptographic keys are numbers, any process that incorporates a cryptographic key will necessarily involve a sequence of mathematical operations such as adding, multiplying, shuffling, or swapping. I will refer to such a computational process as an *algorithm*. An algorithm is essentially a recipe dictating a sequence of operations that must be performed in a specific order. Do this, do that, then this, then that, and so on and so forth. The number we end up with after this process is called the *output* of the algorithm.

The correct output depends on each step of the algorithm being successfully performed, and in the prescribed order.

With a recipe, you don't get your dinner unless you include all the ingredients. An algorithm works the same way: there is no output unless you first put something in. The precise *input* to an algorithm depends on the task the algorithm has been designed to perform. For most cryptographic algorithms, the input includes data requiring protection and a cryptographic key.

Here's the core idea. The cryptographic algorithm is shared by all users of a system (it might, for example, be implemented on every mobile phone connected to a telecommunications network). By contrast, every user has a unique cryptographic key. A user inputs the data and their key into the cryptographic algorithm, which is then used to compute an output that depends on both the data and the key (changing either the data or the key results in a different output). This output is a value that can be exposed to the outside world (for example, it could be transmitted over the air as part of a mobile phone call). Without revealing the key itself, this output provides evidence that whoever computed it must have been able to input the user's key into the algorithm. This is, essentially, how most cryptography works. In the coming chapters, I'll show you how this process can be used to provide a range of different security properties.

Numerical Blenders

Algorithms are recipes. Keys are special, usually secret, ingredients. Since the output of a cryptographic algorithm is released into the wilds of cyberspace, we need to make sure nobody can work out the key by observing the output. In other words, we're happy for someone to inspect the results of our cooking, but we don't want them to be able to identify all the ingredients.

If we're making stir-fry, this is a problem, because the ingredients, although mixed, are barely transformed. We want a crypto-graphic algorithm to obliterate the ingredients. Perhaps a smoothie provides a better analogy, since a smoothie blends ingredients to such a fine pulp that little evidence remains of their original form. The color of a smoothie, however, is still informative. We want the ability to blend inputs so effectively that the output reveals no clues as to what those inputs were. A good cryptographic algorithm should produce textureless, colorless smoothies.

The numerical equivalent of being "textureless and colorless" is *randomness*. Randomness is a surprisingly difficult concept to for-mally define, so I'll avoid a detailed explanation.[12] That said, your gut instincts about what randomness might mean are almost cer-tainly broadly correct. Randomness is about unpredictability. Ran-domly generated numbers have no obvious patterns. Importantly, randomness relates to the unpredictability of numbers *over many occurrences*. For example, if you toss a coin five times and get heads every time, you might be disinclined to accept the outcome as ran-dom. Instead, you might think the coin is biased. But if you get heads, tails, heads, heads, tails, then you readily accept the out-come as random.

In fact, however (assuming the coin is not biased), these two outcomes are equally likely; each has one chance in thirty-two of occurring. What would be very odd would be to get five heads in a row *every* time you tossed the coin five times. Or, indeed, to get heads, tails, heads, heads, tails every time. In fact, if you keep toss-ing the coin for a long time and *any* sequence of heads and tails occurs significantly more often than one in thirty-two times that the experiment is conducted, it is reasonable to conclude that the process is not random. If the coin is unbiased, then each time you commence a new set of five coin tosses, you should have no expecta-tion that any one outcome is more likely than another.

Randomness is a concept intimately linked to cryptography in two important ways. First, secret cryptographic keys should be randomly generated. If keys are not generated randomly, then some keys will be more likely to occur than others, which will help anyone who is trying to work out what they are. This randomness, along with key length, is what makes cryptographic keys so difficult to both guess and memorize. On the other hand, passwords are rarely random, since in most cases passwords forming memorable words, such as *BatMan1988* (or even *B@tM@n1988*), are more likely to be selected than nonsensical passwords such as *8zuHmcA4&$*. This lack of randomness, in addition to their short length, makes passwords weaker than cryptographic keys as a basis for providing security.

Second, and of equal importance, a good cryptographic algorithm should behave like a random number generator.[13] If you encrypt some data, then the result should appear "nonsensical" and lack any meaningful patterns. This apparent randomness can be sent over the internet, with anyone who observes it seeing merely bland numerical fog.

The blending process required to protect our activities in cyberspace is even more demanding. Suppose a chef has a recipe for colorless, textureless smoothies (it's just an analogy, so please don't protest). Taste the smoothie; it's not bad, and it's so well blended that there's no hint of the ingredients. Now suppose the chef tells you the ingredients. Next, the chef secretly mixes a new smoothie, this time adjusting the ingredients a minuscule amount (extra carrot in exchange for less apple). Taste this new one. It's also not bad; in fact, it tastes almost the same as the last one, doesn't it? The chef now challenges you to guess the ingredients of the new smoothie.

Naturally, you would be wise to guess that the ingredients are almost the same as those of the original smoothie. You might not be completely correct, but you're bound to be close. Knowledge of the ingredients of the first smoothie is very useful in determining the ingredients of the second. This sort of relationship, however, is one we don't want in cryptography, so the analogy is no longer effective.

For example, suppose a cryptographic algorithm is used to scramble the balances of two bank accounts with similar balances. We don't want one account holder to be able to deduce the balance of the other's account from an apparent similarity between the two scrambled balances. A good cryptographic algorithm should thus be the equivalent of a recipe so sensitive to ingredients that the minutest of changes (one grate of carrot in exchange for one shave of apple) should result in a smoothie tasting completely different. In other words, a small change to the input of a cryptographic algorithm should result in unpredictable changes to the output. Hence, two almost identical keys, or bank balances, when fed into the same cryptographic algorithm should result in two unrelated outputs. Anyone observing these two outputs will thus have no clue that the two keys, or bank balances, are almost the same.

This is quite enough blending for now. All you really need to know is that good cryptographic algorithms disguise the relationship between inputs and outputs, unless you know the key.[14]

Master Chefs and Secret Recipes

It's relatively easy to toss ingredients into a pan and produce a palatable dinner. Coming up with a recipe that will astound food critics is another matter altogether. In haute cuisine, creating quality recipes is a task for master chefs.

In cryptography, things are no different. It's easy to design a cryptographic algorithm that superficially appears to work but is, in fact, insecure. But it is extremely hard to design a good cryptographic algorithm that withstands the scrutiny of time. Frustratingly, some builders of new technology prefer to adopt homemade cryptographic algorithms. The security weaknesses of do-it-yourself algorithms tend to be discovered within months, rather than years, of deployment, which can be disastrous for the products using them.[15] It takes considerable experience and skill to design cryptographic algorithms that are good enough for widespread modern use.

Having carefully designed a good cryptographic algorithm, how much should a designer reveal about the details? After all, a master chef might well keep their best recipes secret. Should a cryptographic algorithm designer do the same?

We can make at least one case for keeping cryptographic algorithms secret. Suppose a hacker has broken into a computer system and discovered a database whose contents are protected by cryptography. The hacker now needs to work out what the secret key is. If a good cryptographic algorithm has been used, then it should be impossible to work out what this key is just from observing the scrambled database. However, a hacker who knows which cryptographic algorithm has been used has at least a starting point. They could, for example, guess the key and try to unscramble the database using the algorithm. There is some chance, however slim, that they get lucky and this works. But a hacker who does not know the algorithm won't even know where to *begin* the task of unscrambling the database. Use of secret algorithms thus appears to offer a security advantage over use of algorithms whose details are known.

Despite this apparent advantage of secret algorithms, most of the cryptography you use every day to secure your digital activities is based on openly published cryptographic algorithms. You can buy books, or visit websites, that explain exactly how these algorithms work. There are two reasons why openly published algorithms are preferred over secret algorithms.

The first reason is that openly published algorithms can be scrutinized in order to develop public confidence in their strength. Suppose you want to buy a very secure physical lock for an outhouse that you have erected in your garden to store some gold bullion (one can dream). You visit the top locksmith in town to seek some advice. He shows you a range of standard products, based on conventional, quality locks that he has been selling all his working life. The locksmith can show you cutaway models and explain in detail how every bolt and pin of these products operate. However, the most expensive lock in the shop is the gleaming *WunderLock*, a recent addition to his range. You ask how the WunderLock works, and the locksmith confesses he has absolutely no idea, since the details of the mechanism are confidential. He has been told by the manufacturer that the lock is strong and merits the high price tag, but he himself cannot vouch for its quality. Should you buy it?

It might seem tempting. If it is, indeed, an excellent lock, then you will have a security advantage. Every thief in the neighborhood will be dumbfounded at the shiny mystery object on the outhouse door and, with luck, will be foiled in their attempts to rob you. So, purchasing the pricey lock might pay off, but it's a gamble. You're forced to trust the manufacturer that the lock is as secure as claimed. You cannot call on the experience of your local locksmith, or indeed any locksmith. The majority of experts who live and breathe the design and security of locks would be unable to give you any advice on how good a lock the WunderLock really is.

Importantly, this issue is not just about recommendation prior to purchase. Your newly installed WunderLock might do the job nicely for a year or two, until the day you wake up to an empty outhouse. You later read a news story about the antics of clever thieves who have discovered that persistent tapping of the WunderLock with a pin hammer is enough to trigger the bolt. This is a weakness that surely would have been discovered earlier if all the locksmiths in the world had been privy to the details of the WunderLock design. Somebody, somewhere, somehow would have found this out.

Once upon a time, not long ago (perhaps half a century), the few cryptographic algorithms in existence were used mainly in military and intelligence applications. At the time, very few people in the world had any knowledge about the design of cryptographic algorithms. The algorithms used were designed in secret. It is even conceivable that every expert in a particular country could have been party to the design of a secret algorithm. Further, these designers were fully trusted by the select few who relied on these secret algorithms.

These circumstances do not, however, resemble the environment within which we use cryptography today. Two things are significantly different. First, there is an active global community of researchers and designers with expertise in the design of cryptographic algorithms. It is simply not possible to involve this entire community in the design of a *secret* algorithm. Any algorithm whose details are secret is immediately of interest, and an object of potential suspicion, to this community. If the algorithm is not being exposed to the "many eyes" test of open, public evaluation, might there be something wrong with it? Second, we *all* rely on the use of strong cryptographic algorithms. We thus *all* need to trust in their design.[16] Using the cryptographic equivalent of the WunderLock as the basis of security is extremely risky. Why use the cryptographic WunderLock when widely respected and openly evaluated cryptographic algorithms are available?[17]

A second reason we tend not to use secret cryptographic algorithms to support everyday technologies is more fundamental. These days, it's almost impossible to keep secret algorithms secret. Fifty years ago, cryptographic algorithms were implemented in large metal boxes to which few people had access. Today, cryptographic algorithms are implemented in mass technologies. Algorithms implemented in software are almost impossible to keep secret. Hiding the details of algorithms implemented in hardware is also very hard when many people have access to the devices on which the algorithm is implemented. Experts with access to a device can analyze the technology and its behavior in order to establish the details of how the algorithm works—a process known as *reverse engineering*.[18]

Anyone deploying a secret cryptographic algorithm would be wise to operate under the assumption that one day (perhaps sooner than expected), the secrecy of the algorithm will be lost. This is not just contemporary advice based on recent experience. In the late nineteenth century, the esteemed Dutch cryptographer Auguste Kerckhoffs included this maxim among six design principles that he formulated for the design of cryptographic algorithms.[19] This was a time long before algorithms were implemented on machines. In Kerckhoffs's day, an algorithm (which he called a *system*) was something you applied by hand to manipulate written text. More precisely, Kerckhoffs observed: *The system must not require secrecy and can be stolen by the enemy without causing trouble.* He was a wise man.

A Tale of Two Algorithms

I have argued that, for cryptography, keeping recipes secret is not always beneficial, or even possible. This is particularly true when these recipes relate to ubiquitously deployed products.

It is worth reflecting on this conclusion by considering two very different secret recipes, both of which have global reach. The manufacturers of Coca-Cola claim that the recipe for making their soft drink is one of the world's best-kept secrets, and they have an elaborate process for safeguarding it. Having a "secret formula" for Coca-Cola is not unlike trying to protect a mobile phone by using a secret cryptographic algorithm. It is hard to find anyone who has not both drunk Coca-Cola and owned a mobile phone. Keeping the algorithms behind either of these products secret when they are both so prevalent presents a considerable challenge.

Mobile phones were once protected by the use of secret algorithms, because the architects of the first mobile networks believed that this practice offered extra security. However, the secret algorithms used on these mobile phones were eventually reverse engineered and, in some cases, found to be not as secure as originally hoped. Today, mobile operators have decided that the benefits of making their cryptographic algorithms public far outweigh any questionable security gains from keeping them secret.[20] Secret recipes are out of fashion in the mobile telecommunications industry.

So, how has Coca-Cola managed to get away with keeping its recipe secret? The truth is that the Coca-Cola recipe is *not* strictly a secret. The process (the algorithm) for creating a carbonated soft drink is well known. So, too, are most of the ingredients of Coca-Cola, some of which have been surmised by experts. Indeed, several manufacturers now produce soft drinks tasting so much like Coca-Cola that most people cannot tell the difference. What remains a secret is the precise nature of one of the ingredients of the Coca-Cola formula, which is referred to as *Merchandise 7X*.[21] In this respect, the secrecy of 7X is more like the secrecy of a cryptographic key. While the algorithm for making a carbonated soft drink is broadly known, a whole range of different beverages can be produced by replacing 7X with other flavoring agents. Just as for modern mobile phones, while the Coca-Cola algorithm is broadly known, safeguarding Coca-Cola depends on the secrecy of a key.

Algorithms Are Important, but Keys Are Key

It really is essential to recognize the different roles played by algorithms and keys in cryptography.

Algorithms are the engine rooms of cryptography, determining and conducting the necessary computations. As far as most of us are concerned, algorithms run in the background and we never have to worry about them. Even seasoned cybersecurity professionals rarely interact directly with cryptographic algorithms, other than needing to be aware of which algorithms are being used to protect the systems they're responsible for.

Keys are the secrets that the security provided by cryptography depends on. From a security perspective, keys are part of the interface between a technology and its users. Unlike algorithms, which we all share, keys are unique to individual users or devices. Keys are thus things we should all have an acute awareness of. Everyone knows the cryptographic algorithms that we use, but if someone else gets hold of our personal cryptographic keys, then we lose all sense of security in cyberspace.

In using cryptography to support our security in cyberspace, algorithms are important, but keys are key.

3

Keeping Secrets

I n order to recognize the full range of distinct security mechanisms that cryptography provides in cyberspace, it is helpful to
break down the idea of *security* into some core functionalities.
The first of these is the capability to keep secrets.

Confidentiality

When asked to consider the idea of "security" of information, most
people think immediately of *confidentiality*, which is the ability to
restrict knowledge of our (confidential) information to only those
whom we want to have it.

We all have secrets. A secret is not necessarily something
extremely sensitive, whose revelation would lead to humiliation.
Any information about yourself that you don't want to see published
in a newspaper is a secret. Anything you are happy for some people
to know, but not others, is a secret. Your bank account details, your
passwords, and your PINs are certainly secrets. It's likely that your
address, your date of birth, and your family photographs are also
secrets. And what would happen if a stranger walked up to you in

the street and demanded to know the names of your children and
what you had for dinner last night? Would you tell them? If not,
then these are also secrets. We all have information we don't want
everyone to know.[1]

Confidentiality is often associated with the concept of *privacy*,
which is more complex and broadly relates to the desire and ability to exclude information from others. As Eric Hughes argued in
"A Cypherpunk's Manifesto": "A private matter is something one
doesn't want the whole world to know, but a secret matter is something one doesn't want anybody to know. Privacy is the power to
selectively reveal oneself to the world."[2] Security mechanisms for
providing confidentiality can be used to support privacy, but privacy itself is about more than keeping secrets.

Confidentiality is important in the physical world. We provide
confidentiality for written information by sealing it in envelopes,
using trusted couriers, or locking it in filing cabinets. For spoken
information, we control the level of our voice to restrict who can
hear information, or we discuss secrets in closed rooms.

Keeping secrets in cyberspace is a necessity. We need confidentiality whenever we give our personal details to a website;
otherwise hackers attacking this website could acquire them. We
need confidentiality when we make a mobile phone call, to stop
anyone with a simple radio receiver from listening to the call. We
need confidentiality when we make an internet payment, to stop
attackers from learning our bank card details. Put simply, we
need confidentiality whenever we want to store sensitive information on any computer we should not fully trust. Frankly, this
is any computer at all, including your mobile phone and your
car. And we need confidentiality whenever we transfer sensitive data across any network we should not fully trust. Frankly,
this is any network at all, including the internet and your home
Wi-Fi network.[3]

Hide-and-Seek

A child comes home from school with a bad report card that they don't want their parents to see. This information urgently needs a confidentiality mechanism! The child stuffs the report card under a mattress or buries it in a drawer of clothes. In other words, they hide it.

The critical feature of hiding something is that nobody looking around the hiding place should see any obvious indication of the hidden object. The bed still looks like a bed when the report card is underneath the mattress. The clothes drawer appears its usual messy self when the report is hidden under a pile of football shirts.

Digital information can also be hidden in apparently normal digital objects. One technique is to hide information within a digital image. A computer image is made up of hundreds of individual pixels, each of which is too small to be perceived by the human eye. Each pixel is a fixed color. Just as for any other data, the pixel color is identified by a sequence of bits. Some of these bits are important, while others, the least sensitive ones, fine-tune the precise color. Changes to these least sensitive bits are invisible to a human observer; hence these bits can easily be replaced by bits representing some information we want to hide. All observers see a regular image. Someone who knows where to look can retrieve the hidden information.

We've all played hide-and-seek, so we all know that hiding is a risky business, since discovery is always possible. When the bedroom gets cleaned, there is a good chance the report card will be found. Likewise, if someone suspects that a digital image contains hidden information, inspecting the pixel details may uncover the secret.

Hiding information has one advantage over other confidentiality mechanisms. It not only provides confidentiality but also prevents anyone from realizing that a secret exists in the first place.

Until other parents start discussing report cards in the school playground, the errant child's parents don't even realize a report was sent home. Nobody observing a digital image that contains hidden information has any idea that a secret is contained within.

However, hiding the existence of information is only very occasionally an advantage. If your bank decides to send you a confidential paper statement, then both you and the bank want to use the traditional postal service to dispatch the letter, sealed in a normal envelope, rather than agreeing on a hiding place where you will need to go to collect the statement. It doesn't matter, after all, that the mail carrier knows you're receiving a letter from your bank. What is important is that the mail carrier can't look inside the protective envelope. Likewise, when you make a call using your mobile phone, you're not normally worried about keeping secret the fact that you're making a call. It's the content of the call that's confidential.[4] Similarly, when you purchase goods over the internet, it's not the fact that you've made a purchase that's confidential, but rather the details of the transaction.

Indeed, in all these cases, hiding the secret information is not only unnecessary but unrealistic. Where would you hide it? When you make a phone call, you want to send only the data encoding your voice, not some other digital object in which the call information could be hidden. Any digital object in which the data could be embedded would need to be much larger than the secret voice data, which would ultimately make the whole process extremely inefficient to conduct.

In general, hiding digital information is not a particularly useful means of providing confidentiality. The study of information-hiding mechanisms is known as *steganography*, literally "concealed writing."[5] Steganography has certain niche applications. A criminal wishing to hide incriminating material on a computer might deploy steganography to prevent anyone from realizing that such data is stored on the machine.[6] Steganography has uses in the area of digital rights protection, where producers of digital content some-times use steganography to brand content without visibly degrad-ing the content itself. Steganography is also potentially useful for keeping secrets from any political regime that outlaws the use of confidentiality mechanisms. It's hard for an authoritarian regime to prosecute someone for keeping secrets when it cannot detect the existence of these secrets in the first place.[7]

Mainly, however, the most useful mechanisms for providing con-fidentiality are those that keep a secret but do not disguise the fact that the secret exists. This type of confidentiality mechanism can be achieved through cryptography.

Steganography is not cryptography. Indeed, steganography is arguably only really effective as a confidentiality mechanism when the hidden information is itself first protected by cryptography. You use cryptography every day. You rarely, if ever, use steganography.

Cracking Codes

Suppose we have some confidential information we want to send to someone in cyberspace. We have no need to conceal the fact that this information exists; we just want to restrict access to the infor-mation itself. Since anyone might be able to observe whatever we send, we need to mask the information in some way. In other words, we need to send the information in disguise.

How do we disguise information? What we need to do is scramble the original information into a form that makes no sense to anyone who observes it. In other words, we need an algorithm.

Let's look at a very simple example of such an algorithm. Sup-pose the information we wish to protect consists of letters of the alphabet—for example, TOPSECRET. This is called the *plain-text*, since it is the "plain" information before being disguised. The algorithm I will use to illustrate this process is the *Atbash cipher*, which is a method of scrambling letters by reversing the letters of the alphabet.[8] In other words, each plaintext letter to keep confidential is replaced by the letter in the equivalent position of the alphabet written in reverse: A is replaced by Z, B is replaced by Y, C is replaced by X, and so on. The following table depicts the complete algorithm.

Plaintext	A B C D E F G H I J K L M N O P Q R S T U V W X Y Z
Ciphertext	Z Y X W V U T S R Q P O N M L K J I H G F E D C B A

The Atbash cipher algorithm replaces each letter in the top row of this table with the letter beneath it. Hence, the plaintext TOPSECRET is converted into GLKHVXIVG. This latter sequence of letters, which does not make any apparent sense, is referred to as the *ciphertext*.

The ciphertext is what we send to the intended recipient of our secret message. Anyone observing this communication sees only GLKHVXIVG. The recipient, knowing that we used the Atbash cipher to convert the plaintext into ciphertext, now uses the reverse algorithm to recover the plaintext. In other words, the recipient replaces each letter in the bottom row by the equivalent letter in the top row. In this way the recipient successfully removes the disguise and reconverts the ciphertext GLKHVXIVG back into the plaintext TOPSECRET.

How effective is the Atbash cipher as a confidentiality mechanism? The Atbash is considered a very weak mechanism for many reasons, but the most significant one relates to my previous observation about making sure that we do not rely on a cryptographic algorithm being kept secret. I argued, in line with Auguste Kerckhoffs, that we should always assume everyone knows which algorithm is being used, even if, in practice, they don't. Since in this case we are using the Atbash cipher to scramble information, it should be assumed everyone knows that Z replaces A, Y replaces B, and so on. Hence, everyone knows that the ciphertext GLKHVXIVG corresponds to the plaintext TOPSECRET. So much for confidentiality!

The problem with the Atbash cipher is simple. Anyone who knows we're using it also knows exactly how to convert between plaintext and ciphertext, because there's only one way of doing so. The Atbash cipher fails to provide confidentiality because there's no variability in the way it scrambles the data. The real problem with the Atbash cipher is that it's an algorithm without a key.

Algorithms that scramble information without using a key are often referred to as *codes*. While the purpose of a code is usually to transform information in some way, the motivation for doing so tends not to be keeping secrets. Arguably the best-known code is Morse code, which replaces letters by short sequences of dots and dashes.[9] Morse code was designed to convey information by telegraph. The sequences of dots and dashes enable alphanumeric characters to be translated into short and long electromagnetic pulses. This scheme has nothing to do with confidentiality. Indeed, it would be catastrophic if a ship in distress, urgently pulsing the international emergency encoded message "dot dot dot, dash dash dash, dot dot dot" were not able to have this communication successfully decoded by a receiving vessel. This is a ciphertext whose equivalent plaintext everyone needs to understand.

Codes sometimes, misleadingly, appear to provide a veneer of confidentiality. Occasionally, you might be challenged to "crack a code" (indeed, I have lost count of the number of times it has been suggested that my job, as a cryptographer, is to do this). For centuries, Egyptian hieroglyphs presented just such a challenge to scholars researching the history of ancient Egypt. Only in the early nineteenth century did the code behind hieroglyphs once again become understood.[10] Hieroglyphic writing, however, was never designed to provide confidentiality. As ancient Egyptian culture died away, people forgot the details of the algorithm that encoded ideas into hieroglyphs. Rediscovery of this algorithm was all that was necessary to render hieroglyphs meaningful. The ancient Egyptians would surely not have regarded this as a breach of their security.

Another well-publicized code features in the title of Dan Brown's novel *The Da Vinci Code*, a book all about secrets, mysteries, and intrigue.[11] One of the main protagonists in this novel is a cryptographer, Sophie Neveu, who was allegedly educated at my current place of employment, Royal Holloway, University of London. At the time the book was riding high in the bestseller lists, many different media outlets got in touch, wanting to know more about the cryptography used in the book.

Alas, Sophie Neveu's excellent training in cryptography seemed wasted, since there is no real cryptography in *The Da Vinci Code* at all. To unravel the mysteries of the book, Sophie primarily uses her lateral thinking skills to make sense of a number of puzzles. The closest she comes to true cryptography is when she realizes that one of the puzzles consists of ciphertext encoded with the Atbash cipher. Since the Atbash cipher, as you now know just as well as Sophie, doesn't provide confidentiality, she is instantly able to determine the secret message.

So, codes are algorithms that can be used to disguise information, but normally for reasons other than providing confidentiality. If a security mechanism for providing confidentiality is required, then what is really needed is an algorithm with a key.

Redeeming the Atbash

It's time to redeem the Atbash cipher. To convert the basic idea behind the Atbash into something more useful, plaintext letters should be scrambled in different ways. In the Atbash cipher, the *only* way of scrambling is to reverse the letters of the alphabet. Instead, let's make reversing the letters of the alphabet just one of *many* different ways in which the plaintext letters can be scrambled. Indeed, ideally, let's make it one of *any* ways of scrambling the letters. The result is known as the *simple substitution cipher*.

The simple substitution cipher is best also considered as a table, except that instead of the second row consisting of the reverse of the letters of the alphabet, it's a random rearrangement of the letters of the alphabet in which every letter appears once. Just as for the Atbash, the simple substitution cipher algorithm replaces each plaintext letter in the first row with the ciphertext letter beneath it in the second. For example, if the simple substitution cipher is:

Plaintext A B C D E F G H I J K L M N O P Q R S T U V W X Y Z

Ciphertext D I Q M T B Z S Y K V O F E R J A U W P X H L C N G

then plaintext TOPSECRET is scrambled into ciphertext PRJWTQUTP. And if the simple substitution cipher is:

Plaintext A B C D E F G H I J K L M N O P Q R S T U V W X Y Z

Ciphertext N R A W K I L F O C T E Y P V J S D B X H M Z U Q G

then TOPSECRET becomes XVJBKADKX.

Is this progress? In the Atbash cipher, the scrambling algorithm replaces A by Z, B by Y, and so on. The confidentiality showstopper for the Atbash is that everyone knows the algorithm, and hence knows that plaintext A is replaced by ciphertext Z, and so on. In the preceding simple substitution cipher, the scrambling algorithm replaces A by N, B by R, C by A, and so on. Since it should be assumed that everyone knows the algorithm, is there a difference between this and the Atbash cipher?

There's an enormous difference! The critical observation is that the scrambling algorithm in the simple substitution cipher of our last example is *not*: "Replace A by N, B by R, C by A, and so on." The algorithm, which we assume everyone knows, is: "Replace the letter in the top row of the table by the letter beneath it in the bottom row." What everyone does not know is the *precise* table being used. Knowledge of the precise table is what separates those whom we want to understand the plaintext from everyone else. The precise table is the *key*.

Let's look at how this works. You want to send a confidential message to your friend, using the simple substitution cipher. You and your friend first need to agree on a secret key. In other words, you and your friend need to agree on a random rearrangement of the letters of the alphabet. Assume that you are able to do this somehow. Suppose you choose the same key in our most recent example—namely, the rearrangement N, R, A, . . . , U, Q, G. If you want to send the plaintext TIMEFORCAKE, then you look up the table, replacing letters in the top row by letters in the bottom row, to obtain ciphertext XOYKIVDANTK. You send XOYKIVDANTK to your friend, who uses the same table to recover the plaintext TIMEFORCAKE.

Now, let's consider the perspective of an attacker, someone who wants to learn the secret messages. Assume that the attacker knows the algorithm, is thus aware that you're using the simple substitution cipher, and is able to observe any ciphertext you send. Had you been using the Atbash, on seeing XOYKIVDANTK the attacker would immediately be able to work out the plaintext. However, you're using the simple substitution cipher, so all the attacker knows is that the plaintext letters are being jumbled up by means of an unknown rearrangement of the letters of the alphabet. The ciphertext letter X could have replaced any plaintext letter of the alphabet, the letter O could represent any plaintext letter, so could the letter Y, and so on.

How hopeless is the attacker's situation? Well, there is always one option open to the attacker: although they don't know the key, they could try to guess it. Since the key was chosen randomly, the attacker needs to guess a random rearrangement of the letters of the alphabet and hope to get lucky. To find the odds of success, it's necessary to first determine how many random rearrangements there are of 26 letters. This is quite easy to calculate. The first letter can be any of the 26 letters, so there are 26 options. The second letter can be any letter other than the one chosen as the first letter, so there are 25 possibilities. Hence, there are $26 \times 25 = 650$ choices for the combination of the first two letters. The third letter can be any letter other than those chosen as the first and second letters, so there are 24 choices. There are thus $26 \times 25 \times 24 = 15{,}600$ possibilities for the combination of the first three letters. And so on.

There are, ultimately: $26 \times 25 \times 24 \times 23 \times 22 \times 21 \times 20 \times 19 \times 18 \times 17 \times 16 \times 15 \times 14 \times 13 \times 12 \times 11 \times 10 \times 9 \times 8 \times 7 \times 6 \times 5 \times 4 \times 3 \times 2 \times 1 = 403{,}291{,}461{,}126{,}605{,}635{,}584{,}000{,}000$ possible rearrangements of 26 letters. How big is this number? You can save data entry time on your calculator by typing "26" and looking for a button with the ! symbol (referred to as the *factorial* function). If you have a cheap calculator, this request will probably blow the calculator's mind and it will return an error message, indicating that the answer is too large to handle. If you own a slightly more sophisticated calculator, it will indicate that 26 factorial is something enormous. What it won't tell you is that the answer equates to 40,000 times the number of stars in our universe. Put simply, guessing which of the 26-factorial possible secrets was chosen by you and your friend is a lost cause that the attacker should not waste time pursuing.

The Atbash cipher is just one of the 26-factorial possible instantiations of the simple substitution cipher. If you choose your key randomly, then it is very unlikely you will end up using the Atbash cipher—just as unlikely as ending up with either of the other two key tables described earlier. And each of these keys is just as unlikely as the chances of selecting one specific star from 40,000 times the number of stars in the universe. Even if, by an unbelievably rare chance, you did end up with the key corresponding to the Atbash cipher, this scenario is so mind-bogglingly unlikely that the attacker will never guess it happened.

Seen from this perspective, the simple substitution cipher seems to provide confidentiality. But before you rush off to use this cipher to safeguard secrets on your computer, a word of caution: while the simple substitution cipher does indeed have 26 factorial keys, the level of confidentiality it provides is severely limited. The reason is that there is a much easier way for an attacker to determine plaintext from ciphertext than guessing the key. For now, just accept that, unlike steganography and codes such as the Atbash cipher, the simple substitution cipher is a genuine (albeit flawed) example of a cryptographic security mechanism for providing confidentiality.

Encryption

The process of providing confidentiality using a cryptographic security mechanism is known as *encryption*. Any mechanism for providing encryption includes an *encryption algorithm*, which defines the basic process by which plaintext is scrambled, and a key, which provides the means of varying the way encryption is performed. The encryption algorithm takes as input both the plaintext and the key, and defines a process that eventually outputs the ciphertext. In the case of the simple substitution cipher, the encryption algorithm is the process of replacing letters in the top row of the table by letters in the bottom row, and the key is the random rearrangement making up the second row of the table.

The process of reversing encryption is known as *decryption*. In decryption, the ciphertext and a key are input into a *decryption algorithm*, which outputs the plaintext. The decryption algorithm is the process reversing the effect of the encryption algorithm. The decryption algorithm for the simple substitution cipher is the replacing of the bottom letter by the top letter in the table. The encryption algorithm and decryption algorithm are so intimately related to one another that it's common to refer to just the encryption algorithm, leaving the decryption algorithm implied.

Encryption is an extremely important security mechanism for a number of reasons. For one thing, encryption is the security mechanism that cryptography has provided for the longest time. Indeed, historical uses of cryptography by the likes of Julius Caesar, Mary,

Queen of Scots, and Napoleon were only to provide confidentiality by means of encryption. The world wars of the twentieth century, and the subsequent Cold War, all heavily relied on the use of encryption to provide confidentiality for clandestine communications.

Encryption is used widely in modern applications. If you have done any of the following today, then you have used encryption: made a mobile phone call, withdrawn money from an ATM, connected to Wi-Fi, bought something from a website, used a virtual private network to access your work computers from home, watched pay-per-view television, sent a message using WhatsApp, and so on.

While encryption is perhaps the most attention-grabbing use of cryptography, it is worth reminding ourselves that it provides *only* confidentiality. Nowadays, encryption is rarely used without being accompanied by cryptographic security mechanisms that provide additional security properties. For example, encryption of a mobile phone call happens only after cryptography has been used to identify the SIM card on the mobile phone. Encryption of bank card transactions takes place only when accompanied by the use of cryptography to make sure the messages being encrypted have not been modified in transit.

To see why encryption of a plaintext message does not provide guarantees that the received plaintext is the one the sender intended to protect, let's again consider the simple substitution cipher. In one of our previous examples, the plaintext TOPSECRET was encrypted into the ciphertext XVJBKADKX. This process prevents an attacker who observes XVJBKADKX from knowing the meaning of the underlying plaintext.

However, there is nothing stopping the attacker from modifying this ciphertext before it reaches the intended recipient. The attacker could, for example, change one of the letters in the ciphertext. If they changed the first letter from X to J, then the receiver would decrypt this to the plaintext POPSECRET. Has there been a mistake? How will the receiver know? (Perhaps POPSECRET

refers to the mysterious ingredient behind the recipe for Coca-Cola!)
Even though the attacker does not know precisely what impact the
change to the ciphertext has made, the receiver cannot be sure the
plaintext they decrypt is correct.[12]

Vanilla Encryption

Returning to our security mechanisms of the physical world for a
moment, in some ways encryption is a bit like the digital equivalent
of locking written information inside a box. The encryption (and
decryption) algorithm is the digital version of the locking mechanism itself, and the cryptographic key is the digital version of the
physical key.

Importantly, there are different kinds of physical locks. The
most common type of lock is one that requires the same key to both
lock and unlock the box. Analogously, the default (or *vanilla*) type
of encryption is one in which the key used to encrypt plaintext into
ciphertext is the same as the key used to decrypt ciphertext into
plaintext. The simple substitution cipher works in precisely this
way, with the key required to encrypt and decrypt being the random rearrangement represented in the bottom row of the table. An
encryption algorithm in which the same key is used to both encrypt
and decrypt is described as being *symmetric*.

It might at first seem natural for encryption to be symmetric.
Intuitively, any other keying relationship does not appear to make
any sense. How can plaintext encrypted using one key be decrypted
using another? However, recall that physical locks are not always
symmetric. In particular, pin tumbler locks (of the type often associated with the manufacturer Yale) and padlocks are typically
not locked by applying a key at all. These locks are normally just
snapped shut. A key is necessary only for unlocking these locks.
Fascinatingly, and significantly, there are cryptographic equivalents of pin tumbler locks and padlocks. Encryption mechanisms

in which different keys are used for encryption and decryption are referred to as being *asymmetric*.

Until the 1970s, all encryption mechanisms were symmetric. What do Julius Caesar, Mary, Queen of Scots, and Napoleon have in common? They all only ever used symmetric encryption. Even Alan Turing, one of the people whose genius is most associated with the influential role that cryptography played during the Second World War, would possibly have regarded the idea of asymmetric encryption as a bizarre impossibility.[13]

Today, symmetric encryption remains by far the most common type of encryption. You use symmetric encryption when you encrypt all the data on your laptop. You use symmetric encryption when you use Bluetooth. You use symmetric encryption when you use all our favorite previous examples of everyday encryption: Wi-Fi, mobile phones, banking, internet shopping, and so on. In fact, whenever you want to protect data in the form of documents, spreadsheets, web forms, email, voice traffic, and the like, it is symmetric encryption you use to provide confidentiality. Most encryption is symmetric encryption. In fact, all encryption would be symmetric encryption if it weren't for a small problem, which I'll explain in a moment.

The algorithms used to provide symmetric encryption have evolved over time, as knowledge of how to design (and break) good encryption algorithms has improved. This progress has been by no means gradual, with knowledge moving forward in bursts, rather than incrementally.

The symmetric encryption algorithm known as the *Vigenère cipher* was invented in the mid-sixteenth century but was still being used during the American Civil War. It was eventually shown to be fallible to statistical analysis techniques developed in the latter half of the nineteenth century.[14]

The electromechanical *Enigma machines* implemented symmetric encryption algorithms based on electrical contact pins connected to sequences of rotors. These were used for much of the first half of the twentieth century, most famously during the Second World War.[15] The effectiveness of Enigma machines as symmetric encryption mechanisms was swept aside by the communication revolution caused by the development of digital computers after the war.

Prior to the early 1970s, the main users of symmetric encryption were those with the most serious secrets to keep—namely, governments and military organizations. All this changed in the 1970s, with the arrival of commercial computing. It became apparent that there was a business need for symmetric encryption, particularly in the financial sector. At that time, and possibly to an extent today, secret organizations preferred to use secret encryption algorithms, so commercial encryption required a new and open form of symmetric encryption that everyone could use.

In 1977 the US government published a symmetric encryption algorithm called the *Data Encryption Standard*, better known to its many friends as *DES*.[16] This was a truly extraordinary moment in the history of cryptography, as it marked the passing of cryptography as a largely secret business into a subject very much in the public eye. A *standard* is something that experts have evaluated and approved for widespread use. The establishment of an encryption standard was unprecedented and facilitated the use of DES by commercial organizations in the United States, and de facto in many other countries around the world. We now had a symmetric encryption algorithm that ordinary members of the public might interact with as part of their day-to-day lives, albeit sometimes inadvertently.

During the last two decades of the twentieth century, anyone using symmetric encryption to provide confidentiality of data was most likely to be using DES. An exception was any application requiring especially fast encryption of real-time traffic, such as voice data. Symmetric encryption in such environments is often accomplished by special encryption algorithms known as *stream ciphers*, which encrypt each bit of the plaintext data individually and immediately. Stream ciphers are symmetric encryption algorithms optimized for speed and efficiency. In contrast, DES is an example of a much more general class of symmetric encryption algorithms known as *block ciphers*, because they process data in chunks (*blocks*) of bits at a time.

By the late twentieth century, DES was no longer deemed an effective symmetric encryption algorithm, mainly because computing power had steadily increased to the point that DES no longer provided sufficient security. However, DES is such an influential encryption algorithm that it has become embedded in many systems to an extent that removing it completely from some remains hard. There is a decent chance that you have indirectly used a form of DES in the last few days to encrypt some data, especially if you have paid for anything with a bank card.

Made in Belgium

Modern symmetric encryption enlists a range of different symmetric encryption algorithms. The banking networks still heavily rely on DES, but, recognizing that a single application of DES is no longer regarded as secure enough, they tend to encrypt data three separate times by means of an extension of the basic DES encryption algorithm known as *Triple DES*.[17] Increasingly, however, applications requiring symmetric encryption use a block cipher known as the *Advanced Encryption Standard*, or *AES*.[18]

The AES represents yet another milestone in the history of cryptography. In the mid-1990s, it was widely recognized that a new symmetric encryption algorithm was required that could be recommended for use by the increasingly wide range of applications requiring confidentiality.

Several significant changes had occurred in the world of cryptography between the 1970s, when DES was designed, and the 1990s. One was the rise of the internet and the World Wide Web, both of which had increased demand for conducting business, and indeed everyday life, in cyberspace. At the same time there was an increase in the diversity of technologies connecting to cyberspace. When DES was developed, symmetric encryption was intended primarily for dedicated computers within the likes of banking networks, so the design of DES was specifically tailored for implementation on hardware. By the 1990s, there was a demand not just for symmetric encryption in hardware but also for symmetric encryption that could be implemented efficiently in software. There was also a greater range of hardware platforms requiring symmetric encryption. In the 1970s all computers were fairly similar. By the 1990s, there was a requirement for cryptography on both supercomputers and tiny devices such as smartcards (plastic cards with an embedded chip like your credit card).

Another significant change was in cryptographic expertise. In the 1970s, most cryptographers worked for governments or military organizations. Indeed, knowledge of cryptography was largely confined to employees in these sectors. The US government turned to IBM, one of the few commercial companies with an interest in cryptography in the 1970s, for the design of DES. By the 1990s, there was a flourishing community of cryptographers in both academia and the private sector, particularly in telecommunications companies, who were building commercial empires that relied on the effectiveness of cryptography.

The US National Institute of Standards and Technology (NIST) was the agency tasked with procuring a new symmetric encryption algorithm standard fit for the twenty-first century. NIST decided to harness the cryptographic community outside of government by holding an open competition for the design of the new AES algorithm. Recognizing that this new symmetric encryption algorithm would find its way into products all over the world, the AES competition permitted international entries, not just designs from the United States.[19]

This was a radically new approach to designing cryptographic algorithms, and most of the leading experts in symmetric encryption engaged with the competition. My only personal contribution to this process was trying to persuade my Belgian office colleague Vincent Rijmen to rename the candidate algorithm he had co-designed with friend Joan Daemen. I couldn't believe that any algorithm with the name *Rijndael*, crafted from a merger of the inventors' surnames and the fictional valley of Rivendell, could possibly be taken seriously. I was ignored, but the algorithm wasn't. In 2001, the Belgian symmetric encryption algorithm Rijndael became the AES.

The AES is elegantly simple in its design—a feature that makes it efficient to implement and that played a significant role in Rijndael's selection as the competition winner. You might imagine that contemporary encryption algorithms need to be mathematically sophisticated, well beyond the comprehension of nonexperts. It's true that the precise algorithm design details are subtle and require expertise to appreciate, but you might be surprised to discover that the basic idea behind the AES is quite accessible. In order to demystify modern encryption somewhat, I will try to explain (roughly) how AES encryption works.

Recall that an encryption algorithm is a recipe that takes two core ingredients—namely, some plaintext and a key—and mixes them up to produce a ciphertext. The AES algorithm conducts this scrambling operation as follows:

Format the plaintext. The plaintext is first converted into bytes. The first 16 bytes are then arranged into a 4×4 square (4 bytes by 4 bytes).[20] If there is more plaintext to encrypt, then a second square is formed, then a third, and so on. If there's not enough plaintext to complete a 4×4 square of bytes, then the square is filled with redundant information known as *padding*. The plaintext is now ready to encrypt.

Change all the bytes. The first step in mixing up the plaintext is to replace each byte in the square with a new byte that is determined by rules specified as part of the AES algorithm, so that everyone knows how to do this. At the end of this step, a new square of 16 bytes has been formed.

Slide the rows. This second mixing step couldn't be simpler. Each row of the square is shifted along a specified number of positions, with entries that drop off the right end of the row being reinserted back into the left end.

Transform the columns. The 4 bytes of each column are now transformed according to another mixing rule specified by the AES algorithm. Each result is a new column, again consisting of 4 bytes. The overall result is a new square of 16 bytes.

Add the key. Each of the previous steps jumbles the plaintext in a different way, not unlike the way a dealer uses a mix of techniques to shuffle a deck of cards. The key, however, has not yet been mixed into the process. To do so, the AES algorithm specifies how to take the key and define from it a separate 4×4 square of 16 bytes known as a *subkey*. The square of mixed-up plaintext bytes is now added to the subkey square to form yet another square of 16 bytes.

Do it all again. Once a square of bytes that is a blend of the plaintext and the key has been produced, the button on the blender can be pressed again. The latest square of 16 bytes is inserted back into the "Change all the bytes" step, and the entire process is repeated (*Change all the bytes, Slide the rows, Transform the columns, Add the key*). And *Do it all again*, until the AES specifies that everything has been mixed enough. For the most basic version of AES (there are three versions, each with a different length of key), this process is repeated ten times. Each pass through these different mixing operations is known as one *round* of AES.

Output the ciphertext. The final 4×4 square of bytes is our ciphertext.

To decrypt ciphertext back into plaintext, the entire process is performed in reverse.

This is the idea anyway. I've left out a few subtleties, and spared you some details. The reason for spelling out the core idea behind AES is to show that, at its heart, the AES encryption algorithm consists of a series of relatively simple operations, the combined effect of which produces a ciphertext that preserves the confidentiality of the plaintext. Hopefully you agree that AES has a simple, even elegant, design. You should not, however, even for a moment, think that coming up with an encryption algorithm such as the AES is easy.[21]

The AES is used to provide confidentiality in many modern technologies. For example, you probably use it whenever you make a secure connection from your web browser to a website (of course, you don't personally choose to use the AES; your web browser does this for you). The AES has been so well studied and evaluated that it is likely we'll continue to keep secrets by sliding rows and transforming columns for the foreseeable future.

If anyone asks you what Belgium is famous for, now you know. Frites, beer, chocolate, and fictional detectives are fine, but Belgium should be better known for its cryptography.

The Ubiquitous Block Cipher

The AES is not the only block cipher available today for symmetric encryption. A considerable number of block ciphers have been proposed over the years, including some excellent competition finalists that narrowly missed selection as the AES. There are block ciphers named after animals, Norse gods, Belgian beers, and the downright obscure (everyone's favorite is the Hasty Pudding cipher). There are an astonishing number of block ciphers named after fish.[22] However, only a few of these block ciphers are ever deployed in real products, and the AES is arguably the most important of these.

One of the reasons block ciphers are the most common mechanisms for conducting symmetric encryption is that they are so flexible in how they can be implemented. Recall that a block cipher encrypts a block (a group of bits, with 128 bits being a typical group size) of plaintext into a block of ciphertext. We often want to encrypt more than 128 bits, since 128 bits represents only about 16 characters of text. Encrypting longer plaintext by first chopping it up into blocks, and then encrypting each block separately, is not a wise idea.

The main problem is that recurrences of the same plaintext block will always encrypt using a specific encryption key into the same ciphertext block. A commonly occurring plaintext block might thus become recognizable to an attacker who analyzes the frequency of occurrence of ciphertext blocks. Worse, if an attacker somehow discovers the plaintext corresponding to a particular ciphertext block, any subsequent occurrence of that ciphertext block will immediately reveal to the attacker that the known plaintext has been sent again.

To counter this risk, more sophisticated methods exist for encrypting plaintexts of more than one block. These *modes of operation* of a block cipher link together the encryptions of separate blocks in different ways. In doing so, modes of operation enable a block cipher such as AES to achieve different properties, beyond just providing confidentiality. For example, some modes of operation remove the need for padding the final block, other modes enable the detection of changes to the ciphertext, and there are modes of operation specifically tailored for particular applications, such as encrypting hard drives. Indeed, in many applications more suited to the use of a stream cipher, encryption is performed by a block cipher deployed in a special mode of operation that effectively converts it into a stream cipher.[23]

Symmetric encryption is the most common cryptographic means of providing confidentiality, block ciphers are the most widely deployed symmetric encryption mechanisms, and AES is by far the most used block cipher. Consequently, we heavily rely on AES for security in cyberspace.

Does the ubiquity of AES create a problem? After all, biodiverse ecosystems tend to be the healthiest, and reliance on single genetic strains of food crops can have disastrous consequences. Should there not be greater cryptodiversity?

To some extent, reliance on AES is a gamble, but it's a defensible one. Although there will never be an absolute guarantee that AES is secure, a standardized cryptographic algorithm such as AES is scrutinized much more than any other block cipher. As a result, as time goes by without anyone reporting a problem, confidence in AES increases.

There are occasions in life when there is a case for demonstrating individual flair, such as choosing what to wear to a party, or deciding how to decorate a room. When purchasing something purely functional, however, such as a dishwasher, going with a reliable brand and model trumps high fashion any day. In this respect, encryption mechanisms are much more like a dishwasher than like a ball gown. If, one day, an unexpected critical flaw is discovered in AES, then it will be in the whole world's interest to act swiftly to do something about it. Using a less fashionable block cipher might expose you less to this particular danger, but it runs the greater risk that your less scrutinized block cipher is not as secure as you hoped it might be.

The Key-Distribution Problem

Symmetric encryption is a wonderful tool, which we use all the time to keep secrets in cyberspace. However, there is an obvious catch involved with using symmetric encryption. Anyone who scrambles plaintext into ciphertext needs a secret key. But anyone who wishes to unscramble this ciphertext back into plaintext also needs this same secret key. Symmetric encryption works, as long as, somehow, everyone who needs the secret key can get hold of it.

But how is this distribution of secrets accomplished? We can't simply send someone a secret key whenever one is needed, by any old means, because secret keys (by definition) are themselves secrets. Most communication channels in cyberspace, such as the internet, are easy for an attacker to access. What do we normally do when we need to send someone a secret in cyberspace? We encrypt it, of course! And before we encrypt anything, we need . . . a key. You heard right. To send someone a key, we first need a key. It's a sort of cryptographic version of the chicken-or-the-egg dilemma.[24]

When we use keys in the physical world, we rarely have significant problems transporting the keys to where they are required. When we lock something, we are often the ones who need to unlock it later, in which case the keys don't need to go anywhere other than our own pockets. We don't tend to send one another secret messages in locked boxes, so we never have to worry about how someone else is going to get hold of the key to unlock such a box. In other words, we don't come across the significant *key-distribution problem* that users of symmetric encryption face.

Symmetric encryption keys are not always difficult to distribute. In the physical world, on the rare occasion when we need to give someone else a physical key, we normally rely on physical proximity to do so. If you want to lend a visitor your front-door key, you just hand it to them when you meet. If for some reason a meeting is not possible, you leave the key somewhere nearby (say, underneath a flowerpot).

Likewise, some applications of symmetric encryption rely on physical proximity to distribute keys. A good example is a home Wi-Fi network. All devices connecting to Wi-Fi have their connections to the Wi-Fi protected by symmetric encryption. The critical information needed to create the key used to encrypt traffic is the master key used to access the Wi-Fi network. The owner of the network should be able to generate this master key. While the owner has often written the critical password on a piece of paper (which they usually can't find when you ask for it), the password is often more reliably found printed on the box controlling the Wi-Fi network. Any new device wanting to join the network and use symmetric encryption needs to be supplied with this password. This master key can either be typed into the device manually, or it can be installed automatically if the new device is brought physically close to the Wi-Fi box. Both solutions are workable because any device connecting to the Wi-Fi needs to be in close proximity to the box (or the owner).[25]

In the physical world, sometimes we need a new physical key for something. We usually collect new keys from a "trusted party," meaning someone with whom we have at least a business relationship. For example, we normally obtain the key to a new house from the real-estate agent (whether we fully trust real-estate agents is a moot point). Likewise, we collect the key to a new car from the sales center, which we trust enough that we hand over cash for wheels. Many real-world applications of symmetric encryption to protect secrets rely on the use of a trusted party of some sort to support the distribution of keys. We get the symmetric key for our credit card directly from our bank when we're sent the card. We receive the symmetric key on the SIM card of our mobile phone either directly from the mobile-network operator, or indirectly from an agent selling contracts on the operator's behalf. Notably, in both examples we obtain encryption keys well in advance of the time we need to use them.

However, sometimes in cyberspace we need to do something we are rarely required to do with locks and keys in the physical world. In cyberspace, we often need to use locks and keys to share secrets with a stranger. As a concrete example, suppose you decide to purchase a widget from an online store you have never previously visited. Because you want the payment details to be kept confidential from the outside world, you have a sudden need for a cryptographic key. You are not close to the store, so you can't just stop by to agree on a key. Nor do you and the store necessarily have any prior business relationship, during which you could have previously agreed on a key (for example, the store could have equipped you with a loyalty card with a key on the chip). Worse, you want to buy the widget *now* and are probably unwilling to wait for a key to be delivered by some (expensive) physical means.

Sharing a secret with a stranger at first appears an impossible problem to solve. But, like many seemingly impossible problems, cryptography can be used to solve it. To do so, however, a radically different type of encryption is required.

4

Sharing Secrets with Strangers

n the early 1970s there was only one type of encryption: symmetric encryption. By the late 1970s there were two. It is hard to express how truly revolutionary the idea of asymmetric encryption was. Asymmetric encryption directly tackles the symmetric-key-distribution problem by providing a means for two people who have not previously agreed on a secret symmetric key to do so in plain sight of an attacker. Asymmetric encryption seems like magic. And it is. Even more wizardly, it has indirectly facilitated many other amazing things that cryptography can now help us do in cyberspace, such as digitally signing documents, making payments with digital currency, and voting.

A Huge Bunch of Keys

In order to appreciate the power of asymmetric encryption, recall the previous example, in which you unexpectedly needed a key in order to encrypt communications with a website you had previously never visited. What would it take to solve this problem using symmetric encryption alone?

Earlier I observed that you could solve this problem by having a key delivered by some physical means. Either you, or the website, could generate a cryptographic key and then arrange for it to be delivered manually to the other party, perhaps using an express delivery service. All of this would cost you money and, more importantly, time. In the case of buying something online, this idea is preposterous.

An alternative is to share a key with the website before you even connect. Since the key you share with one website must be different from the key you share with another, key sharing would require you to have a key for every possible website you might ever want to visit.

The problem with this idea is the elephantine scale of it. There are over 1.5 billion websites in cyberspace.[1] If you have to store a unique symmetric key for each of these websites, then you will need to store over 1.5 billion secret keys. Given that half the world's population has access to the internet, if an online merchant wants the capability of allowing each user to buy goods from its website, the merchant needs to store 3.5 billion keys.

Intriguingly, it's not storage capacity that's the problem. If each of these 3.5 billion keys were an AES key of 128 bits, then the merchant would need to safeguard 45 gigabytes' worth of keys (a memory stick capable of this amount of storage costs less than a meal for two in a cheap restaurant). What makes this idea such a nightmare is the logistics of managing all these keys. How would we distribute them? How would we keep track of which keys are for which websites? How would we cope with all those new websites created every minute of every day of every year?

A third option would be to have a global key center that everyone on the internet trusted. You could each share a symmetric key with this global key center. This key would be sent to you in advance, perhaps on a smartcard, similarly to the way your bank has conveyed a key to you. When you wanted a key to securely communicate with a website, you could ask the global key center to generate a new key for this purpose. It could send this key to you, encrypted using the key you share with the center. A similar process could be used to send this key to the website.

If only.

First there is a political problem. Who, on the internet, is so trusted by all users that they could provide the services of the global key center? The Americans don't trust the Russians, who don't trust the British, who don't trust the French, who don't trust the Ruritanians, and so on. Perhaps the burden of this role could be passed to the United Nations? It might work, but an even bigger issue is the centralized nature of this architecture. Every time anyone wanted to talk to anyone else, they would first need to interact with the global key center. This requirement would slow all communications down. There would also be catastrophic implications if the global key center became temporarily unavailable, or if it were compromised.

It's worth noting, however, that the key-center solution works perfectly well for smaller organizations. For example, a private company's organizational relationship with its employees makes sharing a key with each employee possible. Further, many companies have their own centralized networks, which make requesting keys from a central key center a workable solution. In this situation, the users are not really "strangers," since they all share a common relationship with the key center through their contract of employment.[2] For large, less structured populations (such as the global internet population), this doesn't work.

The bottom line is this: in general, it's not feasible to use only symmetric encryption when sharing secrets with strangers.

Padlock Madness

To seek inspiration about how we might share a secret with a stranger, consider a somewhat artificial scenario from the physical world. A silly story maybe, but hopefully illustrative.

Suppose you are given the name and address of a stranger on the other side of town to whom you must send a secret written letter. This premise sounds unlikely, so let's make the scenario plausible by conceptualizing the stranger as a lawyer you've spoken to on the phone but are unable to visit, and the secret letter as your last will and testament.

One obvious way of proceeding is to seal the letter in an envelope and put it in the mail. However wonderful the postal system is, one problem with this approach is that an inquisitive employee could steam open the envelope and sneak a peek. A more robust solution would be to place the letter in a briefcase, secured by lock and key, and send the briefcase by courier. But how would the lawyer get the key to unlock the briefcase?

Recall that there are two types of physical locks. While one type requires the same key to both lock and unlock, padlocks allow anyone to lock, but only the key holder to unlock.

Here's a version of the previously described scenario in which padlocks are used to secure the secret letter that you send to your lawyer.[3] First, you place the letter in a briefcase, and then you lock the briefcase using a padlock for which only you have the key. Now you have a courier deliver the locked briefcase to the lawyer. Although trusted to deliver the briefcase, the courier might try to inspect the letter; hence the need to lock it away (cryptographers would describe the courier as "honest but curious").

Upon receiving the briefcase, the lawyer is unable to open it because she doesn't have the key to your padlock. So, she adds a second padlock to the briefcase, this time using a padlock for which only she has the key. She then returns the briefcase to the courier and asks him to take it back to you. The briefcase is now more impregnable than ever, since it is secured by two padlocks, and nobody has the key to both.

On receipt, you unlock your padlock, leaving only the lawyer's lock on the briefcase. You now return it to the courier and ask him

to deliver it, once again, to the lawyer. Exasperated, but undoubtedly happy with the triple fare, the courier escorts the briefcase
back across town. Finally, the lawyer removes her padlock and is
able to open the briefcase to retrieve the letter.

A crazy process maybe, but it works. What's really going on?
The ultimate purpose of the to-and-fro is to secure the briefcase
with a padlock that the lawyer can open. The proposed solution,
fun though it is, seems a rather overengineered means of securely
delivering a confidential letter. However, a worthy refinement saves
a bit of time, some money, and quite a few carbon emissions (unless
the courier is on a bicycle). You could first call the lawyer on the
phone and request a padlock. She could courier the padlock to you.
On receipt, you could secure the briefcase using her padlock, then
courier the locked briefcase back to her.

This padlock-by-courier idea is still a bit clunky, but it's an
improvement on the triple trip. More significantly, it's precisely the
model on which asymmetric encryption is based.

Padlocks in Cyberspace

Alas, a physical padlock requires physical delivery. Suppose, however, that a physical padlock could defeat the conventional laws of
physics and teleport itself instantly to wherever it was required!
We would then have an efficient solution to the problem of how to
share a secret with a stranger in the physical world.

Cyberspace, fortunately, is a place where teleportation is almost
possible. Conceptually, a digital "padlock" could be dispatched with
lightning speed, by email perhaps, and then used to snap shut the
equivalent of a digital briefcase. This idea, if realizable, would
allow us to share secrets with strangers in cyberspace. When we
connect to a website we have never previously visited, all we need
is a digital padlock, which is what asymmetric encryption provides.

A padlock is a lock that, in theory, everyone can close but only the key holder can open. A digital padlock thus needs to be a form of encryption that allows anyone to encrypt but only the designated recipient to decrypt. Since everyone can encrypt and encryption involves a key, the key used for digital padlock encryption will need to be something everyone knows—in other words, a key that is *not* secret. Such a key is known as a *public* key because it can be made publicly available. Consequently, asymmetric encryption is often referred to as *public-key encryption*.

In contrast, the designated recipient should be the only person capable of unlocking a digital padlock. Just as for symmetric encryption, the key used to decrypt will need to be kept secret by the recipient. This key is usually referred to as a *private* key, because it is private to the key holder and not shared with anyone else, just as for a physical padlock key. In the case of asymmetric encryption, the keys used to encrypt and decrypt are thus *different*. Of course, even though the encryption key and decryption key are different, they must be related to one another in some way.

Let's take stock of what asymmetric encryption requires. Anyone can encrypt using the public key, but only the holder of the private key can decrypt. Encryption, therefore, involves a process anyone can perform but nobody, other than the private key holder, can reverse. How is such a process possible?

When you think about it, life is full of examples of things that are easy to do but hard to reverse. A good example is cooking your dinner from fresh ingredients. While it's easy to cook a tasty dinner from scratch, extracting the original ingredients back from the dinner on your plate is normally impossible, since the chemical processes involved in cooking transform and bind them in an irreversible way.

Cooking is not a perfect analogy for asymmetric encryption, because it's *impossible* to recover the original ingredients. In the case of asymmetric encryption, we want it to be impossible for almost everyone, but we do want *someone* to be able to recover these ingredients—namely, the holder of the private key. Decryption is thus possible, albeit only in a special circumstance. Since decryption cannot be impossible, we'll have to settle for the next best thing. For anyone lacking knowledge of the private key, decryption should be *extremely hard* to perform.[4]

An asymmetric encryption scheme needs to be built around something that computers find easy to do but that is extremely hard to reverse. Converting us into internet slaves? Turning us into social media junkies? Making us busier? Losing us sleep? These might all fit the brief, but we need something more precise. We need to find a *computational task* that computers find easy to do but is hard to reverse.

The Blinking Cursor

To get a feel for how an asymmetric encryption scheme could be built, it's worth becoming aware of what *hard* means for a computer. Suppose money is no object. Imagine you have a challenging task you want a computer to perform. You buy a computer, program it to perform the task, and then press the Return key. The computer grinds away for a few hours, which soon becomes days. As weeks and months go by, the computer becomes increasingly hot. Ultimately, smoke emerges from the back. What do you do next? Go and buy a bigger, better computer?

Maybe! But maybe not. Computers are extremely powerful machines and can do amazing things, but some computing tasks quickly get out of control on even the best of computers. If you ask a computer to perform such a task, you might not always see smoke, but you certainly won't see an answer.

To see how this happens, imagine a task that is doable for a human being but takes a bit of effort. Consider the weekly cleaning of a house. How long does this take you? Half a day, say? (I live with someone who would challenge this estimate as being rather optimistic.) Yes, it's work, and it's tiring, but it's a task that can be completed within an acceptable amount of time. Suppose you discover that you are rather good at cleaning houses, and you decide to make a living doing that. You first need to market your business proposition.

One obvious marketing strategy is to contact a few neighbors. The woman next door asks you to clean for her, so now you have half a day of paid work. The family down the road needs a cleaner, and so do both of that family's neighbors. You ring a few more doorbells, and eventually you find six more houses to clean. You now have a full-time job. You could stop now, but you detect there's an even bigger market for domestic cleaning in the local area. You take on an employee, and in a short while you have a small business with several staff. Your fledgling venture into the world of commerce has been a great success. Importantly, your business is steadily growing in a very manageable way.

Now let's consider a slightly different marketing strategy. In this scenario you decide to advertise your services among your friends on a social media site, such as Facebook. Suppose you have 100 friends, and 10 of these friends respond positively. Your weekly calendar is immediately full. Now, let's imagine that, as part of your advertising pitch, you ask your friends to forward the cleaning offer to all *their* Facebook friends. Assuming they each have 100 friends different from yours, and you experience a similar acceptance rate (we're making all sorts of assumptions in this scenario, so let's not get hung up on the details), then your offer of cleaning will have reached an incredible 10,000 people and you'll be inundated by 1,000 requests for house cleaning. Ouch! If you want to pursue this business opportunity, you urgently need to hire 100 cleaners.

Almost overnight, you've gone from being self-employed to

becoming a significant local enterprise. If, heaven forbid, each of these 10,000 friends of friends then forwards your cleaning offer to *their* friends, you'll be marketing to 1 million new customers and can expect another 100,000 cleaning requests. In the blink of an eye, the whole project is out of control. In just two additional iterations of this viral marketing process, you will have 1 billion customers and be cleaning everything from igloos in the Arctic to thatched huts in the Kalahari.

The serious point behind this example is that some tasks scale well as numbers increase, while others spin madly out of control. This behavior applies just as much to computing tasks as it does to house cleaning. Some tasks on a computer are very doable. For example, computers are excellent at adding two numbers together. You can keep feeding your computer bigger and bigger numbers to add together, and it will perform the task as dutifully as a dog fetches a stick. As the numbers get larger, you will eventually reach the limit of your computer's processing capability, at which point it will decline to give an answer. If you insist on adding these giant numbers together, all you need to do is buy a bigger computer. However, some other computing tasks don't work like this at all. Just as in our viral marketing exercise, some tasks rapidly become infeasible to manage on *any* computer. Even when you ask the most powerful computer in the entire world to conduct them, its cursor merely blinks back—not just for a few hours, but for the rest of your life.[5]

A combination of these types of computing tasks is precisely what is necessary in order to accomplish asymmetric encryption. The encryption algorithm needs to be a manageable computation, so that any computer can perform it. On the other hand, without knowledge of the private key, any computer that tries to run the decryption algorithm should end up displaying a helpless, blinking cursor—as your brain would do, if tasked with finding 100 million cleaners by tomorrow afternoon.

The Prime Factor

Not many people truly understand the role of cryptography in protecting computer systems (you are, of course, well on your way to becoming a notable exception), but one thing that does seem widely recognized is that the security of computers has something to do with prime numbers, or (more simply) *primes*.[6] While primes are used throughout cryptography, their role in asymmetric encryption algorithms is what has garnered them the most attention.

Primes are whole numbers (greater than 1) with a very simple arithmetic property: the only two numbers dividing a prime without leaving a remainder are 1 and the prime itself. The smallest prime is 2 (it is the only even prime, since 2 divides all other even numbers without remainder). Also prime are 3, 5, and 7. But 9 is not a prime, since 3 divides into 9. The next two odd numbers — 11 and 13 — are prime, but 15, also divisible by 3, is not. This pattern continues forever because there are infinitely many primes.

Primes are, in a sense, the basic building blocks of all whole numbers, since every whole number can be formed by multiplying some primes together. For example, $4 = 2 \times 2$, $15 = 3 \times 5$, $36 = 2 \times 2 \times 3 \times 3$. In fact, for every whole number there is only one collection of primes that can be multiplied together to form the number. For example, $100 = 2 \times 2 \times 5 \times 5$. No group of primes besides 2,2,5,5 can be multiplied together to make 100. The primes 2,2,5,5—which are known as 100's *prime factors*—thus form the unique "DNA" of the number 100.

This singular connection between a number and its prime factors forms the basis for the most famous asymmetric encryption algorithm: *RSA*, named after its inventors, Rivest, Shamir, and Adleman.[7] The relationship between a number and its prime factors creates exactly the types of computational tasks that were earlier identified as necessary in order to accomplish asymmetric encryption: going in one direction, it's manageable; going in the other, it's a circuit-board burner.

The doable direction is multiplication. A computer can multiply any two primes. Hopefully, your schooling has left you also capable of multiplying primes. Try multiplying the following primes, in order, and preferably in your head (reach for pen and paper only if required!): 3×11, 5×13, 7×23, 11×31, 23×23, 31×41.

How was this experience for you? You probably took a little bit longer on each multiplication as you progressed, but each calculation surely took you less time than it takes to make a cup of tea.

With the help of pen and paper, you could surely multiply even more impressive primes. Go on—what's 23,189 multiplied by 50,021? (Really work this out. You'll need the answer in a moment.) Using techniques very similar to those you learned in school (if you failed to complete the previous task, then you've simply forgotten, as opposed to never having known), computers can multiply truly enormous primes together. In this sense, multiplication is an easy computing task. As the numbers get larger, the time taken to complete the computation increases, but it's a feasible task and an answer can be obtained.

The reverse of prime multiplication is to be given a number and asked to compute its prime factors. Let's assume a starting number that consists of *two* primes multiplied together. The question is: *Which* two primes? This doesn't feel like it should be a mind-boggling, brain-blowing challenge, does it? Surprisingly, this computational task rapidly veers out of control on a computer. As the numbers get larger, a point is reached, counterintuitively quickly, when even the world's most powerful supercomputers, such as China's Sunway TaihuLight with its almost 100 petaflops* of processing power,[8] display the likes of a blinking cursor or spinning wheel of death.

---

* 100 petaflops = 100,000,000,000,000,000 operations per second.

To get a feel for how factoring becomes so difficult so quickly, use the wondrous computer in your own brain to try to determine the two prime factors for each of the following numbers: 21, 35, 51, 91, 187, 247, 361, 391. Note how much longer you take (and how your brain increasingly hurts) as you progress through these simple examples.

Did you give up before the end? These are very small numbers in the general scheme of things! What about 83,803? Or, more significantly, 1,159,936,969? If you still have the piece of paper where you recently demonstrated your multiplication skills, you will have discovered that 1,159,936,969 = 23,189 × 50,021. Would you have ever, otherwise, been able to work it out? Given that the most obvious factorization tactic is to try dividing by the smallest prime (2), then by 3, then by 5, and so on, and given that there are 2,586 primes to try before you reach 23,189, I doubt it.[9]

Yet, on the cryptographic scale of things, 23,189 and 50,021 are very small primes. The primes recommended these days for use in RSA are more than 450 digits long.[10] Despite the magnitude of these primes, you can easily use a laptop computer to multiply them together. However, if you give the answer to the Sunway TaihuLight and ask it to find the two prime factors—blink, blink, blink, . . .

A Digital Padlock Based on Factoring

For its security, the RSA asymmetric encryption algorithm relies on the difficulty of determining prime factors. Without going into the specific details, the basic idea is as follows.

If you want to create a digital padlock, you first generate two enormous primes, each on the order of 450 digits long. These primes must be kept secret and essentially form your private key (in fact, your private key is something that can be worked out from these primes, not the primes themselves, but this is a detail). Only you can know what these two primes are.

You now multiply the two primes together. The approximately 900-digit result of this multiplication, alongside another value, is your public key. You can tell all your friends your public key; you can display it on your website; you can print it on your business card. It doesn't matter who sees your public key. The difficulty of determining the prime factors of a number means that, although the two primes are hardwired into the public key, nobody owns a computer powerful enough to work out what they are.

There's a little bit of undergraduate-level mathematics behind the full details of how RSA encryption really works,[11] but we can skip that. What's important is that anyone who wants to send you an encrypted message must first obtain your public key (which is relatively straightforward, since it's not a secret). To encrypt a message to you, they begin by encoding the plaintext as a number (there are standard ways of doing this). The encryption process essentially consists of a series of multiplications involving the plaintext and your public key.

Since computers can multiply numbers, encryption is doable. After you receive the ciphertext, you can apply the decryption process. Decryption is also doable, since it, too, involves a series of multiplications, this time involving the ciphertext and your private key. Anyone else who intercepts the ciphertext and tries to make sense of it needs to somehow undo the encryption process without knowing the private key. However, the only known method of reversing RSA encryption involves determining the two prime factors associated with the public key. Since no computer appears able to do this in a reasonable amount of time, RSA is believed to be a strong mechanism for providing confidentiality.

Some of the language that I just used merits further unpacking. First, I argued that no computer can determine prime factors *in a reasonable amount of time*. Note that I did *not* say that determining prime factors is *impossible*. Because it's not; it is possible. As noted earlier, trying to divide by every prime from 2 onward will eventually result in the two prime factors being found. Given the computers used today, however, the human race is more likely to face extinction, or at least to evolve into a different species, before all the possible prime factors of a 900-digit number have been tested.[12] Note that this argument is based only on the computers we use *today*; a more accurate security assessment needs to take into account the computing capability we expect to have in the future.

A perhaps more alarming issue is that it is only *believed* that no computer can find prime factors efficiently. The claim that determining prime factors is hard can be based only on what we know, not on what we don't know. A more accurate version of this claim is that, even with the smartest techniques known today, determining prime factors seems to be hard. This doesn't mean that some child genius, or indeed artificial intelligence, of the future won't come up with a new method of determining prime factors. Such a method would have catastrophic consequences for any technologies relying on RSA. For the security of many of the things we do in cyberspace today, the possibility just doesn't bear thinking about. Except it does, and I will, before the end of this book.

A Reliance on Hard Sums

While a design for a new symmetric encryption algorithm scratched on the back of an envelope is unlikely to end up passing the stringent security requirements of an AES competition finalist, neither might it be disgracefully insecure. As a result, many symmetric encryption algorithms have been proposed, particularly block ciphers. Although the majority have eventually been found wanting, a decent number have had no significant flaws found in their design and are, at least in theory, available for use.[13]

In contrast, there have only ever been a handful of serious proposals for asymmetric encryption algorithms. Creating a digital padlock requires rather counterintuitive properties. A computing task needs to be found that is easy to do and hard to reverse, but possible to reverse if you know a special piece of information. Not many such computing tasks are known.[14]

The concept of asymmetric encryption was first suggested in the 1970s. The idea was conceived independently in both the secret governmental world of GCHQ (Government Communications Headquarters) in the UK, and the public academic world of Stanford University in the US. The secret discovery came first, but in true British style, an idea that would help to drive a computing revolution in the 1990s was quietly set aside. Interestingly, in both cases only the *idea* of asymmetric encryption was initially proposed, not a concrete example of an actual asymmetric encryption algorithm. Indeed, in both cases it was other researchers who followed up on the initial idea by proposing how asymmetric encryption could be realized. Most extraordinary of all, in both GCHQ and academia, researchers seeking an example of an asymmetric encryption algorithm essentially came up with the idea of RSA.[15]

This tells us two things. First, finding examples of asymmetric encryption algorithms is difficult. Second, RSA is, in some sense, a "natural" solution. Mathematicians throughout history have extensively studied the problem of finding prime factors of a number, so it's an obvious computational task around which to try to design asymmetric encryption. Importantly, it's also a simple problem to understand, which helps foster wider confidence in RSA. As a result, RSA was by far the most important asymmetric encryption algorithm of the late twentieth and early twenty-first century, being widely adopted by almost all applications requiring asymmetric encryption.

That said, RSA is not the only asymmetric encryption algorithm you might come across. At least one other asymmetric encryption algorithm, based on a mathematical concept called *elliptic curves*, is used fairly widely. While the security of RSA encryption relies on the difficulty of computing prime factors, the security of elliptic-curve encryption depends on the difficulty of working out something called *discrete logarithms*.[16]

This direct linkage to a specific computational problem is both the great strength and potential weakness of asymmetric encryption. The security of a block cipher can be likened somewhat to building an intricate series of barricades. To access the plaintext, an attacker needs to tunnel under a wall, cut some barbed wire, choose which of several secret pathways to follow to the next barricade, climb over a slippery mound, swim a ditch, and fight their way through a field of head-high maize. To make the block cipher more secure, more barricades are stacked until it is believed that an attacker will not be able to fight their way through.

In contrast, the security of asymmetric encryption is connected to the computational problem around which the algorithm is designed. If the problem is well understood and widely believed to be difficult, which is the case for seeking prime factors, then confidence can be placed in the security of the associated asymmetric encryption algorithm. But if, for some reason, the computational problem turns out not to be as hard as everyone hoped, the algorithm is doomed. This situation is more like wearing a protective suit made from material believed to be bulletproof. If it really is bulletproof, we're fine. If it's not, beware of loud bangs.

This uncertainty, at least partly, explains why the world has been somewhat conservative about adopting new asymmetric encryption algorithms based on less well studied computational problems than factoring and computing discrete logarithms. At the end of this book I will look to the future and discover that this is a conservatism we're going to need to overcome as soon as possible.

Problems with Padlocks

As you've seen, creating a digital padlock is possible. Asymmetric encryption enables us to establish confidentiality on a link between our computer and a website we have never previously visited. We first obtain the public key of the website, which could, for example, be prominently displayed on its home page. The public key then enables us to send encrypted data to the website. Brilliant and elegant!

Alas, not quite. Unfortunately, there are two difficulties with this concept of a digital padlock, and they are both significant. Neither are showstoppers, but they are party poopers. The approaches used to address them dictate the ways in which asymmetric encryption is used today in real systems.

The first problem is inherent even in the physical scenario that I used to motivate asymmetric encryption. Remember the lawyer and the hyperactive courier? I argued that an efficient solution to sending a confidential physical letter to the lawyer was for the lawyer to first courier a padlock to you. There's a catch here that I glossed over. A courier shows up at your home, rings your doorbell, and hands you a package containing a padlock. This might work, but what happens if the courier is dishonest? After all, the courier could have discarded the lawyer's padlock and replaced it with one of his own. You lock the letter in the box, believing that only the lawyer can unlock it. Unfortunately, in reality, only the courier can unlock it. The problem here is that you cannot be sure the padlock you are given is the padlock that genuinely belongs to the lawyer.

This scenario is analogous to obtaining a public key from a website. Can you really be sure the public key on a website is the genuine one for communicating securely with the business you think owns the website? Maybe the website was hacked. Is this even the correct website for the business you think you're conducting a transaction with? The history of fraud and other evils in cyberspace is full of examples of innocent users failing to distinguish fake websites from genuine ones. Asymmetric encryption relies on the assumption that you have the correct public key before you encrypt anything. If this is in doubt, all bets are off.[17]

Addressing the problem of determining the validity of public keys means we must establish procedures for reliably linking people and organizations to public keys—a task that is surprisingly difficult. Like many technologies, cryptography works brilliantly until you involve human beings. We might be clever, innovative, creative, and eager to embrace new ideas, but we can also be lazy, selfish, manipulative, and naive. Manufacturing a secure padlock is one thing. Finding a reliable and honest courier service is quite another. I'll return to this thorny issue when I later consider how cryptography gets broken.

However, assuming we can find a way of placing some faith in the correctness of ownership of a public key, there is yet another problem, this time a technical one. All the asymmetric encryption algorithms we know today are slow. By *slow* I don't mean "like a snail." What I mean is this: *relative to symmetric encryption, asymmetric encryption is slow.* If you encrypt data using AES, then there is almost no delay. When you encrypt data using RSA, there is a slight delay, although you, personally, probably won't notice it. For example, RSA encryption on a laptop might take a few thousandths of a second. Who cares? Such a delay, however, matters to a website deluged by millions of requests for secure connections. All these thousandths of a second start to add up to real seconds, resulting in delays noticeable by humans.

Once upon a time, delays of seconds did not matter. In Laurie Lee's England of the 1920s, as portrayed in *Cider with Rosie*, Rosie would have merrily initiated an RSA encryption (had RSA been invented, and had she had any device on which to use it!) and then headed off to milk the cow and churn some butter, delighted to get back some ciphertext in an hour or two's time.[18]

In today's frenetic world, seconds are important. Stock prices rise and fall in the flutter of an eyelid. Consumers abandon shopping carts if their screen fails to respond promptly. Commuters hurtling through an automated ticket barrier don't have fractions of a second to spare before the travelers behind thunder into them. Everything needs to happen *now*. This need for speed applies particularly to something like encryption, which nobody really *wants* to do, but which is done out of necessity. This means that encryption had better be very, very fast.

The Best of Both Worlds

Symmetric encryption is fast, but it has a particularly challenging key-distribution problem. Asymmetric encryption is slow but conveniently allows encryption keys to be downloaded from websites. Each type of encryption has a positive feature that nicely complements the other. How can we harness the benefits of both types of encryption while overcoming their drawbacks?

If we return now to our favorite scenario, here's the answer: The courier delivers a physical padlock from the lawyer. You first take a conventional key (the type of key you use to both lock and unlock). You place the confidential letter in a box, which you lock with the conventional key. You then place the conventional key itself into a smaller box, which you lock with the lawyer's padlock. Now, you courier both boxes to the lawyer, who first opens the small box, and then uses the key it contains to open the larger box. This analogy is getting sillier, the more we complicate it, so instead, let's focus on websites, where this solution makes far more sense.

Here's the idea, which is often called *hybrid encryption*. You want to secure a confidential connection to a website. You first obtain the public key of the website. You'd love to use this public key to encrypt your data, but sadly, asymmetric encryption is slow. So, you generate a symmetric key and speedily AES-encrypt your data by using this key instead. You then RSA-encrypt the symmetric key by using the public key of the website. The process might, indeed, be slow, but all you are encrypting here is a small piece of data—namely, a symmetric key. At about 128 bits, this is likely to be much smaller than all the data you really want to protect over the communication channel to the website. Finally, you send the two items of encrypted data to the website. The website first (slowly) decrypts the RSA ciphertext to recover the symmetric key. The website then (speedily) decrypts the AES ciphertext by using the symmetric key. It's the best of both worlds.

When asymmetric encryption is used in everyday technologies, it is almost always deployed as part of a hybrid encryption process. Hybrid encryption is commonly used, just as described, to secure the connection between two computers, such as when a web browser connects to a website. Hybrid encryption is also typically used for securing email, where a symmetric key is asymmetrically encrypted by using the email recipient's public key, and then the body of the email is symmetrically encrypted by using the symmetric key.[19]

It's a Miracle; Get Me Out of Here!

Asymmetric encryption is miraculous; there is no better word to describe it. For centuries, cryptographers had to live with the symmetric-key-distribution problem. They did not imagine there would turn out to be a cryptographic solution to it. The idea of a digital padlock is revolutionary, as it enables strangers to secure communications with other strangers. In the late 1990s, asymmetric encryption enabled confidentiality to be provided to the increasing number of fledgling World Wide Web users. You could argue that the success of the web is, at least in small part, down to the miracle of asymmetric encryption.

However, the two issues identified earlier regarding the use of asymmetric encryption should never be underestimated. Reliably linking users to their public keys *is* a complex process. And asymmetric encryption *is* slow. Around the year 2000, asymmetric encryption began a rapid descent on the famous Gartner Hype

Cycle[20] from the "peak of inflated expectations" to the "trough of disillusionment," as the booming, and then busting, dot-com businesses realized that asymmetric encryption was a miraculous beast with a sting in its tail. What they didn't realize is that you should never use asymmetric encryption, even in its hybrid form, unless you truly must.

The core issue is this: the only times you genuinely need to use a digital padlock are when you are operating in a relatively *open* environment, where you don't have full control over the wider system (including the users and the underlying network). This is precisely the case when we browse the web, or send emails around the globe. If, on the other hand, you are in a *closed* environment, where you can exert control over the system, then you don't need asymmetric encryption at all.

Choose your favorite user of encryption technology. Choose banks. Mobile phone companies. Car companies deploying electronic keys. Issuers of smartcards for transportation ticketing. Controllers of a Wi-Fi network. In all these examples, there is an entity that has control over users of the system, the network being used, and, most importantly, a managed process by which symmetric keys can be distributed. Whenever you can control users and easily distribute keys, there is absolutely no need for asymmetric encryption. If you can encrypt quite happily by using only speedy symmetric encryption, this is precisely what you should do.

Asymmetric encryption should be regarded as a tool solving a very specific problem: how to share a secret with a stranger. Solutions to achieving this seemingly impossible task might well have their drawbacks, but what matters is that they're possible, and available to use whenever (but only whenever) we strictly need them.

5

Digital Canaries

The second core component of security, following confidentiality, is *data integrity*, which provides evidence that information has not been altered. During your typical day in the physical world, you relied on several integrity mechanisms, such as envelope seals and banknote holograms. However, you also relied on context to provide integrity, such as believing in the integrity of prescribed medication because it resembled genuine medicine and was sold to you by someone who looked like a pharmacist. In cyberspace, context is a far less reliable basis for assessing security. Ensuring integrity in cyberspace requires some tools.

The Unreliability of Data

When considering what is meant by *security* of data, people usually think about confidentiality. Since we all have secrets, the provision of confidentiality usually tops cryptographic shopping lists. But should it?

Consider your bank account for a moment. However much, or

little, is amassed there, you probably don't want everyone to know the balance. You might be concerned about unsolicited approaches from marketers, offering luxury products if it is high or loans if it is low. You might also be worried about others speculating about your lifestyle. It seems entirely reasonable to want to keep details of a bank balance confidential.

What if, however, you had to choose between keeping your balance secret or ensuring it was correct? Hopefully, you will never be faced with such a ridiculous choice, but what if you were? A mistakenly high balance might be welcome, but could you cope with one that was inaccurately low?[1]

Unlike the written word, data on computers is prone to becoming accidentally corrupted. This can happen at any time. Data can be accidentally altered while it is being either written to or read from memory. It can be damaged while being processed by an application, or when being transmitted over a network, particularly a wireless one. It can even change during storage, while simply sitting around doing nothing other than aging.

Much more concerning, however, is deliberate manipulation. Data is very easy to alter. In just a few seconds of unauthorized access, a "data vandal" can wreak havoc with a company's annual-return spreadsheet or change the ending of a novelist's latest work. Careful addition of a single zero to your bank balance might propel you to financial security; deletion of a zero could be your ruin.

Data integrity provides assurance that data has not changed since the point at which it was created legitimately. Crucially, a data integrity mechanism cannot prevent data from corruption. What a data integrity mechanism *can* do is indicate when it seems likely that the data has changed in some way.[2] A data integrity mechanism can serve as a warning, just like a canary falling off its perch in a Victorian coal mine.[3]

Degrees of Integrity

The concept of data integrity is not as clear-cut as confidentiality, since there are nuances. As a result, a range of different security mechanisms provide data integrity.

One nuance is the severity of the perceived threat to integrity. Some security mechanisms identify only accidental changes to data, but not deliberate changes.

Another nuance is whether data integrity should include identification of the source of the data, meaning whoever created the data in the first place. We expect such assurance with many everyday uses of data. For example, when you transfer money, you expect the recipient to be sure it's you making the transfer. Rather than providing assurance that data has not changed since the point at which it was legitimately created *by whomever*, this assurance is stronger, verifying that data has not changed since the point at which it was legitimately created *by an identifiable source*. For this reason, this stronger notion of data integrity is sometimes known as *data origin authentication*.

A third nuance concerns the entities to which data integrity should be demonstrable. In many situations, such as when one person sends a file to another, only the recipient needs the ability to verify the integrity of the received data. For digital contracts, however, it is extremely important to be able to demonstrate data integrity to someone else as well, such as a judge resolving a future dispute.

Coming up soon are examples of data integrity mechanisms appropriate for providing these many different degrees of data integrity.

Fake News

It is worth noting that while data integrity is all about making sure information is correct, in the sense that it is unchanged, this is not the same as a consideration of whether information is *true*.

To appreciate the difference, think about the concept of *fake news*,[4] where misinformation is presented as fact. It's easy for a journalist to fabricate a fake news story and release it into the wild jungles of online media. Fake news is well suited to cyberspace, since the lack of physical context surrounding a digital news story makes it harder for people to determine its truth.[5] A fake news story might well be an untrue story, but as long as readers receive the fake news story that the journalist intended to write, I would argue that data integrity has been preserved. A data integrity mechanism enables readers to detect whether any changes have been made to a story since it was originally created. In this sense, a fake news story can be shown to be correct (as written), even though it is untrue. In other words, readers can be assured that the story is precisely as fake as the day it was penned.

This confusion between truth and correctness arises because the traditional concept of *integrity* has different meanings.[6] One definition is "the quality of being honest and having strong moral principles," both of which seem to be somewhat lacking in the world of fake news. Honesty and morality are qualities best assessed by human beings, not machines—which means that cryptographic data integrity mechanisms can do little to support them. However, the term *integrity* also means "the state of being whole and undivided." This is the notion of data integrity that I'm considering here. Cryptography can be used to detect whether data has remained whole and undivided since the moment it was created. Ironically, this means that cryptography can be used to protect, but not prevent, fake news.

Integrity or No Integrity, That Is the Question

To confirm the whole and undivided nature of data, we first need an accepted source of the "truth" about what state the data *should* be in. Do we have data integrity or not? Where should we turn for the answer?

The most obvious option is to identify a specific source we can trust enough to act as an integrity reference point. If your friend says something is true and you trust your friend, then you tend to believe in the integrity of what they tell you.[7] Another common approach is to defer trust to a higher authority of some sort. If you're not sure how to spell a word, for example, you might consult an authoritative source, such as the *Oxford English Dictionary*.

In reality, matters of trust are often less clear-cut. For example, if you download software from a website, you will often see some data displayed on the website called an *MD5 hash*.[8] This value enables you to verify whether the software you download is exactly the same as the software the website thinks it's making available to you. This verification process works only if you "trust" the website—not just that the website has good intentions, but also that it has good cybersecurity processes in place and could not possibly have been hacked. The website is offering itself directly as a point of trust for providing integrity. Trust me, or don't trust me; the choice is yours.

Most cryptographic mechanisms for supporting data integrity rely on specific sources of trust. These sources are typically linked to keys. I'll explain shortly how this works for a few different cryptographic data integrity tools. However, there is another possible reference point for data integrity. Rather than relying on a specific source, we might regard something as correct because *everyone says so*.

In 2016, the relatively lowly English soccer team Leicester City confounded the pundits, and almost everyone with even a passing interest in the sport, by winning the English Premier League. But how does anyone know *for sure* that this happened without having been there when Leicester City was awarded the trophy? Should you believe it to be correct because you read about it in a newspaper? Or saw it on television? Or because your trusted Uncle Angus told you? Should you contact the English Premier League directly to seek confirmation in writing? No, most people accept that Leicester City won the trophy because they consistently heard about it from everyone, and everywhere. Rather than relying on a specific source for the integrity of this information, we rely on the fact that all the sources agree. Leicester City was the winning team because the world agreed it to be so.

There is an increasing interest today, for a variety of reasons, in integrity mechanisms that use a more global type of reference point. These include technologies such as Bitcoin (more on this shortly), which enables the integrity of a digital currency without the need for a single trusted bank.

Integrity Checks

One way of checking correctness of information is to seek corroborative evidence. Determining the integrity of information during a court case usually means seeking information from multiple sources, then establishing which aspects of this information are agreed upon. Scientists determine the integrity of experimental results by rerunning past experiments. Ideally, we make up our minds about the integrity of information by evaluating evidence received from different sources, all of which we trust to varying degrees.

In many situations, however, we cannot afford the luxury of seeking supporting evidence. When our web browser is communicating with an online store, there is no alternative source of integrity to consult regarding the integrity of the data being exchanged. Decisions about the integrity of data need to be made immediately, on the basis of the current communication session, and need to be resolved efficiently, without delay.

Think, for a moment, about how we approach this problem in

the physical world. An example of important written information requiring an assurance of integrity is a transcript listing a job applicant's academic qualifications. In extreme circumstances, a potential employer could personally call the applicant's teachers in order to directly confirm the validity of a transcript, but this would be an inefficient means of verifying integrity.

More commonly, the transcript bears an official stamp or seal.[9] The real purpose of the seal is to indirectly state that *the integrity of the information on this piece of paper is assured by the creator of this stamp*. The stamp itself is small, containing much less information than the transcript, yet it vouches for the integrity of the entire document. The employer only has to scrutinize the stamp and, if satisfied, can assume that the information in the rest of the document is likely to be correct.

In many other situations as well, a small piece of information is used as a verifiable representation of the integrity of a larger piece of information. Perhaps the most widespread means of providing assurance of integrity is the handwritten signature. Interestingly, signatures are used in several different security contexts, but perhaps the most common use of a handwritten signature is to vouch for the correctness of a longer document. When you sign a letter or a contract, you are really confirming that you're happy with the integrity of the information contained therein. Anyone relying on the contents of the signed document will assume, on checking the validity of your signature, that you were happy with the document's integrity at the time of signing.

Stamps and handwritten signatures are compact seals of approval of the integrity of a written document. However, their effectiveness also relies on the materiality of the document itself. An unscrupulous job seeker could try to modify the grades on a transcript and hope that a potential employer will not notice the change. Likewise, a fraudster could sign a letter and then later modify the contents. Cumbersome legal procedures, such as keeping duplicate copies of a contract at a lawyer's office, are perhaps the only means of countering such fraud.

The main problem with compact assurances of integrity, such as stamps and signatures, is that they have a static form; they don't change each time they are used. The stamp on the transcript is precisely the same on both the original transcript and the one the fraudster modified. The handwritten signature on the letter remains the same, no matter how many modifications are subsequently made to the contents. Indeed, in the physical world, it's hard to imagine how it could ever be otherwise. This is one reason context is so important to the provision of integrity in the physical world.

The digital world presents an amazing opportunity to do much better. Information in the digital world is represented by numbers. Since numbers can be combined and computed, it is possible to do something in the digital world that's unthinkable in the physical world: we can design means of assuring the integrity of data that are not just compact and easy to check but also *dependent on the data itself*. In other words, we can produce a digital stamp on a transcript that will cease to be valid if the transcript changes. While we lose physical and contextual integrity in cyberspace, we can use data integrity mechanisms that are more sophisticated than those of the physical world.

The Evil Librarian

Let's start with a simple data integrity mechanism designed for information consisting of numbers. The *International Standard Book Number* (*ISBN*) is a universally recognized means of uniquely identifying a published book (in fact, you'll find one printed on the jacket of this book).[10] For example, the must-read title *Dachshunds for Dummies* by Eve Adamson (John Wiley, 2007) has the ISBN 978-0-470-22968-2. The ISBN identifies this title precisely. Should anyone else choose to write a book with the same title, it will have a different ISBN. The ISBN is particularly useful for librarians and booksellers, who can be sure they are accessing the correct title by referencing it.

That said, "Dachshunds for Dummies" trots off the tongue, and keyboard, much more readily than does "978-0-470-22968-2." Even if you spell *dachshund* incorrectly, most computer spellcheckers will automatically rectify your error. You probably won't be so fortunate if you mistype one of the digits of 978-0-470-22968-2. For this reason, each ISBN has a built-in integrity check, designed to make it likely that errors will be detected. While the first twelve digits of an ISBN form the unique serial number, the purpose of the last digit is to verify the integrity of the first twelve. This final *check digit* is computed from the others by means of a simple calculation: add the digits in positions 1, 3, 5, 7, 9, and 11 to 3 times the sum of the digits in positions 2, 4, 6, 8, 10, and 12; then subtract the last digit of the answer from 10. The answer is the thirteenth digit of the ISBN. Check our example: $(9 + 8 + 4 + 0 + 2 + 6 = 29)$ is added to $3 \times (7 + 0 + 7 + 2 + 9 + 8 = 33)$ to get 128, whose last digit is 8, which, subtracted from 10, is 2.

Whenever an ISBN is entered into a computer, the thirteenth digit can be automatically recomputed. If an error has occurred in any of the first twelve digits, it is highly likely that the result of the calculation will not be the thirteenth digit of the ISBN. For example, if the fourth digit in our example is mistakenly entered as 1 rather than 0 (resulting in the incorrect 978-1-470-22968-2), then the check-digit calculation yields 9. Since the thirteenth digit is 2, something is wrong. There is a small chance that an error could go undetected and, unluckily, the check digit would compute correctly anyway (for instance, if we made two mistakes and wrongly entered the ISBN in our example as 978-1-470-22968-9), but in most cases errors are flagged.

Importantly, the ISBN is not designed to cope with intentional errors. If a manipulative librarian decides to make deliberate changes to an ISBN, then this mechanism offers no protection. For example, suppose a librarian changes the twelfth digit of the ISBN in our example from 8 to 7. If this is the only change, then 978-0-470-22967-2 will be flagged invalid because the check digit does not compute correctly. However, anyone can compute what the thirteenth digit should be, so an evil librarian simply has to calculate what the correct check digit is for the twelve digits 978-0-470-22967. Since 29 plus 3 × 32 is 125, whose last digit is 5, the correct check is 10 − 5 = 5. To avoid detection, the librarian should thus alter the final digit to 5, resulting in a valid ISBN of 978-0-470-22967-5, which happens to correspond to the sister title *Chihuahuas for Dummies* (perish the thought that such a horrendous crime might ever be committed).

Librarians are generally not evil, as we all know. The ISBN integrity check mechanism is extremely lightweight and designed to cope with only accidental errors. Nonetheless, we rely on numbers like the ISBN for many aspects of our lives, and including a lightweight integrity check as part of these numbers is better than having no integrity check at all. Integrity check digits computed using similar calculations are included in the likes of credit card numbers, social security numbers, and the numbering system for European locomotives.[11]

Toward Stronger Integrity Checking

The check digit included as part of the ISBN is very basic. However, integrity check digits share a few important features with stronger cryptographic integrity mechanisms that are worth commenting on.

Most fundamentally, unlike stamps on a physical transcript, check digits serve as compact representatives of the data being protected because they are computed *from the data itself.* For a particular data item, such as a book number, there will be only one correct check digit. However, because there are many fewer possible check digits (only ten) than book numbers, there will inevitably be many ISBNs with the same check digit. This is not a problem per se, but it is the reason that an erroneous ISBN might not be detected, since an incorrect number's check digit could compute correctly. Adding extra check digits could reduce this risk, but at a cost of reduced efficiency (in this case the ISBN would have to become longer). Likewise, cryptographic integrity mechanisms sometimes allow such a trade-off between security and efficiency.

It is worth reemphasizing that check digits don't *guarantee* the detection of errors; rather, they detect errors with a known probability of success. Nor do they prevent errors from occurring (realistically, no mechanism based solely on a data computation would be able to do this) or correct errors that have occurred. These observations apply just as readily to cryptographic integrity mechanisms.

Unfortunately, check digits have a property that is highly undesirable in stronger cryptographic integrity mechanisms. Because the ISBN check digit is computed simply by adding multiples of the first twelve digits together, it is straightforward to predict how changes to the first twelve digits of an ISBN will affect the value of the check digit. This means it is easy to determine how the check digit changes if, for example, we alter one digit of an ISBN or add two ISBNs together. It also makes it very easy to predict when two ISBNs will have the same check digit.

That said, booksellers and librarians don't care about the predictability of check digits. Nor does anyone ever want to add two different social security numbers together. Check digits work just fine for these examples.

The Cryptographic Swiss Army Knife

Integrity check digits are the "store brand" data integrity tool. If you are willing to pay a little bit more, where the currency in this case is a combination of complexity to implement and time to compute, then the integrity mechanism you should use is a cryptographic *hash function*.[12]

A hash function inputs data of any length and outputs a short integrity check for this data known as a *hash*, or *digest*. Somewhat unusually for a cryptographic tool, no key is involved in this process. Just like a check digit, a hash is much smaller than the underlying data and is computed directly from it. If we want to detect whether a file has suffered accidental changes while being transmitted across a network, for example, then the sender of the file can first compute a hash of the file. The sender transmits both the file and its hash to the receiver. In order to check the integrity of the file arriving at the destination, the receiver computes the hash of the received file and compares it with the sent hash. If they match, the receiver concludes that the file did not accidentally change en route.

Where a hash differs from a check digit is in the process used to compute it. While a check digit is calculated in a very simple way from the data, a hash is computed by a cryptographic algorithm. Recall that I previously compared cryptographic algorithms to blenders. This analogy works quite well for encryption, since an encryption algorithm mixes a set of ingredients into a blended form with no loss of mass. In other words, the ciphertext is a randomized version of the plaintext but remains (approximately) the same size as the plaintext. A hash function also blends the underlying data, but it outputs something much smaller than the data itself. A hash function is more like a juicer: the ingredients are pulped, but what is eventually output is much smaller in quantity than what was put in.

The main advantage of a hash over a check digit is that the cryptographic process used to compute a hash obscures the connection between the data and its hash. In contrast to a check digit, changes to the data being hashed result in unpredictable changes to the hash. Even if you change just one bit of information in a file, for example, the resulting hash will bear no apparent relationship to the hash of the original file. In addition, unlike for check digits, it is extremely difficult to find two different files with the same hash.

Hash functions turn out, perhaps surprisingly, to be one of the most useful tools that cryptographers have ever invented.[13] Unlike encryption, hash functions aren't much use on their own. However, they are used in all sorts of other ways to support more complex cryptographic operations. For this reason they are sometimes described as the "Swiss Army knives" of the cryptographic tool kit.

For starters, they can be used as a sort of cryptographic "glue," to bind different data items together. Because hashes of data are essentially unpredictable, hash functions can also be used to generate random numbers. Since they compress data, hash functions are often used as central components of other cryptographic mechanisms, including digital signatures, to improve efficiency. Another use of hash functions is to protect passwords. And the Bitcoin cryptocurrency scheme is built from multiple uses of hash functions, which means that hash functions help to drive the economy of the Dark Web. I will discuss all three of these latter uses of hash functions in due course.

Integrity in the Presence of Malice

Unfortunately, a hash function on its own cannot provide integrity in any situation where there might exist an attacker capable of deliberately changing data. While an evil librarian is unlikely to gain much from manipulating ISBN check digits, the same cannot be said for an attacker who observes a file and its hash being sent over the internet. If the attacker wants to change the file without detection, all they need to do is modify the file and then compute the new hash for the modified file. When the receiver retrieves the modified file, this new hash will be verified as being correct. This situation arises because, just as anyone can compute the check digit of an ISBN, anyone can compute a hash of some data.

There are two approaches to dealing with this problem. The first is to make sure the hash is communicated to the recipient of the file by means that an attacker cannot manipulate. Suppose you want to send a file to a friend. First, you email the file to your friend. Your friend then telephones you and asks what the hash of the file should be. Since a hash is a short piece of data, it is easy to read over the phone. Your friend then checks the hash of the file they received from you and compares it with the hash you've just told them.

In many situations, however, it is either impossible, or at least inconvenient, to employ a separate means of protecting the hash of some data. In these cases the idea of a hash function needs to be adapted to make it impossible for everyone to be able to compute the hash of some data. Fortunately, there is an obvious way of doing this. Remember, a hash function is a cryptographic algorithm that simply compresses data into a smaller hash *without using a key*. The solution to preventing everyone from being able to compute a hash is thus to include a key, somehow, in the hash computation process.

On the Origin of Data

The next product upgrade in our data integrity store is a *keyed hash function*. Suppose you and your friend agree on a secret cryptographic key. You append this key to a file and then compute a hash on the combined file and key. You now send the file (without the appended key) and this hash to your friend, who appends the shared secret key to the received file and recomputes the hash. If this recomputed hash matches the sent hash, your friend concludes that the file is unmodified.

This process should protect the file against an attacker who makes deliberate changes. The attacker can intercept the file during transmission and make any changes they like. What they cannot do is compute a new hash that will be valid for the modified file. Although they know the contents of the modified file, since they don't know the secret key they cannot compute the hash of the key appended to the modified file. Any alteration of the file will thus be detected.

The basic idea here is excellent. Alas, however, it does not quite work, for a variety of technical reasons, none of which I will bore you with here.[14] In practice, special hash functions are used that incorporate the secret key in a more sophisticated manner than simply appending it to the data. These hash functions are more commonly referred to as *message authentication codes*, or *MACs*. One of the most popular MAC algorithms is known as *HMAC*[15] and is built directly from a hash function (hence the "H"). Other MAC algorithms are built in different ways, including *CMAC*,[16] which is built from a block cipher (hence the "C").

In fact, MACs are one of the most important cryptographic mechanisms used to protect everyday applications in cyberspace. The reason MACs are so useful is that the introduction of a key not only enables protection against an attacker who deliberately manipulates data but also strengthens the level of integrity protection to enable the provision of data origin authentication, which I introduced earlier. When the receiver of a file successfully verifies a MAC on the file, the key also provides evidence of the source of the file itself. Whoever computed the MAC on the file must know the key, and the receiver knows that the specified sender is the only other entity who knows this key. The file must thus have originated with the specified sender.

You have undoubtedly used MACs many times without realizing it. They provide data origin authentication (and hence data integrity) for bank transactions, card payments, Wi-Fi communications, secure web connections, and many other applications. Indeed, it is relatively unusual to symmetrically encrypt data without also adding a MAC of the data. Confidentiality and data origin authentication are so commonly required together that a number of special *authenticated-encryption* modes of operation of a block cipher have been proposed in order to both encrypt and compute a MAC on data in one go. These authenticated-encryption modes are increasingly popular and are likely to become default choices in the future.[17]

Anything You Can Do, I Can Do

In terms of providing strong data integrity in the form of data origin authentication, you would think, surely, that MACs are the perfect tool. They can detect the tiniest changes to data, whether accidental or deliberate; they can be used to determine the sources of data; they are widely deployed in many of the most vital applications of cryptography. What's not to like?

A MAC provides the receiver of a file with assurance that the file is unmodified. This is sufficient assurance for most applications in the real world. But it's not the strongest notion of data origin authentication that we could ever ask for. To see why, ask yourself this question: Does a MAC allow *anyone* to be sure that a file is unmodified and came from the specified sender?

Consider using a MAC to protect a digital contract being sent over the internet. The MAC allows the receiver to be confident that the contract came from the sender. But what happens if the sender and receiver later argue about the contract? If they call in a third party to resolve their dispute, the receiver might present the MAC as evidence that the sender originated, and by default agreed to, the contract. The sender, on the other hand, could argue that no such thing happened and that the receiver created the contract and its MAC without any involvement of the sender. This problem arises because of the symmetric capabilities of both sender and receiver. The third party can certainly conclude that the file originated with a holder of the MAC key. But which one? Was it the sender or the receiver who created the MAC? They both have the key, so either could have computed it.[18]

This example reveals an inherent problem with using symmetric cryptography to provide data origin authentication. Because a symmetric key is shared between, in this case, a sender and receiver, anything one can do, the other can also do (not better, just equally). Therefore, the receiver can confirm the sender as the originator of a received file, but the MAC does not enable anyone else to be so sure.

Thus, MACs are excellent cryptographic mechanisms for providing data origin authentication, unless you want to demonstrate the authentication to someone else. If this yet stronger ability to provide data origin authentication to a third party is required, some asymmetry needs to be introduced into the keying arrangements of a MAC so that only one person has the ability to create a MAC. Fortunately, you already know all about asymmetric keys—don't you?

Digital Anti-padlocks

Most physical integrity mechanisms have a property not provided by check digits, hash functions, or MACs. Sealing a document with an official stamp or writing a signature on a contract might not prevent anyone from subsequently modifying the contents, but both of these integrity-assuring mechanisms provide undeniable evidence of who created them. The stamp on an academic transcript is an authoritative linking of the transcript to the issuing institution. A handwritten signature on a contract essentially states: "The signatory was here." In contrast, anyone can compute a hash, and anyone who holds the symmetric key can compute a MAC.

The ability to link an integrity check to a unique source is sometimes called *nonrepudiation*, because it prevents whoever created an integrity check from denying they did so. Nonrepudiation is the premium version of data integrity, and it is needed wherever an attacker could manipulate data and where the source of data may need to be proved to a third party. These are strong requirements and call for a powerful cryptographic tool.

Nonrepudiation requires a cryptographic mechanism producing an integrity check that anyone can verify as uniquely linked to the creator of this check. If you think about it, this is almost the opposite of what a padlock does. Remember that a padlock allows anyone to lock something up in such a way that only the key holder can unlock it. What is required is a sort of "anti-padlock," which allows only a key holder to create an integrity check that anyone can verify.

Can we use our knowledge of how to build digital padlocks to create a digital anti-padlock? The good news is that we can. The concept of a digital padlock, enabled by asymmetric encryption, can be adapted to create a cryptographic mechanism for providing nonrepudiation. Since this mechanism links data to a unique source in much the same way that a handwritten signature does, it is known as a *digital signature*.

Digital Signatures

The principle behind a digital signature is to use an asymmetric encryption scheme somehow in reverse. By *reverse*, I mean swapping the roles of the public and private keys. In asymmetric encryption, the sender encrypts their plaintext data by using the widely available public key of the recipient, who then decrypts the ciphertext by using the private key that, critically, only the recipient has access to. To create a digital signature, the sender *encrypts* the data by using their private key, and the recipient verifies the integrity of the data by *decrypting* it using the sender's public key. Only the sender can create this digital signature, because the signature relies on the sender's private key. Anyone can verify this digital signature, because verification requires the sender's public key, which is not a secret. This is the idea anyway.

In practice, things don't work quite so simply. For one thing, most asymmetric encryption algorithms need to be slightly reworked to facilitate this reversal. Perhaps more fundamentally, however, digital signatures are an integrity check, not a means of providing confidentiality. Since the data is not secret, it is reasonable to assume that whoever needs to verify the digital signature will also be sent the data itself. An integrity check should thus accompany the underlying data, just as a handwritten signature is an addition to a document. If the data were simply "encrypted" in order to produce a digital signature, the signature would end up being a "ciphertext" as large as the data itself. Compared to the compactness of check digits, hash functions, and MACs, digital signatures would be clumsy and inefficient.[19]

The crucial observation is that to create a digital signature, it is not necessary to "encrypt" (a better verb in this case is *sign*) the entire data. It suffices to sign a compact representation of the data—something small that depends on every bit of the data. If you've been paying attention, you should remember that we have a great cryptographic tool for this! A digital signature is typically created by first using a hash function to generate a hash of the data; then this hash is signed using the sender's private key. Anyone can then verify this digital signature by first computing a hash of the data and then checking whether the "decryption" (let's call this *verification*) of the digital signature results in the same hash. If it does, then whoever is verifying this digital signature learns several things. Let's go through them one by one.

First, the verifier is assured of data integrity. If an attacker has modified the file in transit, the hash of the modified file will be different. The attacker can compute this modified hash, but what the attacker cannot do is produce a new valid digital signature on the modified hash, because they don't have access to the original sender's private key.

Second, the verifier is assured of data origin authentication. The only circumstance in which the digital signature could be "decrypted" via the sender's public key to the correct hash of the data, is when the sender's private key was used to create the digital signature. So, the verifier knows that the data originated with the sender.

Third, we have nonrepudiation. Anyone can verify this digital signature, since all that's needed is knowledge of the sender's public key. Importantly, the sender cannot deny signing the data, since only they know the private key corresponding to the public key used to verify the signature.

Game, set, and match.

Digital signatures are top-drawer data integrity mechanisms; in terms of the strength of the data integrity offered, they really can't be beaten. However, you don't get the best without paying for it. Hopefully, you'll have already noticed that using digital signatures costs the same as asymmetric encryption. First, we have the problem of determining the validity of public keys, in this case public verification keys. Second, digital signatures are slower to compute than are other data integrity mechanisms, because they rely on computations similar to those of asymmetric encryption.

Just as for asymmetric encryption, it is probably wise not to deploy digital signatures unless you really need the strength of integrity they offer. As noted, MACs suffice for many of our daily uses of cryptography. In some sense, digital signatures are to integrity what asymmetric encryption is to confidentiality. In the types of open environments where we tend to need asymmetric encryption, we also tend to need digital signatures. For example, most secure email systems give users the options to encrypt email (using hybrid encryption) and/or digitally sign email. Your Wi-Fi, on the other hand, uses symmetric encryption and MACs because it's a closed environment where sharing keys is simple.

Ironically, however, one of the most significant uses of digital signatures is to address the primary problem with using them in the first place! Digital signatures form an important component of the most common method for validating public keys, whether those are public keys to support asymmetric encryption or digital signatures. More on this later.

Digital Signatures Are Not Signatures

The term *digital signature* conjures up the image of some sort of futuristic cyber hand signing digital data. It is tempting, therefore, to claim that digital signatures are the cyberspace equivalent of a handwritten signature. Tempting, maybe, but the analogy is treacherous. While they indeed share certain features, digital signatures are very different beasts. Perhaps they should really be described as *nonrepudiation mechanisms*, but that doesn't have the same ring to it!

In many respects, digital signatures are superior to handwritten signatures. By far the strongest advantage of digital signatures is that they are computed directly from the underlying data. If the data changes in any way, then the digital signature changes. Therefore, *every version* of a document has a different digital signature. Sure, you have your "I'm in a hurry but you don't really need to read this" signature for the delivery driver, and your "I can do really nice handwriting when I want to" signature for your passport application, but in general, handwritten signatures vary only slightly from document to document.

Another positive feature of digital signatures is that they can be reproduced with precision. If the same data is signed a second time using the same signature key, then the same digital signature will be produced. This feature has the potential to provide strong evidence in a court case. Handwritten signatures do not have such absolute accuracy, and sometimes they require experts to determine whether two handwritten signatures are the same.

However, there are some disadvantages of digital signatures. Most significantly, digital signatures rely on a cryptographic infrastructure, which requires good key-management practices and reliable technology. If there are weaknesses in this potentially costly infrastructure, then digital signatures become ineffective. For example, if someone manages to steal another person's signature key, the thief will be able to create digital signatures appearing to originate from the victim. Handwritten signatures require no such infrastructure and are, quite literally, portable.[20]

The Wisdom of the Crowd

It's time to think again about who, or what, we rely on in order to determine data integrity. Is this data correct or not? What helps us decide? We can verify the MD5 hash of a downloaded file by checking it against the one displayed on a website. This verification works, as long as we trust the website. We can verify the MAC on a received file by locally recomputing it. This verification also works, as long as we trust that the sender is the only other person with a copy of the key used to compute the MAC. We can verify the digital signature on an email message by applying the appropriate public verification key to the signature. This verification works as well, as long as we trust that the public verification key is the one belonging to the sender of the email.

All of these examples rely on some very specific trusted roles. The effectiveness of the MD5 hash requires trust in the implementation and management of the website. The MAC requires trust in the distribution and secrecy of MAC keys. The digital signature requires trust in the distribution and secrecy of private signature keys, as well as trust in the authenticity of public verification keys. What do we do when trust of this type is lacking?

One option, which I introduced earlier when considering Leicester City's year of glory, is to trust the integrity of some information if *everyone* says it is correct. We must be a little careful with this argument, however, since much depends on who "everyone" really is.

The citizens of North Korea, for example, are subject to very strict information control. They have few means of communicating with the outside world, and their ability to freely exchange information with one another is limited through press control, surveillance, and travel restrictions. North Korean citizens are also required to tune in to daily radio broadcasts from the governing regime. As a result of these measures, they undoubtedly believe many things that most of us would not, largely because what everyone agrees on is the result of an information control operation, tightly managed by their political leaders.[21]

North Korean state broadcasts may not always be factually correct, but because the government controls information within the country's borders, the political messages received by North Korean citizens do have integrity in the sense that the information North Koreans absorb is unchanged from the information they were intended to receive. The fact that everyone receives this same information, and most citizens believe it, helps to reinforce integrity. The *truth*, as noted during our discussion on fake news, is quite a different matter.

Societies more democratic than North Korea are not always in a much better position to assess the correctness of information.

Traditional media, social networks, and search engines are all known to create *filter bubbles*, where experiencing a consistent message from multiple sources influences a user's beliefs.[22] A user may come to trust in the integrity of some information because "everyone" seems to say it is correct. In these examples, however, the notion of "everyone" is often restricted in ways that the user may not appreciate or understand. Readers of a particular newspaper often have shared political beliefs, social networks are self-selecting because most people choose friends with whom they share interests, and search engines are driven by algorithms heavily influenced by a user's previous behavior (search history, visits to web pages, etc.). "Everyone," in these instances, might be only a few people and will most likely be unrepresentative of the population at large.

The web encyclopedia Wikipedia provides another interesting example. You read it on Wikipedia, so it must be correct, right? Some people scoff at the very idea that anyone would trust Wikipedia, while others regard it as a reliable source of information. The important thing to recognize is that almost anyone can create and subsequently edit a Wikipedia web page. The information displayed on Wikipedia evolves over time through a process whereby users read, contest, and correct the entries. It could thus be argued that a Wikipedia page eventually represents a consensus of what "everyone" says. The problem with this argument is that some Wikipedia pages are scrutinized extensively, while others are rarely visited. For each individual page there is thus a very different notion of who "everyone" is. As a result, the quality of information on Wikipedia is highly variable.[23]

As we've seen, the perceived wisdom of the crowd comes with hazards. The correctness of information depends very much on which crowd is used. Nonetheless, especially when there's no central point of trust on which to base integrity, the idea of using a global reference point for integrity is highly compelling. Does anyone doubt that Paris is the capital of France?

We cannot always depend on "everyone" being sufficiently excited about some particular information that its integrity becomes globally recognized. Nor can we always wait for integrity to grow over months and years in the manner of information on a Wikipedia page. So, how do we use this idea of a global reference point to support the integrity of day-to-day information, such as precisely how much bitcoin you own? How do we find a crowd whose wisdom can be universally relied on?

You Are Your Bank

How much money is in your bank account? Don't tell us! But consider how you establish the integrity of this number (whether positive or negative). How do you really know your correct bank balance? Whether you like it or not, the ultimate answer to this question is that you need to trust your bank. The bank is the authoritative source of your balance. You are welcome to dispute the details, but frankly, if you don't trust your bank, then you should move your money elsewhere.[24]

For some types of information, however, there might not be any single authority we can trust. Or we might not *want* such a central point of trust to exist. An example is the Bitcoin digital-currency scheme.[25] Its main purpose is to emulate the perceived freedoms of cash. These include the lack of necessity of having a relationship with a bank, and the relative anonymity of conducting transactions. Digital cash can be facilitated by a single central bank, but all users need to trust this bank.[26] The alternative, which Bitcoin uses, is to simulate the role of a bank without actually having one.

What do banks do anyway? In terms of currency management, the most important role of a bank is to serve as a trusted witness of transactions into and out of your account. In doing so, your bank acts as the definitive source of truth regarding the integrity of your account balance. It's not easy to be a trusted bank; the bank has to work hard to establish the necessary authority to have such trust placed in it. To accomplish this status, a bank must engage in multiple interrelated activities, including managing the bank brand, adhering to financial regulations, subjecting itself to financial audit, managing personnel, and using numerous physical and cybersecurity mechanisms (banks are avid users of cryptography).[27] All this effort ultimately protects the financial information that the bank oversees. You can think of this information as being represented by a *centralized ledger*, containing the accounts of the financial data of all the customers for whom the bank is responsible.

If we cannot have a bank witnessing transactions, then who will do it? The answer is "everyone." The idea of a *distributed ledger* is to do away with the need for an official centralized version of (well, anything really, but let's stick to banks for now) all financial transactions and replace it with an entirely open ledger that everyone keeps a copy of. In other words, you don't need a bank, because you, and everyone else who has money, *are* the bank.

At first, this seems a fairly mind-blowing idea. Every Bitcoin user maintains their own version of the ledger of all transactions, which represents the true state of Bitcoin finances. While a distributed ledger is simple to propose, the practical challenge is clear. This concept will fly only if everyone agrees on the ledger's contents.

Clearly, it's not possible for every Bitcoin user to sit down each night with the entire day's Bitcoin receipts (accompanied by a large glass of wine) and check the validity of each transaction in order to establish which bitcoins have gone where. Fortunately, computers are more efficient at this type of task. It remains, however, a formidable challenge to develop and manage an agreed-on, but distributed, version of the Bitcoin ledger. The solution that Bitcoin deploys is ingenious, and it's built almost entirely from cryptography.

The Bitcoin Blockchain

Bitcoin uses the idea of a *blockchain* to facilitate a distributed ledger. It's worth emphasizing that although distributed ledgers and blockchains are often treated as being synonymous, simply because of the high profile of Bitcoin, which uses the latter to enable the former, a distributed ledger does not necessarily have to be based on the use of a blockchain.

The users of Bitcoin form the Bitcoin network. A Bitcoin user maintains as many Bitcoin "accounts" as they like. Each account is identified by a *Bitcoin address*, which is just a cryptographic public key that can be used to verify digital signatures. Importantly, while a Bitcoin address is unique to its owner, it does not explicitly identify the owner. This masking provides Bitcoin's anonymity. A Bitcoin transaction consists of a digitally signed statement (cryptographically signed with the private signature key of the payer) that a certain amount of bitcoin should be transferred from the payer's Bitcoin address to the payee's Bitcoin address.

Each time a Bitcoin transaction is conducted, the details are made available to everyone else on the Bitcoin network. You can think of Bitcoin, therefore, as a whole bunch of individual transaction statements that are all flying around the Bitcoin network. Since new transactions are continuously being made, at a rate of one every few seconds, the challenge is to manage all this information in a sufficiently organized manner that every user can agree on what has been happening.

A *block* is a collection of Bitcoin transactions (roughly the equivalent of ten minutes' worth of Bitcoin payments). Whenever a new block is formed and approved, it is "glued" to the previous blocks, thus forming an ever-growing *chain* of blocks. This growing collection of blocks, bound to one another, forms the Bitcoin ledger that everyone has to agree on. Since each block consists of data, digital glue is required to join the blocks. Digital glue? With luck, you may recall that binding data together is one of the many important uses of a hash function, the great Swiss Army knife of cryptography.

It would be anarchic if every user in the Bitcoin network were constantly forming new blocks and trying to bind them simultaneously to the blockchain. How would a single agreed-on version of the blockchain ever emerge? The cunning solution to this problem is to make the forming of a new block rather difficult, but not impossible. The effect is that new block creation is slowed down to approximately one block every ten minutes.[28] This pace is fast enough to ensure that transactions find their way into the Bitcoin ledger fairly soon after they are conducted. However, it is also slow enough that a new block has time to propagate through the Bitcoin network and become accepted by the majority of Bitcoin users before the next block is created.

The process of creating a new block, which lies at the heart of Bitcoin, is called *mining*. This term reflects the fact that forming a new block takes considerable effort. The mining task is to collect some floating Bitcoin transactions that are not yet in a block of the current blockchain, verify that they're in the right format, and then cryptographically bind them together. As part of this process, the miner must attach some data known as a *header* to the start of the new block. This header includes an indication of which block the miner believes is currently at the end of the blockchain (and to which this new block should be attached), as well as a cryptographic "summary" of all the transactions in the new block. However, the header also must include something else, and this something else is what makes new blocks so hard to mine.

Recall that hash functions are cryptographic "juicers," which compress data that is input into a smaller number (a hash). If you hash some data, then make even a tiny change to the data, the hash of the modified data will have no apparent relationship to the hash of the original data. In other words, the hash of some data appears to be randomly generated. Therefore, if you want to find some data with a *particular* hash value, the only thing you can do is keep trying to hash different things until you get lucky.

This is precisely the challenge presented to a bitcoin miner. The miner must include a randomly generated number in the block header that results in the hash of the entire block header having a particular property. As soon as the miner has gathered a sufficient number of transactions to form a block, they have to try out different random numbers in the hope that one of them will result in the header of the new block having the right hash. This is a somewhat frantic process, because all around the Bitcoin network, rival miners are also attempting to form a new block. The first to do so will "win." But what's the prize?

Nobody sane would expend the considerable resources required to mine a new block just for the fun of it. Mining involves not just trying out the odd random number or two, but trying out millions and millions of them. So many, in fact, that you must have considerable computing power to be a successful bitcoin miner.[29] A miner who successfully creates a new block is thus paid a financial reward—in bitcoin, of course.

Once a new block is formed, the users of the Bitcoin network are all notified, and each user adds the block to the version of the blockchain that they currently believe to be correct. Each user is able to check the validity of this new block and can be reasonably sure that their version of the blockchain is the same as everyone else's. They are only *reasonably* sure, though, because it's possible for two different blocks to be found at approximately the same time by different users of the network. In this case, two different versions of the blockchain will be forming, each extended by a different block.[30]

This problem is unavoidable, but resolvable. As soon as the *next* block is found, one of these two versions of the blockchain will become further extended. Whenever a user of Bitcoin encounters two possible different versions of the blockchain, and one is longer than the other, the user rejects the shorter one. In practice, every Bitcoin user can be almost certain that within half an hour of being conducted, most transactions are included in a universally accepted version of the blockchain (only the very end of the block-chain might vary, and any differences will soon be sorted out).

Blockchain This, Blockchain That

Bitcoin is a wonderful cryptographic construct. An account is associated with a cryptographic key, transactions are digitally signed statements, formation of new blocks requires the solving of a cryptographic challenge, and the Bitcoin blockchain is crypto-graphically bound together by hash functions. This is why Bitcoin, alongside the hundreds of other similar digital-cash technologies now in circulation, is often described as a *cryptocurrency*.[31] How-ever, it's important to remember why we are discussing Bitcoin. The Bitcoin blockchain is, first and foremost, a security mecha-nism for providing data integrity—in this particular case, the integrity of Bitcoin transactions.

The Bitcoin blockchain is not without its flaws. For one thing, the amount of computer time and energy required to form new Bitcoin blocks has raised serious questions about whether bitcoin is an environmentally sustainable currency. From time to time, the cost of mining Bitcoin blocks exceeds the value of the new currency generated. As noted earlier, however, using a blockchain the way Bitcoin does is not the only way a distributed ledger can be instantiated.

Distributed ledgers have much wider potential applications than just to digital cash. They could, at least in theory, be used to protect any data that is not confidential but requires absolute integrity. Instead of Bitcoin transactions, the data protected in a distributed ledger could concern any form of formal record keeping, such as legal contracts, supply-chain details, or government registers.

As we have seen, distributed ledgers have the distinct advantage of providing data integrity without requiring a centralized point of trust. However, we should be cautious about rushing to place everything in a blockchain, or any alternative form of distributed ledger. The architecture of blockchains and distributed ledgers is very different from the traditional architecture, in which integrity is provided by the data being secured in protected, centralized databases. Distributed ledgers represent a significant change to the way most data is protected today. While distributed ledgers are a fascinating idea, the purposes (beyond Bitcoin) for which they ultimately prove effective as data integrity mechanisms remain to be seen.

The Integrity of Integrity

It's easy to underestimate how important integrity is to the functioning of our daily lives. In the physical world, integrity is often provided implicitly. In cyberspace, however—a place where data is relatively simple to manipulate—the explicit provision of data integrity is paramount.

Data integrity mechanisms cannot stop data from being altered, but they can warn us when such modification has occurred. Which data integrity mechanism you choose depends on what you realistically imagine could go wrong. Friendly environments, such as the book cataloguing of a public library, require only lightweight data integrity mechanisms. Hostile war zones (like the internet!) require strong data integrity mechanisms such as MACs and digital signatures. If you have no single place you can go to establish the trust necessary to provide data integrity, then you can consider deploying a distributed ledger.

Data integrity mechanisms work. For this reason, as long as appropriate data integrity mechanisms are used, criminals do *not* tend to manipulate the value of a bank transfer as you make it, or change the wording of an email as you download it from your web-mail provider, or remove previous transactions from the Bitcoin blockchain. They *don't* do these things because they *can't* do these things, at least without being caught out.

However, data integrity mechanisms can only tell you that data has not been altered since the point at which it was created by . . . a MAC key holder or a signature key owner or the possessor of a Bitcoin address private key—whoever they are.

Good cybercriminals don't waste their time trying to manipulate integrity-protected data. A far better strategy is to appear to be someone they're not. If you are fooled regarding the identity of someone you're talking to in cyberspace, then the integrity of any data they subsequently send you is worth very little. As valueless as a bitcoin, perhaps, when all you want to know is heads or tails.

6

Who's Out There?

I t's important to be able to keep secrets and have ways of recognizing changes to data. However, neither of these capabilities addresses what is perhaps the greatest peril in cyberspace. Every day, thousands of people are fooled because of how easily cyberspace facilitates impersonation. Use of cryptography alone cannot address this problem, but there are ways in which it can help.

Woof Woof

A famous 1993 cartoon from the *New Yorker* is often cited to illustrate the issue of anonymity on the internet.[1] It features two dogs, one of which is sitting at a computer, paw on keyboard, looking down at his companion and barking: "On the internet, nobody knows you're a dog." It's a great cartoon. Isn't it funny (both "ha ha" funny and "peculiar" funny) that dogs could be using the internet without our knowing! However, the unexpected success of this cartoon is that, in an apparently harmless way, it captures a sinister truth.

Dogs, clever though they are at retrieving bits of sausage from under the sofa, lack any ability to wrestle with a keyboard. Much as we'd really love them to be, dogs are not on the internet. So, who is?

Consider this story: Chloe is twelve, and a big fan of a social media platform that allows users to easily record and share short video clips of themselves on their phone, dancing to short excerpts from their favorite artists. All her friends have accounts, and they post almost every day. Fortunately, Chloe is a sensible girl and has parents who are aware of some of the potential dangers of social media and the internet. They have advised her to share her videos only with people she regards as friends in the physical world. She does not permit "friends of friends" to see her work, because Chloe has been warned that her friends may not be as careful as she is about who can see videos. All seems good until Chloe's account is audited one evening by her parents.

"Are you just sharing with your friends?" they ask.

"Yes," replies Chloe.

"Are these all friends who you really know in real life?"

"Yes. I mean, almost," says Chloe. "There's this dog, and it's really funny, and it has its own account, so I'm following it. The videos are great; do you want to see one?"

"In a moment, perhaps," reply the interrogators, "but are you friends with this dog?"

"Well," confesses Chloe, "I was following the dog, and the dog asked if it could follow me, so I said yes. I mean, it's a dog, and its videos are really, really funny; this is my favorite one . . ."

Here's the real truth behind the *New Yorker* cartoon. On the internet, not everyone thinks carefully enough about the implications of the fact that you're *not* a dog.

The Need to Know Who

Think about the things you do each day in cyberspace. Before you do many of them, you have to, either explicitly or implicitly, answer a question such as: *Do you have an existing account?* Or: *Have you registered?* Indeed, even first accessing cyberspace typically requires answering such a question. Have you ever wondered why?

For one thing, most things we do in cyberspace relate somehow to a commercial service. Cyberspace might be an intangible, abstract concept, but it's facilitated by equipment, networks, and services operated by human beings, which all cost money to provide. Commercial providers of these components often need to determine who's out there so at least they know where to send the bill.

Even seemingly free services in cyberspace must be paid for. We almost always have to register for free services, and then pay for them by submitting personal data and exposing ourselves to commercial advertising. These service providers need to know who's out there so that they can correlate the data they're collecting, and the ads they're pitching, to the profile of the user of the service.[2]

Another reason for determining who is out there is that a great deal of information in cyberspace is intended for a restricted audience. Few workplaces would function smoothly if everyone always knew everything. In sensitive sectors of government and the military, strict control of access to information is particularly important. Hopefully, you have configured the privacy settings of your social media account to control who sees what. In cyberspace, wise data owners need to know who is out there before deciding whether to release data to them.

So, given that dogs such as wire-haired dachshunds are not in cyberspace, who *is* out there? The safety of many activities in cyberspace depends on how accurately we can conjure up an answer. The problem is that in cyberspace, getting an accurate answer is very hard. Chat rooms, social media networks, and online dating services would be much safer environments if we could reliably answer this most vexing of questions.

Human versus Machine

The process of *entity authentication* attempts to determine who is out there. The word *entity* is deliberately abstract. The different ways that entity authentication can be provided depend, at least in part, on whether the entity is controlled by the pulsing of a heart, or by a clock driving the processing of a microchip.

Let's consider one way that entity authentication can be provided in the physical world. A traveler approaches a border control point. The immigration officer must determine whether to permit the traveler to enter the country. The traveler is asked for, and presents, a passport.

A passport is a document containing a range of physical security mechanisms. Modern passports feature holograms, special ink, and computer chips, and they include biometric information about the person to whom they are issued.[3] These mechanisms are designed to make the passport hard to forge, and to bind the passport to the intended bearer. The passport is a token, which is the result of a fairly laborious administrative process, designed to make it hard for passports to be inappropriately issued to the wrong people. The immigration officer is likely to admit the traveler if the passport seems to be valid and the traveler appears to be the person it was issued to. Importantly, it is the *combination* of both human and passport that the officer takes into consideration. Border control officers are just as unlikely to admit a traveler who cheerily announces their name but has no passport, as they are to approve a person who submits a valid passport but is wearing a paper bag over their head.

In cyberspace, it is easy enough to create tokens that play a role similar to passports. You are undoubtedly familiar with presenting the likes of passwords, bank card numbers, or other security tokens in order to access services in cyberspace. These were almost certainly acquired after some administrative process, sometimes as minimal as supplying an email address, designed to link you to a particular service. In cyberspace it is relatively easy to present the token, but much harder to demonstrate the presence of the person to whom the token was issued. Alas, we've all got paper bags over our heads in cyberspace.

Of course, entity authentication is not always so important. Border control deals with admitting real human beings, with all their flesh and flaws, into the country. It matters who they are. For much of what we do in cyberspace, it matters less. A web retailer might love to know who is using its website so that it can profile visitor browsing behavior, but it can derive value from visitor data without accurately identifying every human being who views its web pages.

Note that precisely which entity matters is not always obvious in cyberspace. A mobile phone company wants to know where to send the bill. The entity the phone company wants to authenticate is thus the account holder, who is not necessarily the human using the phone, as is true when a parent buys a phone for a child. The mobile phone owner, on the other hand, does not want an opportunistic stranger who discovers a lost phone on the seat of a train to be able to use that phone. The entity that the owner is more concerned about is thus the person who uses the phone.[4]

Even more confusing is our own perspective on who is out there. We're often under the impression that humans directly communicate with one another in cyberspace, with computers merely acting as humble facilitators. This is, however, largely an illusion.

Everything that happens in cyberspace is really an interaction involving computers, in most cases one computer communicating with another. The perception that human beings are at the end of any interaction in cyberspace is slightly dangerous, since often they are not. Even if your phone is in your hand, it is capable of doing all sorts of extraordinary things without asking you. Most of these are benign, even desirable, such as checking for updates or retrieving messages from a server. However, your phone certainly has the potential capability, if you're not careful, to be used to clean out your bank account and wire the balance to a stranger.[5]

Even when humans are involved palpably in a digital communication, a problem arises from the fact that (for now, at least) human beings are not computers, and computers are not human beings.[6] Every time you interact with cyberspace, you are not strictly at the end of the line of communication. Your computer is.

To see this, consider just about the simplest possible interaction with cyberspace. You're sitting in front of your computer typing an email. You do so by forming your thoughts into words, and then transferring these words to your computer by pressing letters on a keyboard. You are certainly present during this interaction and are undoubtedly communicating directly with your own computer. What could possibly go wrong here? Surely, *you* are out there.

In most cases, everything will be fine, but much *could* go wrong. After you have pressed the symbols on your keyboard, your computer takes over. You, the human, are no longer part of the process. A whole sequence of invisible operations takes place, beginning with matching keyboard characters to digital codes, before this data is submitted for processing by applications running on the device. If your computer is working properly, then everything is rosy. But if your computer has been infected by *malware* (an undesirable program such as a computer virus), then your computer could do some things you do not intend. For example, your computer could store what you type and send this information to someone who is conducting surveillance of your activities.[7] It could also suppress or alter the information you type, resulting in a different email being sent. You may well have been there, but it's what your computer does that really matters.

The fact that a computer could behave differently from the way a human user expects, or indeed conduct tasks that the human user is unaware of, is something attackers often exploit. We cannot prevent this gap between humans and devices, so we have to manage it somehow. One method that you will undoubtedly have encountered is the *captcha* (a term that derives from the phrase "completely automated public Turing test to tell computers and humans apart"). Captchas are used to test the presence of a human by setting tasks that machines are currently less effective at, such as deciding which alphabetic characters are suggested by an almost illegible squiggle, or which of a series of photographs features a building that could plausibly be a shop.[8]

Love them or loathe them (the smart money is on the latter), the need for captchas is symptomatic of the gap between human and machine. At the very least, we need to keep this gap in mind whenever we're wondering who is out there.

"Hello from the Other Side"

Try screaming "Hello, who's out there?" into cyberspace. Even if you hear back a faint "It's me," what value can you possibly place in an answer from the void?

Any comprehensive answer has two important components: the first relating to identity, the second relating to time.

Just as discussed for physical security mechanisms, the only way to distinguish one entity from another in cyberspace is to equip the entity with a special capability distinguishing it from the crowd. There are many different ways this can be done, and these vary, depending on whether the entity you have in mind is a human or a computer.

Humans can be given a tangible object. To test presence, a human could be asked to demonstrate that they have this object. In cyberspace, objects can be things such as smartcards, tokens, and even phones, the possession of which represents evidence of the human's presence. Of course, the biggest problem with using only possession of objects for entity authentication is that objects can be lost or stolen.

Humans are, themselves, objects. The field of *biometrics*[9] is based on extracting characteristics of a human and using them to provide entity authentication. Biometrics vary in their effectiveness, but some have become well established. Air travelers and convicted criminals will be familiar with fingerprinting and automatic face recognition, both of which can also be deployed in cyberspace. Biometrics are less easily lost or stolen, at least directly from the humans they represent.[10] However, biometrics are simply physical measurements converted into digital values. If the digital values are compromised in some way—for example, the database storing them is stolen—then serious problems arise. You've been asked to change your password many times, but what could you do if someone asked you to change your fingerprint?

By far the most common approach to entity authentication in cyberspace is to base it around the special capability of knowing something that others don't. This technique can be used to authenticate either humans or computers. A significant advantage of the latter over the former is that computers tend not to have problems remembering complicated things, such as strong passwords or cryptographic keys. Most of the ways cryptography can be used to support entity authentication are based on secret knowledge being the distinguisher.

Because these different approaches to entity authentication all have their own strengths and drawbacks, it is not uncommon in cyberspace to require that multiple techniques be applied together. A classic example of *two-factor* entity authentication is to present both a bank card (tangible object) and a PIN (secret knowledge) to a point-of-sale terminal in a store. In this case it is really the *presence* of the bank card that's being tested for, since the card contains a chip that stores the cryptographic keys used to protect the transaction. However, the knowledge of the PIN provides an extra layer of authentication by demonstrating that the human who knows the PIN is also present. Two-factor authentication thus attempts to authenticate two different entities at once: the card and the human owner. Unfortunately, banks are not so thorough when we buy things online without the use of a point-of-sale terminal.[11] As a result, this type of *card-not-present* transaction is where most fraud happens.[12]

Note that entity authentication is not always explicitly about *identification* of who is out there. For some applications, it suffices to establish that whoever is out there is *authorized*[13] to do something. For example, many cities now support payment for public transportation using "pay-as-you-go" smartcards that have pre-loaded value. The ticket reader on the train needs only determine whether there is enough credit on the card to open the barrier and permit the traveler to pass. It is not strictly necessary to *identify* the traveler, although some systems may do this for other reasons, such as journey profiling.

The second component to answering our scream into cyberspace relates to time. If you shout "Hello, who's out there?" into a deep, dark chasm and hear back "It's me," then is "me" a living, breathing person? Or might it be a recording? One of the challenges facing investigators of kidnappings is to determine whether hostages are still alive when videos of them are released. Since this issue can be just as important to the kidnappers, it used to be common practice for such videos to feature hostages holding newspapers to prove that the video was recorded after a displayed date.[14]

This inclusion of evidence of *liveness* can be just as important in cyberspace. In this aspect, biometrics have a built-in advantage over the likes of passwords. While a victim can be forced to reveal their password and then be thrown down a well, good biometric technology requires a response to "Who's out there?" from a living body.

However, as previously discussed, entity authentication is more often required for a device than for a human. Since information from the past can easily be recorded and then *replayed* in cyberspace, what is really needed is that an answer to the question "Who's out there?" include evidence that the response is genuinely new. This is often referred to as evidence of *freshness*, rather than of liveness. Intriguingly, as will be discussed shortly, cryptography can be used to provide evidence of freshness without explicitly incorporating clock-based time.

Strong entity authentication mechanisms should thus indicate freshness, as well as establish either identity or authorization (or both). However, the most common entity authentication mechanism that you use every day in cyberspace—supplying a password—does not do so. This is just one of many reasons why it is so flawed as a means of establishing who is out there.

Agonizing Passwords

In cyberspace, it seems impossible to do anything without supplying a password. Passwords have become the default means of offering some kind of evidence of who might be out there. When you log on to a website (or indeed a computer or an app), you typically need to supply a username and a password. Passwords are liked because they appear to be an easy means of providing entity authentication. Passwords are loathed because, in many ways, they're not. Elizabeth Stobert has referred to *the agony of passwords*, and we all instinctively know what she means.[15]

The real reason you should be wary of passwords is that they are very weak entity authentication mechanisms. You are probably familiar with some of the criticisms of passwords, but it's worth identifying their two most critical flaws.

First, passwords are relatively easy for someone else to acquire. An attacker could get hold of your password in many different ways. An attacker who happens to be physically nearby could simply watch you type a password into a computer—a process some-times referred to as *shoulder surfing*—or perhaps obtain it from a note stuck on the wall of your office. But even if the attacker is not nearby, there are still plenty of options. Sometimes passwords are passed across a network such as the internet in the clear (in other words, unencrypted). A clever attacker thus simply needs to watch your communications in order to obtain your password.

An attacker could also try to guess your password, since pass-words are rarely chosen well. The vast majority of passwords are either easily acquired personal information or simple modifications of dictionary words. Worse, many technologies come with well-known default passwords that a user is supposed to change at the earliest opportunity, but in practice often they don't know how to do that, or they don't care or bother to.

Second, passwords have longevity. Since passwords are a bit of a nuisance to set up, you tend to use a password for an extended period of time. Indeed, for many applications you may have never changed your password. Since passwords don't incorporate any notion of freshness, if someone else acquires your password, you're potentially in a whole lot of cyber trouble.[16]

One password might be useful to an attacker, but many pass-words form a treasure chest. One place where large numbers of passwords potentially exist is on the computer of someone who asks you for a password. For example, an online retailer might ask you to log in by supplying a password before you complete a purchase. This arrangement is convenient for them, since they can store your personal data (which could include payment-related data) and link your visits. This means that somewhere on the retailer's computer system reside a whole bunch of passwords. The database contain-ing these passwords presents a lucrative target for attackers to seek out. And they do, sometimes successfully.[17]

Fortunately, any respectable organization using passwords to authenticate its customers will not maintain a database containing passwords, thanks to cryptography.[18] All the organization really needs is evidence that whoever is logging in knows their password. Cryptography enables the organization to verify this without requiring knowledge of the password itself. To do so, what is necessary is a database containing some means of checking whether supplied passwords are correct—in other words, a database of integrity checks for passwords.

Hash functions are candidates for this purpose. Here's the idea: When you first create an account, you supply the organization with a username and password. The organization hashes this password and stores the hash next to your username in a database. Whenever you log in, you resupply the username and password. The organization hashes the offered password and then checks its database to see whether this hash matches the one next to your username. If it does, then it's you.

For this purpose, a hash of a password is as good as a password. If the supplied password is not correct, then its hash will not match the one in the database. Importantly, however, anyone who manages to access the database will not learn the passwords from the hashes stored there. When passwords are managed in this way, *nobody else* knows your password—even the administrators of the password system. Notice that if you forget your password, nobody is able to retrieve it for you and you're forced to reset it. Hash-protected passwords are like days. You can always start a new one, but you can never be given back one you've carelessly lost.

Revenge of the Reference Book

Username—easy. Password—um . . . While this might be you trying to log on to one of your accounts in cyberspace, it is also the conundrum faced by an attacker. In the absence of anything better, at this point the attacker might as well just guess.

The beauty, and ultimate ugliness, of passwords is that they are memorable. The need for your brain to readily recall a password tends to place a limit on how complex a password can be. As noted earlier, the *Oxford English Dictionary* contains less than 300,000 words. Even allowing for clever morphs of words using other keyboard characters to replace letters, on a cryptographic scale of things there are only so many possible passwords that the attacker needs to try.

Here's a real attack on passwords: The attacker establishes a list of candidate passwords. The obvious stuff, such as *password, test, abc123*, and *justinbieber*, can go at the beginning, followed by the 300,000 dictionary words, and then all their close relatives, such as *ju5t1n81e8er*. An attacker with nothing but guesswork to go on just starts firing away. However, an attacker who has much more usefully managed to access a database containing hashes of passwords starts hashing away. This latter, more powerful attacker is in a position of strength. All the attacker needs is for one of the candidate passwords on the list to hash to the same value as *one* of the hashes in the database. As soon as this happens, the attacker knows a username and password that will let them log on to the system. This is called a *dictionary attack*, since the list used is essentially a dictionary of passwords.

Dictionary attacks can't be prevented. Using passphrases instead of passwords can make them harder to carry out, but do you do that? Good on you if you answered yes. Passphrases are harder to remember and take longer to type, and the chances of making an error as we enter them is much greater than for passwords. Many ingenious methods have been proposed for choosing more complex passwords,[19] but the majority of password users simply won't follow any advice that makes life even harder than it already is, regardless of the potential security reward. If you can't stop something from happening, the next best thing is to discourage it. This brings us to one of the most surprising uses of cryptography that you engage with on a daily basis.

Cryptography is a complete nuisance, as any computer system engineer will tell you (although *nuisance* is probably not the precise word they would use).[20] Conducting cryptographic operations costs time and energy. If a systems engineer can get away without using cryptography in their system, then they certainly will do so. Security is the enemy of performance, they will tell you. Cryptography slows systems down. Now *there's* an idea!

Most cryptographic algorithms are designed to be computed as quickly as possible. However, to protect against a dictionary attack there is a distinct advantage of using a cryptographic tractor rather than a Ferrari. Instead of using a normal hash function to store hashes of passwords, a deliberately "slow" hash function could be designed that takes, say, one second longer to compute than a typical password hash takes (an operation that would normally take a tiny fraction of a second). Slowing down the experience of logging in by one second would be barely noticeable to a system user. However, if an attacker had a password dictionary of 64 million passwords (dictionaries of this size are available for purchase on the internet), then deliberately delaying each hash computation by one second would slow the time required to perform a complete dictionary search by 64 million seconds, which is about two years. To proceed, the attacker would need to be either extremely patient or very determined.

Cryptographic algorithms designed for the purpose of behaving like slow hash functions are sometimes known as *key-stretching algorithms*.[21] Organizations often deploy several layers of different key-stretching algorithms to protect their passwords, making life even harder for an attacker with a password dictionary. Use of these algorithms does not make passwords any stronger as a means of providing entity authentication, but key stretching helps to deter one of the most dangerous ways of defeating passwords.

Too Many Passwords

Passwords for this, passwords for that. Make sure this one is at least eight characters, make sure that one includes upper- and lowercase characters and at least one number or other symbol. It's frustrating, isn't it? Worse, a typical "top ten" internet safety tip is that you should make sure all your passwords are *completely different*.

There's a good reason to have different passwords for each of the various websites and applications you log on to. Suppose, instead, that you use one password for everything. No matter how wonderful this password is, the security of your only password depends on how well the system with the poorest security looks after it. Your bank may well do an excellent job at password management, but does the website of the small campsite you booked online last year care quite so much about security?

Are *your* passwords all well chosen and distinct? Really? Truly? If you make claims to such password sainthood, then either you're deceiving yourself or cryptography is helping you.

The best option for anyone struggling with a proliferation of passwords is to deploy a *password manager*. These come in many flavors, including both hardware and software versions, but the basic concept is the same. Password managers address the three core challenges of choosing different strong passwords for each application you use, and later remembering them. A good password manager will generate strong passwords on your behalf, securely store them, and then automatically recall them whenever they are required.

Generating and recalling strong passwords is much simpler for a computer to do than for a human, since a computer is unburdened by cognitive biases and has almost flawless memory. A password manager securely stores all these strong passwords in a local database and then encrypts the database with a key. So far, so good.

There are two issues to resolve now. First, whenever you're asked to supply one of your passwords, the key to decrypt the database is required. Where is this key? Second, the purpose of all these passwords is to provide entity authentication of you, the human user. A password manager consists of software running on your computer (and may also include a piece of hardware). How do these stored passwords get linked to you?

Different password managers deal with these two questions in different ways, but arguably the most common answer, to both, is to use a password—what else? You activate the password manager by entering a password, and the key to the database is computed from this password. A password to protect passwords; has anything really been gained?

To an extent, it has. The challenge of managing many passwords has been reduced to the difficulty of managing one password. This is a much easier problem to deal with. Yes, the password to the password manager should be strong. Yes, you need to be able to remember it. Yes, you must make sure this password is kept secure. But it's only *one* password.

Of course, it is also a single point of failure. If your password manager is compromised, then everything is lost. Some password managers thus deploy stronger entity authentication techniques to link you to your passwords, including biometrics or the use of two-factor authentication. However they work, the bottom line is that password managers use encryption to make passwords simpler to manage, but they don't really make the fundamental problems of passwords go away. Password managers treat the symptoms but not the cause.[22]

Masquerade on Masquerade

Whether you like it or not, passwords are not going away anytime soon as a means of providing entity authentication. Because passwords are entrenched as a security mechanism but also weak, they tend to be the point of vulnerability exploited by so many of the frauds in cyberspace.[23]

Recall that I previously mentioned several different ways an attacker could acquire your password, assuming you're not using a state-of-the-art password manager. There is another, perhaps even more straightforward, technique: the attacker could simply ask you for it.

This strategy might seem unlikely to succeed, but *phishing* attacks work in precisely this way. A phishing attack is often launched under the cover of an official-looking email from the likes of your bank or system administrator, asking you to do something for security reasons, such as resetting your password. If you proceed, then in most cases you follow a web link taking you to a spoof website run by the fraudster, which will first ask you for your current password (a common requirement to enable a password reset). You type in your password and then . . . bye-bye password, or credit card number, or whatever other important security information the criminals were seeking.[24]

Getting hold of your password can be the start of endless mischief in cyberspace, since, from the perspective of any website or application relying on your password for entity authentication, *you are your password*. The fraudster can now do anything your password enables you to do.

Matters would be made even worse if you were subject to a phishing attack on the password you use for your password manager. We'd all like to imagine that the type of savvy person who deploys a password manager would not fall for such a trick. Suppose, however, that you receive an email purporting to be from the company who sold you the password manager technology, asking you to enter your password in order to activate an upgrade of the password manager software (a request that no reputable company would send you). You wouldn't enter it, would you? If this catastrophe unfolds, then whoever is behind the phishing attack can now potentially do *everything* you can do in cyberspace.

It is worth reflecting on the underlying anatomy of this type of fraud. An attacker conducts a masquerade (as, say, your bank) in order to perpetrate another masquerade (as you). The core problem arises through your failure to authenticate the source of the original phishing email and/or any website you are subsequently directed to. You are possibly fooled by (weak) data integrity mechanisms that made the original email appear genuine (logos, use of appropriate language, plausibility of the request, etc.). The problem, in our cryptographic parlance, is that a semblance of data integrity is not sufficient to provide strong entity authentication. Because of your failure to ask "Who's out there?" during the phishing attack itself, the next time one of the websites you visit asks "Who's out there?" the answer might be you, even when you're not.

A friend of mine opened a bank account in the US in the 1990s and was asked what password he wanted. To my friend's great surprise, the teller wrote his response down in a notebook. Let's be frank; nobody manages passwords like this anymore. At least, they shouldn't! Thanks to cryptography, nobody other than you should ever know your passwords. You should enter passwords only when you are absolutely sure you're talking to a legitimate service in cyberspace.

Perfect Passwords

I've been giving passwords, deservedly, quite a hard time. But now let's take an entirely different approach. If we could reinvent the world, what would a perfect password look like?

A perfect password should be unpredictable, in order to be as resistant as possible to guessing and dictionary attacks. In other words, it should be randomly generated. A perfect password should be used only for logging in to one system and not shared across multiple applications. A decent password manager can facilitate both of these requirements. However, a perfect password should also be of no use to an attacker who acquires it, by whatever means (shoulder surfing, use of a keylogger, observing the network the password is sent over, etc.). Hmm . . . how could a perfect password be devised?

It's certainly possible to take a step in this direction. No doubt you have occasionally, perhaps far too often, been asked to *change* your password. This is another of the frustrating aspects of password management. You have just succeeded in memorizing a complex password with all those funny characters, and then some well-meaning security expert recommends you *change* it? Bothersome maybe, but regular password change reduces the risk of some threats to passwords, such as dictionary attacks, as well as potentially limits the impact of an already compromised password (which you might not even be aware has been compromised).[25] Use of a password manager can make regular password changes less painful, but it doesn't make the process entirely painless. Nor does it create a perfect password, since a stolen password is still useful to an attacker until the next time it is changed.

Suppose an attacker observes a password. The only way to make this information completely useless to the attacker is to ensure that this password is never, ever used again. A perfect password must therefore not just be used to authenticate to only one system; it must be used only *once* to do so. Every time a perfect password is used, it must then be changed.

Fortunately, cryptography can be used to enable perfect passwords. Indeed, there is a very good chance you use a perfect password every time you authenticate to your online bank. It's worth knowing how this idea works in practice.

The first important aspect of a perfect password is that it should be generated randomly. True randomness is difficult to achieve, since it commonly requires a physical process, such as the tossing of a coin or the rolling of dice. More practically, computers extract true randomness from white noise produced by, for example, the oscillations of a transistor. However, as previously observed, one of the fundamental properties of any good cryptographic algorithm is that its output *appears* to be randomly generated. A cryptographic algorithm can never produce true randomness, since there is one sense in which the output of a cryptographic algorithm is predictable. If you encrypt the same plaintext, using the same key, and the same encryption algorithm, you always get the same ciphertext. Similarly, if you hash the same data, using the same hash function, you always obtain the same hash output. By contrast, when you toss a coin, the outcome can never be predicted.

However, this predictability of a cryptographic computation does not matter if we make sure that the data input into a cryptographic algorithm is different every time. Different input to a cryptographic algorithm should result in different output. Ensuring different input each time the algorithm is computed thus means that the output of a cryptographic algorithm can be used as a perfect password.

Here's the idea behind the use of perfect passwords to authenticate to your online bank: the technologies that banks use vary. One fairly common approach is to issue customers a small device called a *token*.[26] Some tokens just have a display screen, while others resemble a pocket calculator. Whatever form of device is used, the bank is really equipping you with a cryptographic algorithm and a key. The algorithm is common to all customers of the bank, but the key is unique to you. The bank maintains a database of all keys issued to customers.

When you authenticate to your bank, the token computes a perfect password by using the algorithm and the key. The token displays the password on the screen. You send this password to the bank, which then repeats the computation, using its own copy of the key. If the two outputs match, the bank is convinced that it's you out there. More precisely, the bank is sure that whoever is out there must have access to the cryptographic key that was sent to you. If someone else has stolen your token, then there could be a problem, so many banks also incorporate other layers of authentication (for example, some tokens themselves ask "Who's out there?" by requesting that you first enter a PIN).

The passwords produced by the token are cryptographically generated, hence random enough. The algorithm is normally specially designed for generating random passwords, but there is no reason why, at least in theory, it could not be an encryption or MAC algorithm. What is most important is that the input supplied to the algorithm is used for only one password computation. The next time the bank asks you to authenticate, the input to the algorithm should be different. In this way, every time you log in to the bank, the password will be different.

Note that the input to the algorithm on your token does *not* have to be secret. The only secret in this system is the key that you share with your bank. What must be true is that the input is known to both you and your bank, and this input changes each time the bank asks who is out there. What do you and your bank both know that changes every time you're asked to authenticate—that changes every *time*?

Many tokens include a clock and work by using the current time as the input to the cryptographic algorithm. Token technologies without a keypad use this technique, typically computing a perfect password every thirty seconds or so and then displaying it on the screen. The bank customer sends the bank the current displayed password as evidence that they have the key (token) currently in their possession. Of course, clocks do stray over time, but the lag on an individual token can be monitored and compensated for by the bank.[27]

The time is just one example of a piece of nonsecret data that can be known at the same time by two entities in different corners of cyberspace. If it's not possible to use clocks, one alternative is to maintain a notion of artificial time by using a counter. In this case, the bank and token each use the counter to keep track of the number of times that authentication using the token has occurred. The latest count is used as the shared nonsecret input to the algorithm. After each authentication attempt, both the bank and the token increment the counter so that they share a new nonsecret value.

This is also how many remote keyless entry systems for cars operate. The "bank" in this case is your car, and the "token" is your car key fob. Both the car and the key fob share a cryptographic algorithm and a secret key. They also each maintain a counter. Every time you press the button to open your car, the key fob computes and wirelessly transmits a perfect password to the car. The car verifies the correctness of the password, before releasing the door catch.[28]

There is another way of facilitating perfect passwords that does not require the synchronizing of clocks or the maintenance of a synchronized counter. The flexibility offered by freedom from a need to synchronize is the reason that this alternative approach underpins not just some perfect password tokens, but also the way entity authentication is performed when you access your Wi-Fi, visit a secure website, or do many other things.

Digital Boomerangs

An indigenous hunter stealthily creeps up to the edge of a coastal swamp in eastern Australia. The distant ducks dabble unaware. The hunter reaches back and launches his boomerang. It curves around the far shore of the wetland before spinning back, low over the water. The ducks take flight, while the boomerang spirals back into the hunter's hand.[29] This scene might seem irrelevant to the discussion at hand, but cyberspace is constantly buzzing with digital boomerangs. Indeed, we couldn't reliably do half the things we do in cyberspace without them.

To understand why, let's consider our hunter once again. Suppose the hunter is blind (which makes boomerang throwing an even more dangerous sport than it already is). Further, let's suppose that instead of seeking dinner, the hunter wishes to use the boomerang to learn something about his surrounding environment. This is precisely why we throw digital boomerangs into cyberspace.

Although our hunter can't see the boomerang as it flies, one thing he can be fairly sure of is that the boomerang returning to him must be the same boomerang he threw (unless one of his friends decides to play an elaborate prank). However, if you launch some data into cyberspace and it later comes back to you, it is less clear that this is *exactly* the same data. The returning data could, for example, be a copy of identical data you sent sometime in the past. For this reason, normally we toss only freshly generated random numbers into cyberspace. Because these numbers are new and randomly chosen, it is extremely unlikely that a copy of them has ever been sent into cyberspace before. Just like the hunter, we are thus assured that when this random number returns, it must indeed be the random number we recently sent.

Despite his blindness, our hunter might be able to deduce information about the environment when the boomerang returns. Suppose some pungent melaleuca trees fringe the far shore of the swamp.[30] As the boomerang flies low over these bushes, it picks up traces of their scent. The blind hunter might now be able to learn something about where the returned boomerang has been from its smell. Note, critically, that the hunter can make this deduction because the returning boomerang has been modified (in this case, ever so slightly) from the boomerang that was thrown.

Like the hunter, we are completely blind in cyberspace. When we send random numbers into cyberspace and they return, we have absolutely no idea where they have been. However, one advantage that data has over boomerangs is the ease with which it can be modified. If random numbers can be transformed in a manner that identifies who modified them, this information can be used to determine precisely where the returning random number has just been. In other words, digital boomerangs enable us to work out who is out there.[31]

This principle, often referred to as *challenge-response*, is readily implemented using cryptography. Going back to our online banking tokens, if the token has a keypad, then we can use challenge-response instead of relying on a system clock. In this case, the bank generates a fresh random number and sends it to the customer of the bank. This is the *challenge*. The real challenge the bank is issuing is: "Show me what you can do with this new randomly generated number." The customer enters the challenge into their token, which then uses its key and cryptographic algorithm to compute a *response* displayed on the token screen. The customer sends the response back to the bank, which then checks whether the same response is obtained when the bank processes the challenge using the algorithm and its own copy of the customer's key. The bank hurls a random number into cyberspace and gets back a modified version, transformed in a way that only the customer should be able to do. The digital boomerang returns and, crucially, the bank knows where it has just been.

The Importance of Challenge-Response

The principle of challenge-response is vital to security in cyberspace. Most practical processes involving cryptography feature some throwing of digital boomerangs.

Thus far I have mainly presented cryptography as a set of tools, which provide properties such as confidentiality, data integrity, and entity authentication. In practice, most uses of cryptography involve more than one party and more than one tool. Challenge-response provides a good example: The bank generates a challenge (almost certainly using a cryptographic random number generator) and sends it to the user, who enters it into the token. The token then applies a cryptographic algorithm to the challenge in order to compute a response, which is sent back to the bank, which recomputes the response locally and then verifies whether the received response from the token matches the response computed locally by the bank.

Most cryptography occurs in a flurry of send this, do that, check this, encrypt that, send it back again, and so on. The whole caboodle is normally referred to as a cryptographic *protocol*, which dictates the precise procedure everyone needs to follow for the cryptographic tools used in the protocol to deliver the desired security. In fact, a cryptographic protocol is essentially a cryptographic algorithm whose operations are carried out by a number of different entities.

Many of the cryptographic protocols you regularly use incorporate challenge-response. For example, whenever you use your web browser to connect to a remote website where you intend to process sensitive data, such as when you make online purchases, access webmail, or conduct online banking, your web browser and the web server (the computer hosting the web page) are hopefully using a cryptographic protocol known as *Transport Layer Security* (*TLS*) to talk to one another.[32] One of the first steps of TLS is that your web browser and the website each send a random number to the other.

However complex the rest of a cryptographic protocol is, the reason many protocols begin with sending a randomly generated challenge to elicit a response is that establishing who is out there is perhaps the most fundamental part of any security process in cyberspace. The TLS protocol negotiates choices of cryptographic algorithm and establishes keys that can be used to encrypt and protect the integrity of subsequent communications between your web browser and the website you're visiting. Why bother doing this unless you can be sure of the identity of the website you're trying to securely connect to?

The security protocols used by Wi-Fi similarly determine keys for protecting the data flowing between a device and the network, but there is no point in going to this trouble if the device is not permitted to access the Wi-Fi network or if the Wi-Fi network is not genuine. Most cryptographic protocols begin with entity authentication, and most entity authentication commences with some sort of challenge-response.

Mister Nobody

Knock knock. Who's there? *Mister!* Mister who? *Mister nobody!* As with most playground games, deep therein lies a hidden truth. Sometimes we want to respond to "Who's out there?" in cyberspace with "I'm not telling you; mind your own business!"

The antithesis of entity authentication is *anonymity*. People desire anonymity in cyberspace for many reasons. It's most natural to seize on negative motivations for anonymity, such as to conduct criminal activities or espionage. In many situations, however, anonymity is desirable for more constructive reasons. Citizens of despotic regimes might wish to remain anonymous when they criticize the government. Journalists might desire anonymity. More mundanely, someone browsing a website might wish to remain anonymous to prevent the website from recording their personal information, or to restrict the site owner's ability to conduct user profiling and targeted advertising. Indeed, the concept of anonymity has been argued to be a human right that supports the broader and more fundamental right to personal privacy.[33]

You might imagine that anonymity is the default state of existence in cyberspace. After all, the entity authentication mechanisms that I've described thus far are all motivated by the apparent ease of masquerade in cyberspace. You can't see who's out there, so maybe you should implement some perfect passwords to find out? The truth is that it's easy to be *kind of anonymous* in cyberspace. True anonymity is much harder to achieve.

You probably feel anonymous when you're in cyberspace. It feels like you, the device you're interacting with, and everything beyond is an unknowable void; nobody is with you, nobody can see you, nobody knows who you are. Indeed, you can easily pretend to be someone else. When the ticketing website annoyingly forces you to register with them, you smugly type "Mickey Mouse" into the name box and become a cartoon rodent. It's not unlike the anonymity you feel when you get behind the wheel of your car: it's just you, a box of bamboozling technology, and the open highway.

There is a negative side to this perception of anonymity. Many people experience a reduction in their natural reserve and their natural desire to conform to behavioral norms. Anonymity appears to unleash some less attractive aspects of personality, which are otherwise constrained.[34] You may have experienced this phenomenon in your car, where a degree of anonymity has led you into conflict with other drivers in a way that doesn't happen when you walk among other pedestrians on a busy city street. Car drivers hit their horns in situations where pedestrians apologize. In extreme cases, car drivers behave very badly, leading to incidents of road rage.

Apparent anonymity unleashes extraordinary demons in cyberspace. Our use of cyberspace for everyday communications has made a raft of societal ills easier to perpetuate, and has given them a much wider reach. Harassment through vitriolic remarks (*trolling*), cyber bullying, and cyber stalking is on the rise, partially facilitated by the perceived anonymity of cyberspace.[35] Sometimes these acts are carried out by people who are known to their victims but whose inhibitions have been reduced in cyberspace. But people who are consciously trying to be anonymous in cyberspace often are guilty of the worst offenses. Just look at the extraordinary comments following articles in online newspapers and magazines. Some of the remarks are deeply disturbing, with the worst normally posted under aliases.

One car driver badly harassing another (for example, tailgating or driving in a dangerous fashion) might well think their apparent anonymity will protect them from prosecution, but that's not necessarily the case. Cars, after all, have registration numbers that can be reported and traced, and roads are often watched by CCTV cameras that can be consulted during an investigation. Cyberspace is no different.

In fact, from an anonymity perspective, cyberspace is a considerably worse environment. Each device accesses the internet using a unique address, which acts as an identifier of the connection and sometimes the device itself. Infrastructure companies, such as mobile operators and internet service providers, often log network activity. Computing devices typically have a range of features that can be used to identify them on the basis of their specific hardware and software. Almost every action in cyberspace leaves a trace, and many of these can be used to unmask a casual attempt to remain anonymous.[36]

You must make an effort if you really want anonymity in cyberspace. Just as cryptography provides some of the strongest mechanisms for *not* being anonymous in cyberspace, it also enables some of the best methods for achieving anonymity.

Peeling Onions

The best-known technology for supporting anonymity in cyberspace is *Tor*. This tool does not provide perfect anonymity (whatever that might mean), but it provides sufficient anonymity to make it a technology of choice, not just for political dissidents and online black-market vendors, but also for ordinary users who have a need for privacy in cyberspace.[37]

Tor consists of a special web browser and a network of dedi-cated *routers*, which are essentially delivery centers. Routers are a standard component of the internet. Normal traffic (not using Tor) includes the unique internet addresses of both the sender of data and the intended receiver, and data travels from sender to receiver by being passed from one router to another until the destination is reached. This addressing information is not secret, so all these intermediate routers can easily see who is sending data and where it is going. Indeed, the whole point is for routers to be able to see addressing information; otherwise they don't know where to direct the data on the next hop of its journey.

The challenge in providing anonymity is how to give routers enough information that they can keep passing the data toward the destination, without revealing the full information about who is sending what to whom. This sounds like a job for encryption, but if you just encrypt the addressing information, then nobody knows where the information needs to go. The Tor solution is both simple and ingenious.

Here's the analogy: You're a whistle-blower who wants to send a document to a journalist. You want to do this urgently and anony-mously. You could seal the document in an envelope with the jour-nalist's address and call a courier, but then the courier has the potential to "de-anonymize" you, since they are aware of the address of both sender and receiver. To address this de-anonymization prob-lem, Tor establishes a network of "safe houses."

To deliver the document using Tor, you first randomly select three safe houses from the Tor network. You seal the document in an envelope with the journalist's address. You then seal this enve-lope inside another envelope, addressed to the third safe house, which is then sealed in an envelope addressed to the second safe house, which is then sealed in an envelope addressed to the first safe house. Now you call the courier. The courier delivers this well-padded packet to the first safe house. Here the first envelope is removed, revealing the address of the second safe house. The first safe house now calls a new courier, who takes the parcel onward. A similar process happens at both the second and third safe houses. At the third safe house, the destination address is revealed, and the final courier delivers the remaining envelope to the journalist.

This scheme might sound contrived, but it is very effective. No safe house or courier is aware of both who sent the parcel and who is supposed to receive it. The first safe house and courier know where it came from, the third safe house and courier know where it is going, but nobody knows both these things. In Tor, the safe houses are routers, and the envelopes are layers of encryption. Data sent using Tor is encrypted in three layers, with each router stripping off one layer of encryption before passing it on. This process is sometimes referred to as *onion routing*, since it is analogous to a chef peeling off the layers of an onion.

Anonymity is a fascinating aspect of cyberspace, for the reasons previously discussed, and many more. However, there are many polarized views of anonymity in cyberspace. The negative aspects of anonymity[38] have led some to regard it as one of the greatest scourges of cyberspace. Others see anonymity as the defining feature of cyberspace freedom.[39] As I will discuss later in greater detail, because cryptography provides the best means to facilitate anonymity in cyberspace, cryptography itself is often either demonized or celebrated.

Who's Who?

My analysis of who is out there has been a bit simplistic. I talked about the separation between human and computer, but reality is even more complex.

What is a human in cyberspace? Most people have many different personas in cyberspace. You, the human, are undoubtedly represented by different aliases and user accounts across the range of services you use in cyberspace. Some people even have different accounts with the same service. Which of these is the "real" you? All of them? Some of them?

Who else, apart from a human, can be out there in cyberspace? It can be a laptop, a phone, a token, a key, a network address. It could also be a web server, a network router, a computer program . . . The possibilities are almost endless.

Matters are going to get even more confusing in the future. The vast majority of humans are rarely far from their mobile phone, making phones an attractive device on which to base authentication. Modern mobile phones are capable of securely storing keys and computing sophisticated cryptographic algorithms. Humans are not just more reliably carrying computers, but the future could see humans *becoming* much more like computers. Advances in health monitoring make it likely that human bodies of the future could be implanted with small computing sensors. More ominously, like it or not, there are projects exploring how to connect human brains to cyberspace.[40] Meanwhile, computers themselves are getting better at behaving like humans. Computers are already thinking more like humans as progress in artificial intelligence and in processing large data sets enables machines to anticipate, and even surpass, human decision-making. Advances in robotics make it likely that a cyber human of some shape and form might be with us soon.

What all this means for the future of entity authentication, heaven knows. Whatever technologies we end up using in future cyberspace, however, the core question of who is out there is not going to go away. Whoever asks this question needs to think carefully about who "who" is. Who do you *need* to know is out there? Human, token, account, key? And when you get your answer, who's the "who" that replied? Similarly, when you're asked who's out there, who answers on your behalf? You or your phone? It would be wise to know, since, if you misplace your phone, you really should be aware of the extent to which you've also lost your "cyberself."

Who is out there? The answer might be complicated, but, to be secure in cyberspace, we ought to know.

7

Breaking Cryptosystems

t's time to take stock. Cryptography provides all sorts of clever tools: encryption mechanisms control who can access information, integrity mechanisms detect whether information has been altered, and entity authentication mechanisms indicate who we're communicating with. These cryptographic tools are all fine in theory, but the crucial services they deliver need to work effectively in real systems if we're all going to be secure in cyberspace. Building real systems is notoriously difficult, so we must consider how cryptography can be transformed from just a fascinating idea into something that really makes us secure in cyberspace. The best way to consider how to get practical cryptography right is to think about what could go wrong.

Nuts and Bolts Are Not Enough

Cryptography works. At least, it should. Yet you will hear stories about cryptography being "broken." The communications of Mary, Queen of Scots, and Napoleon were ultimately revealed, despite their use of cryptography. Much of the traffic protected by German Enigma machines was eventually decrypted by the Allies, giving the Allies a huge advantage toward the end of the Second World War. The cryptography used by new technologies is all too often found to have significant weaknesses. And forensic investigators are sometimes able to get around the cryptography protecting data on a seized mobile phone. How do these apparent failures of cryptography keep occurring?

Good cryptographic algorithms are very hard to design, so it might be tempting to conclude that failures of cryptographic protection are all down to weaknesses in the cryptography itself. But this is very rarely the case.

It's worth recognizing the precise role that cryptography plays in keeping information secure, both in cyberspace and elsewhere. Cryptography provides a range of security mechanisms, each designed for a very specific purpose. For example, encryption scrambles data into an unintelligible form. This sounds useful for providing confidentiality, but there's something of immense importance that anyone relying on encryption needs to be aware of, yet might ignore at their peril. Scrambling the data is the *only* thing encryption does.

Let's think about what encryption does *not* do. Encryption does not come with a guarantee that the encryption algorithm used has been correctly coded or integrated into the technology it is trying to protect. Encryption doesn't control who has access to the decryption key. Likewise, encryption plays no role in the protection of data either before it's encrypted or after it's decrypted.

The best way to consider the protection provided by cryptography is to appreciate that cryptography can only ever be used as part of a wider *cryptosystem*. This includes not just the algorithms and keys, but also the technologies on which the cryptography is implemented, the devices and processes that manage the cryptographic keys, the wider procedures for handling the data being protected, and even the people who interact with all of the above. When cryptography breaks, what has really happened is that some part of the cryptosystem has failed to work as intended. Problems with the cryptographic techniques used are not ruled out, but chances are the issue lies elsewhere.

Cryptography is vital for most of the security technologies that we use today in cyberspace. It provides, if you like, the nuts and bolts around which a secure system can be built. In the case of building a steel bridge across an estuary, nuts and bolts are essential, but they're not enough. And if, heaven forbid, the bridge falls down, the reason is not usually that the nuts and bolts didn't do their job.[1]

Using State of the Art

By all accounts, Julius Caesar was an avid user of cryptography. It's reported that whenever he was concerned about the confidentiality of written information, he used encryption to disguise it.[2] The algorithm Caesar used has come to be known as the *Caesar cipher* and consists of shifting the letters of the alphabet a certain number of positions. The size of the shift is the key, and it is reported that Caesar habitually used a shift of three (encrypting A to D, B to E, and so on).

The Caesar cipher tends to be the first encryption algorithm encountered by students in a cryptography course. It's used as an illustrative example, before the students are informed how weak it is. The Caesar cipher is far too simplistic, for it leaks information about the plaintext, it has only twenty-six possible keys, and the key is revealed if just one plaintext and matching ciphertext are known. The Caesar cipher is how *not* to encrypt your bank account. How naive was Caesar?

Julius Caesar was many things, but naive he was not. A canny politician, defiant military commander, and ultimately authoritarian leader of the Roman Republic, Julius Caesar was a man who undoubtedly had secrets to keep. His use of any form of encryption in the BC era can only be regarded as visionary, and indicative of a man who was well aware of the value of information and how to protect it. It has been pointed out that the majority of Julius Caesar's enemies were probably illiterate. The few who were not were extremely unlikely to be aware of encryption. If they intercepted Caesar cipher ciphertext, they would have been bamboozled. Julius Caesar knew what he was doing. The Caesar cipher was state-of-the-art encryption, and it almost certainly did the job that he required it to do. Hail, Caesar!

In the late sixteenth century, Mary, Queen of Scots, and her fellow Babington Plot conspirators cooked up their own encryption algorithms in order to keep their communications confidential (and what could need confidentiality more than plans to oust Queen Elizabeth I?).[3] The problem for Mary was that neither she nor her friends were versed in the cryptographic cutting edge. Had Mary digested Italian cryptographer Giovan Battista Bellaso's 1553 treatise *La cifra del Sig. Giovan Battista Belaso*, then the world might have been a very different place. Instead, Mary relied on a series of bespoke algorithms that were not dramatically advanced from the Caesar cipher. Pitched against the might of Elizabeth's sixteenth-century intelligence agency, Mary never stood a chance. Elizabeth employed Thomas Phelippes, who was essentially a cryptographer and, notably, Arthur Gregory, who was an expert at undetectably interfering with the seals of letters.[4] There is a salutary reminder there, for all of us, that confidentiality and data integrity are often both required when information needs protection.

The good news is that, today, strong cryptographic algorithms are readily available for everyone to use. Since the 1970s, cryptographic expertise has blossomed beyond the domains of the government and military. Several significant international standards specify cryptographic algorithms, including the AES, that are believed by the wider community of expertise to be extremely secure.[5]

You'd like to believe that the technologies we use every day in cyberspace were using these wonderful state-of-the-art cryptographic algorithms, wouldn't you? Well, most do, but by no means all. There has been a sad history of new technologies adopting their own do-it-yourself cryptographic algorithms. This approach has been taken for a variety of reasons, some of which have a degree of legitimacy, such as the fact that certain algorithms are designed to optimize performance on specific technologies, but in many cases the cause is simply ignorance. These contemporary ventures into Mary-Queen-of-Scots cryptography have almost all ended badly, although, truth be told, not enough beheadings have taken place as a result.[6]

The lesson for us today is simple. When it comes to choosing a cryptographic algorithm, whether for confidentiality, data integrity, or entity authentication, choose the state of the art. Cryptographic algorithms are the core component of any cryptosystem, and there is no excuse for not using the best available algorithms. If a widely respected algorithm is being used and a cryptosystem fails, then the problem will almost certainly lie elsewhere.

Knowns and Unknowns

When experts recommend a cryptographic algorithm as state of the art, they're saying, of course, only that they *believe* this to be so, from what they know about cryptography. There are no guarantees that any algorithm is secure, and there never can be. When speculating about uncertainties, it is not unhelpful to benchmark against former US secretary of defense Donald Rumsfeld's legendary taxonomy of the knowable.[7]

Cryptographic algorithms are designed with primarily the *known knowns* of algorithm security—in other words, available best practice—in mind. Mary, Queen of Scots, lost control of her information because she was not sufficiently versed in the known knowns of the day. Her encryption algorithms shared one particular undesirable property with the simple substitution cipher we encountered earlier—namely, that when a specific key is used, the same plaintext letter (in the case of the simple substitution cipher) is always encrypted to the same ciphertext letter. Since some plaintext letters occur much more commonly than others within any language, some ciphertext letters will occur much more often than others. Careful analysis of how frequently ciphertext letters occur thus permits an informed guess as to what the underlying plaintext letters are. With a bit of intelligent trial and error, it can be surprisingly easy to use this type of *frequency analysis* to determine the full plaintext. Puzzles of this sort are now often published in magazines and are trivial to solve by computer.

Frequency analysis is just one of many attack techniques, most of which are much more sophisticated, that designers of contemporary cryptographic algorithms should be aware of. By Mary's time, knowledge of frequency analysis had led to the adoption of more complex encryption algorithms, including Giovan Battista Bellaso's Vigenère cipher, which ensures that different occurrences of the same plaintext letter are encrypted as different letters in the ciphertext.

For Mary, frequency analysis belonged to an uncertainty category that Rumsfeld, with privileged access to the most powerful intelligence agency in the world, presumably felt was not of relevance to him. It was an *unknown known*, something she could have (perhaps should have) known about but did not. The risk of unknown knowns has dogged the public use of cryptography since its emergence in the mid-1970s. Prior to this time, cryptography was very much an activity in the domains of governments and the military, where it was shrouded in secrecy.

When the DES algorithm was first published in the late 1970s, there was no doubt that the intelligence community knew far more about cryptography than the rest of us did. This exclusiveness led to worries (probably unfounded) that the DES algorithm might be subject to attacks that intelligence agencies, but not everyone else, would know about. In fact, it turned out there were some unknown knowns of this type, but it appears these were used to strengthen the security provided by DES, not weaken it.[8] By the time the AES competition (discussed in Chapter 3) was launched, the gap between secret and public knowledge about cryptography had shrunk.

Today, public expertise in cryptography is so extensive that the chances of there being significant unknown knowns with respect to cryptographic algorithm design are lower than ever before, although the intelligence community almost certainly will know some things that the public community does not.[9] It was notable that among the deluge of Edward Snowden's 2013 revelations about the exploitation of cryptosystems by intelligence agencies, very little suggested that these agencies held an upper hand in the analysis of cryptographic algorithms.

Rumsfeld acknowledged the existence of *known unknowns*, things that he knew US intelligence did not know with respect to Iraq's alleged weapons program. Several known unknowns hang over cryptography like dark clouds. Cryptography is based on an important premise. It's not *impossible* for an attacker to work out plaintext from ciphertext, or find a decryption key, or factor a large number, or forge a MAC, or find an input that hashes to a particular hash value, or accomplish a host of other things. Rather, it's *hard* to do these things. And the perceived level of difficulty of these tasks relies on assumptions about how much computing power an attacker can expend on the problem.

The first difficulty is that we know that powerful attackers of cryptography are out there, but we don't know who they are or how powerful their computers might be; we can only make an informed guess. Second, and more awkward, we know that computers are getting faster and faster, but we don't know how powerful they will be in the future. Fortunately, there are some rules of thumb about the rate of improvement in computing power that can be used to make predictions, but these will only ever be best guesses.[10] Because of these two known unknowns, cryptographic algorithm design tends to be extremely conservative, assuming the existence of much more powerful attackers than are probably ever likely to be out there. Better safe than sorry.

The real cumulonimbus hanging over cryptography, however, is quantum computing. We *know* it's coming. We *know* it will impact contemporary cryptographic algorithms (to quite varying extents). We *don't know* the time frames. We *don't know* how realistically the theory can be converted into practice. Quantum computing is an issue that will impact the cryptography of the future, so I'll discuss this later.

Which brings us, finally, to Rumsfeld's greatest fear: *unknown unknowns*. Could the cryptographic algorithms we use today suddenly succumb to an unexpected breakthrough that completely compromises their security? Hopefully not, but we can never be sure. The world of cryptographic algorithm design is not often shaken by such surprises, but there is past precedent.

In 2004, at one of the leading cryptography research conferences, Wang Xiaoyun, a then relatively unknown Chinese researcher, delivered an informal paper that described a devastating attack on MD5, one of the principal hash functions in use at the time.[11] While this attack did not immediately threaten all applications using MD5, of which there were a great many, it exposed the fact that MD5 was *significantly* weaker than everyone had assumed. Most attack techniques improve steadily over time, but breakthroughs of this type are rare. A previously unknown unknown was now known, kick-starting a process that eventually resulted in the development of entirely new approaches to designing hash function algorithms.

How to Save the World

Here's cryptography in action, as often witnessed on television dramas (and the likes of James Bond movies).

Two intelligence agents sit tensely in a car, careering through busy city streets in a race against time. The driver is panicking and urgently talking to base. The passenger, the geeky agency computer analyst, has just inserted a recently purloined memory stick into a laptop computer. "What's on there?" asks the driver. "It's encrypted," responds the analyst. "Can you break the code?" asks the driver. The analyst wrestles with the keypad while mysterious symbols dance across the screen, purses his lips, and slowly exhales. "I've never seen this means of encryption before; it's unbelievably complex. Whoever wrote this knew what they were doing," he says. "But can you crack it?" fires back the driver, as a timer on the screen hurtles second by second toward zero hour. The analyst grimaces and clatters his fingers over the keypad once more. The camera focuses on the laptop, where a digital Niagara of jumbled data is pouring down the screen. The driver runs a red light, overtakes a bus, and narrowly evades a head-on collision with a motorcycle. The analyst taps away at the keyboard, muttering to himself, eyes like saucers, staring in wonder at the festival of ciphertext on screen. The driver decides to take a shortcut and makes a sudden right turn, finding the way blocked by a garbage truck. The car screeches to a halt, and the driver sighs with despair as the timer enters the final seconds of its countdown. The analyst gasps, "I've got it!" And the world is saved, again.

Either the analyst has knowledge of an otherwise unknown unknown about cryptography, or (to get to the point of the issue as succinctly as possible) this is . . . nonsense.

What just happened? The cryptographic expert in the passenger seat reports that the encryption algorithm is unfamiliar. How did they work it out? Ciphertext from any decent encryption algorithm should appear to be randomly generated, so you shouldn't normally be able to determine which algorithm was used to encrypt it just from idle inspection. But let's set this problem aside. By somehow being able to deduce that none of the encryption algorithms he is familiar with have been used, the analyst is informing us that the algorithm is unknown to him. Since the analyst also indicates that whoever encrypted the data knew what they were doing, it is safe to assume the analyst has not extracted the decryption key from the memory stick (otherwise the key management is so poor that they certainly did *not* know what they were doing). So, the analyst knows neither the algorithm nor the key. Where, then, did the plaintext just come from?

There is only one conclusion. The analyst has, somehow, been able to try every possible algorithm and, for each of these algorithms, every possible key. *Every possible algorithm?* How many possible encryption algorithms could there be? It's not even worth trying to reason about this; the number is so large that this capability can be safely dismissed.[12]

Let's be clear. If you acquire a ciphertext and you don't know which algorithm was used to produce it, then there's very little you can do to analyze it (assuming it has been generated by a good encryption algorithm). However, for all the reasons previously discussed, most modern uses of cryptography involve following standards that precisely specify the algorithm used. In most cases, therefore, it is entirely reasonable to assume that the algorithm is *known*.

So, let's amend the plot of our spy drama. "It's encrypted," responds the analyst. "Can you break the code?" asks the driver. The analyst wrestles with the keypad while mysterious symbols dance across the screen, purses his lips, and slowly exhales. "I'm guessing they've used extremely strong encryption—probably the AES. Whoever encrypted this knew what they were doing," he says. "But can you crack it?" Ticktock, ticktock, ticktock . . . The car screeches to a halt, and the driver sighs with despair as the timer enters the final seconds of its countdown. The analyst gasps, "I've got it!"

I don't think so.

Key Length Matters

Julius Caesar was undoubtedly aware of it. The Babington Plot conspirators appeared to recognize it. Even you, having read thus far, are surely convinced of it. Surprisingly, some designers of new security technologies underestimate it. The screenwriters of intelligence thrillers, on the other hand, often choose to ignore it.

Key length matters. In other words, the number of possible keys has a significant bearing on the security of a cryptographic algorithm. You can never have too many, but you can certainly have too few.

Twenty-six, for example, is not enough! Good for Caesar maybe, but not for protecting your mobile phone calls. Mary, Queen of Scots, however, with her extended version of the simple substitution cipher, was in a much better position with respect to key length. Her encryption algorithms had substantially more keys than the simple substitution cipher had, which itself already had plenty of keys. Mary's key length was close to being acceptable today. The take-home lesson here is clear. Key length matters, but it's not *all* that matters. Having a sufficient number of possible keys is no guarantee that your head will remain fixed to your body.

Key length matters because there is an unsophisticated attack that can be launched against every cryptographic algorithm. This attack works, no matter how well the algorithm blends the input data into ciphertext, MAC, or whatever. An *exhaustive key search*[13] simply tries out every possible key. To work, however, two things are required. The algorithm must be known, and there must be some means of determining when the correct key has been found.

Let's return to our revised fictional drama and consider an exhaustive key search against symmetric encryption. The analyst has some ciphertext, and he wants to know the underlying plaintext. He knows (or makes an informed guess) that the encryption algorithm used was AES. He doesn't know which key was used. In the absence of any further information, his only option is to try out every possible key, one after the other. Guess a key, decrypt. Guess another key, decrypt. Guess another key, decrypt. And so on, and so on, and so on. Assuming the plaintext is not random, it should be easy to determine when the correct key is found because, hopefully, the screen of unintelligible ciphertext will transform into a map depicting the plans for an upcoming terror plot. But can the correct key be found in time?

I'll be perfectly frank. If the correct key for an AES ciphertext is chanced upon just minutes into an exhaustive key search, then the analyst has been lucky beyond all credible belief. How long would it really take to find the correct key? In most cases, it won't be necessary to try out *every* key (this would be just as *unlucky* as our intelligence analyst was fortunate). On average, the correct key will be found about halfway through the search of all possible keys. Had the encryption algorithm been the Caesar cipher, then the analyst could easily work through all twenty-six possible keys, most likely finding the correct key after about thirteen attempts. He could almost do this by hand, but his laptop will perform this exercise instantaneously. But what about a *real* encryption algorithm?

For the sake of this exercise, let's (impossibly) upgrade our analyst's laptop to a supercomputer capable of processing 100 petaflops (100,000,000,000,000,000 operations per second). The AES has—wait for it—a minimum of 340 billion billion billion billion (that's 340 undecillion for the more numerate of you) keys. A crude calculation suggests that an exhaustive search of AES using this supercomputer will take, on average, 50 million billion years to conduct.[14] This is, unfortunately, just a bit longer than television program schedules tend to permit. If the future of the world relies on a successful exhaustive search of AES, then we're all doomed.

Key length matters, with length typically measured by how many bits long the key is. The minimum AES key length on which the last calculation was based is 128 bits. There are two important aspects to key length, each of which merit further attention. These are perhaps both best illustrated by a consideration of DES, the encryption algorithm that would have been used, had our spy drama been set in the latter decades of last century.

The first is the sensitivity of key lengths. The DES has a key length of 56 bits, which is slightly less than half the key length of the AES. This does not mean that the AES has just over double the number of keys that the DES has. If the length of a symmetric key is increased by a single bit, then the number of possible keys is doubled. So the AES has 5 sextillion (5,000 billion billion) *times* more keys than the DES! Just think about that for a moment.

The second issue is how recommended key lengths evolve over time. When the DES was first released in the late 1970s, some people worried that its 70 million billion keys were not quite enough. It was estimated that a machine could be built for $20 million that could search all these keys in less than one day.[15] However, this machine was never built, and it has been suggested that, in any case, such a device would have melted before completing its search.

Fast-forward two decades, and a DES key was found in just under half a year by a distributed exhaustive key search conducted by computers all over the world, joining efforts over the fledgling internet.[16] Such an achievement had been unthinkable in the late 1970s. For two decades, DES was the state of the art in encryption, with such a search deemed computationally infeasible. But as time moves on, technological capability only ever gets better. The AES was born from the realization that the key length of DES had become a liability. Today, our supercomputer that takes 50 million billion years to find an AES key could find a DES key in less than the time it takes to hard-boil an egg.

Of course, nobody is claiming that AES will be good for 50 million billion years. Computers will continue to advance, so recommended key lengths need to factor this into account. Since nothing can be done to prevent exhaustive key search, we have to make sure there are so many keys that, within reasonable time frames, exhaustive key searches are, in all likelihood, impractical to complete. Key lengths matter, even if giving them proper consideration spoils a movie.

It Ain't What You Do
(It's the Way That You Do It)

Napoleon Bonaparte learned, admittedly the hard way, that using good cryptography is important. In 1811 he commissioned the design of a state-of-the-art encryption algorithm, known as *Le Grande Chiffre de Paris*. This algorithm was designed to counter frequency analysis. By using techniques such as encrypting the more common plaintext letters into many different ciphertext letters, as well as masking common letter combinations using dummy characters, this somewhat clunky—but effective—encryption algorithm had the potential to defeat the cryptographic experts of the British army and its allies.

Within one year, Le Grande Chiffre was broken. Twelve months later, Napoleon's forces sorrowfully retreated from the Iberian Peninsula. They had just lost a war in which, unbeknownst to them, their encrypted messages had all been read by the British. Within two years, Napoleon was *"en vacances"* in Saint Helena. What Napoleon never understood was that using a good cryptographic algorithm does not guarantee you security. Just using such an algorithm matters, but so does the *way* you use it.

Napoleon's forces used strong encryption, but they used it carelessly.[17] Their biggest mistake was to regularly encrypt only parts of messages. An efficiency saving, maybe, but a devastating security error. By sending bizarre combinations of plaintext mixed with ciphertext, the French handed a free gift to British intelligence. With sections of the plaintext known, the British analysts could make informed guesses about what the remaining plaintext was, then correlate those guesses against previously intercepted communications. It would not have taken much time to deduce the entire key of Le Grande Chiffre.

The cryptographers working to overcome the German Enigma machines during the Second World War benefited from all sorts of different kinds of carelessness in the use of cryptography. For example, many plaintext messages started with predictable words or phrases. Similarly, the key in Enigma machines consisted of a number of mechanical settings, some of which were "lazier" choices based on the physical layout of the machines, and thus more commonly selected. None of these were enough to break Enigma on their own, but a steady accumulation of knowledge about how Enigma machines could be misused certainly helped in the process of breaking them.[18]

We are far from immune to such problems today. For example, if modern block ciphers are not used appropriately, they can be subject to various attacks, including frequency analysis. The AES, a state-of-the-art encryption algorithm, does not encrypt letter by letter, but it will always encrypt the same block of plaintext data into the same block of ciphertext data. Frequency analysis on blocks of data (which can represent many letters) is much more difficult than on single letters, but blocks can still be analyzed in this way. For example, if a database were (naively) encrypted entry by entry, including a field for "child's favorite food," then among the most commonly occurring ciphertexts would be the encryption of *pizza* (and, you can be sure, not the encryption of *brussels sprouts*).

The AES has encrypted *pizza* to perfection, but our use of the AES allows the plaintext *pizza* to be deduced without the encryption algorithm being broken.

The pizza problem can be remedied in various ways, all of which involve attending to the way AES is used rather than tinkering with the algorithm. For example, if a random number is included alongside each database entry, the ciphertext associated with the word *pizza* should become different for each entry. More generally, as mentioned earlier, block ciphers are normally deployed via modes of operation that use a variety of techniques to ensure that the same plaintext block is not transformed into the same ciphertext block every time.[19]

Selecting a cryptographic algorithm is one task. Using it securely, quite another. Today, we don't just have cryptographic standards specifying algorithms, but also standards advising on ways in which algorithms should be used. The *Grands Chiffres* of the twenty-first century can easily become as ineffective as Napoleon's if used inappropriately.

Following the Protocol

Cryptographic mechanisms are rarely used in isolation. Whenever you use cryptography, you are normally engaging in a cryptographic protocol involving different cryptographic mechanisms being used to deliver separate security properties. For example, when making a secure web connection using the TLS protocol discussed earlier, your web browser uses one mechanism to conduct entity authentication of the web server, another to keep the exchanged data confidential, and yet another to provide data origin authentication (sometimes the latter two are combined). The TLS protocol decrees exactly what needs to happen when, and in what order. If just one step of the protocol is not successful, then the entire protocol should fail. For example, in TLS, if the web server is not authenticated, then the protocol should end without a secure session being approved.

Mary, Queen of Scots, suffered a catastrophic protocol failure because *all* of her security mechanisms were compromised. She relied on an encryption algorithm that Thomas Phelippes could break. Wax seals were used to protect the integrity of the ciphertext itself. Had this integrity mechanism worked, then even though Phelippes could overcome the encryption, his obvious breaking of the seal in order to inspect the ciphertext would have alerted Mary. But Arthur Gregory could open wax seals without detection, so Mary's data integrity mechanism also failed. Worse, Phelippes could do more than decrypt her ciphertexts. His knowledge of the system was so complete that he could also forge apparently genuine messages.

In the closing stages of the Babington Plot, Phelippes was able to forge a message from Mary to Anthony Babington, requesting the names of the chief conspirators.[20] Upon receiving an apparently unadulterated message in correctly encrypted form, Babington would have erroneously assumed that it came from Mary (remember that the use of encryption does not guarantee the strong notion of data integrity introduced earlier, called data origin authentication). As it turned out, this last security failure had no bearing on proceedings, since Babington was seized before he had time to reply. Six weeks later, Babington was hung, drawn, and quartered, and within months, Mary had her own neck trimmed.

Even if strong cryptographic algorithms are chosen to implement the mechanisms used in a well-designed cryptographic protocol, the overall cryptographic protection might not be realized if the protocol is not followed correctly. Suppose, for example, the web server authentication step in the TLS protocol is mistakenly omitted or, more likely, not conducted properly. In other words, your web browser has, for some reason, failed to confirm that it is communicating with the genuine web server you believed you were

connecting to. If the rest of the protocol is followed, then the end
result could be that you establish a secure connection to a rogue
web server. This secure connection prevents outsiders from reading
the encrypted traffic, or trying to modify data sent over it, which
are two of the goals of the TLS protocol. But who is at the other end
of this connection?[21] Well, you have no idea.

Perhaps the biggest challenge is that good cryptographic protocols are notoriously hard to design. The reason is partly that
the interaction of the various different components can sometimes
have unintended consequences. An example of a poorly designed
protocol was the *Wired Equivalent Privacy (WEP)* protocol for
securing early Wi-Fi networks. The WEP protocol used a stream
cipher called *RC4*, which was arguably strong enough at the time
of WEP design.[22]

The design of the WEP protocol had many problems, though—
perhaps the most critical being that WEP specified an unusual
means of making sure the encryption key used to provide confidentiality of Wi-Fi messages was constantly changed. Although
changing this key is good practice, the technique used in the WEP
protocol was flawed. As a result, an attacker who observed the communications on a WEP-protected Wi-Fi channel for long enough
could work out the main key used to protect the network and ultimately decrypt all traffic sent over it.[23] This weakness in the WEP
protocol was not immediately obvious, but it proved fatal. Modern
Wi-Fi networks use more carefully designed protocols to protect
the information sent over them.[24] (To be on the safe side, if you are
using old Wi-Fi equipment, perhaps it would be best to check!)

Mind the Gap

Picking strong algorithms, with appropriate key lengths, and
deploying them in sound cryptographic protocols is an excellent
start to making cryptography work in practice. But it is no more

than a decent launching pad. Thanks to standards, and increased recognition of the importance of using state of the art, modern cryptographic systems suffer from fewer weaknesses than older systems did because of poor design. However, they still fail. The reason is that design on paper is arguably the simplest part of the process of making cryptography work in practice. It's what happens next that tends to go awry.

The first problem is that there's a chasm between design and implementation. In 1997, security specialist Bruce Schneier made some astute observations about the implementation of cryptography, which remain true today:

> There is an enormous difference between a mathematical algorithm and its concrete implementation in hardware or software. Cryptographic system designs are fragile. Just because a protocol is logically secure doesn't mean it will stay secure when a designer starts defining message structures and passing bits around. Close isn't close enough; these systems must be implemented exactly, perfectly, or they will fail.[25]

Schneier's argument was that cryptographic algorithms and protocols are very special components of security systems. Great care needs to be taken during implementation to make sure that the cryptographic design described on the label is precisely the cryptographic design delivered in the box.

Since 1997, much has been learned about building secure implementations. More is known about how to write secure software, and more is understood about how to incorporate and use secure hardware components to strengthen the security of systems. But, at the same time, we use cryptography in more and more products, and not all product developers are well versed in secure implementation techniques, or inclined to employ them. Because of budgetary constraints and urgency to complete development, some products end up having flawed cryptography. As computer security expert Thomas Dullien observed in 2018: "Security is improving, but insecure computing is growing faster."[26]

Despite all the wisdom, and despite the implementation horror stories of the past, there remains a gap to be minded between the cryptography of battle plans and the cryptography of frontline action.

Attacking down the Blind Side

In December 1995, as a fledgling cryptographic researcher, I was sitting in a sweltering office at the University of Adelaide, reading the posts of sci.crypt, an early internet newsgroup about all things cryptographic. In 1995, it was still possible for one person to be broadly aware of all the topics that cryptographic researchers were investigating. Indeed, if you worked in the public domain, it was still possible to know most cryptographers.

The post that really caught my attention was entitled "Timing cryptanalysis of RSA, DH, DSS," by Paul Kocher (independent cryptography consultant). Kocher was claiming to have broken RSA, among other public-key algorithms. RSA broken? He must be bonkers! So I read on:

> I've just released details of an attack many of you will find interesting since quite a few existing cryptography products and systems are potentially at risk. The general idea of the attack is that secret keys can be found by measuring the amount of time used to process messages.[27]

This sealed it for me. Kocher was clearly insane.

Paul Kocher had just announced an unknown unknown. He had not broken the RSA algorithm, which, if we allow for increases in key length due to improvements in computing power, remains as secure today as it was in 1995. He was announcing that implementations of RSA previously believed to be secure were not. The problem was not careless mistakes, resulting in flawed implementations. Kocher was announcing a completely new way of attacking implementations of cryptographic algorithms. It was an attack down the blind side. Implementing cryptography has never been the same since.

Kocher had done something that nobody outside of the intelligence community had previously imagined possible. He had access to an apparently secure device, such as a smartcard, that contained an RSA private key. For such devices, it should not be possible for anyone to read the key that is stored on it, but it should be possible to ask the device to use the key to conduct cryptographic computations (think about your credit card; you clearly don't want a salesperson to be able to extract any keys stored on the chip, but you do want their payment terminal to be able to process your transaction using these keys).

This is precisely what Kocher did: he instructed the device to conduct RSA computations and then closely scrutinized what happened next. In particular, he measured in detail the minute differences in the timing of certain operations as the device crunched its way through RSA decryptions of different ciphertexts. By cleverly selecting which ciphertexts to analyze, and which operations to measure, Kocher was able to eventually determine the private key used to conduct the decryption operations.[28] Amazing!

Kocher's *timing attacks* opened up an entirely new area of cryptographic study. If you could discover a private key simply by measuring the timings of the device on which the key was being used, what other unexpected ways might there be of discovering private keys? This is just one example of a number of *side channel attacks*, all of which exploit different aspects of the implementation of cryptography to leak information about the secret keys on which cryptography relies. Other examples include detailed analysis of the power consumed by a device as it performs cryptographic operations, the electromagnetic radiation that the device emits, and the way a device behaves when deliberately given faulty information.[29]

Most side channel attacks require an ability to possess a device on which cryptography has been implemented and subject it to a form of repeated "torture" until its secrets are revealed. In a previous world where cryptography was implemented only on enormous computers sitting in special rooms in the basements of buildings, side channel analysis did not seem relevant. Today, however, when cryptography is on the devices in your pocket, side channel analysis presents a real threat. An attacker who manages to get hold of your device can then interrogate it to obtain your secrets.

This is why, hand in hand with investigations on the effectiveness of side channel attacks, ways of protecting implementations against them are being developed. Since side channel attacks are subtle, so, too, are the approaches to masking against them. This is yet more evidence, if any was really needed, of just how tricky it is to securely implement cryptography.

How to (Really) Save the World

Take two.

Two intelligence agents sit tensely in a car, careering through busy city streets in a race against time. The driver is panicking and urgently talking to base. The passenger, the geeky agency computer analyst, has just inserted a recently purloined memory stick into a laptop computer. "What's on there?" asks the driver. "It's encrypted," responds the analyst. "Can you break the code?" asks the driver. The analyst wrestles with the keypad while mysterious symbols dance across the screen, purses his lips, and slowly exhales. "They're using AES encryption," he says. "But can you crack it?" fires back the driver, as a timer on the screen hurtles second by second toward zero hour. "I just have," states the analyst, calmly. "They used the factory default key. What idiots," he adds. "You can't do that!" complains the driver. "We haven't even made it to the great scene with the garbage truck!"

Take three.

. . . "What's on there?" asks the driver. "It's encrypted," responds the analyst. "Can you break the code?" asks the driver. The analyst wrestles with the keypad while mysterious symbols dance across the screen, purses his lips, and slowly exhales. "They're using AES encryption," he says. "But can you crack it?" fires back the driver, as a timer on the screen hurtles second by second toward zero hour. The analyst grimaces and clatters his fingers over the keypad once more. Ticktock, ticktock, ticktock . . . The driver decides to take a shortcut and makes a sudden right turn, finding the way blocked by a garbage truck. The car screeches to a halt, and the driver sighs with despair as the timer enters the final seconds of count-down. The analyst gasps, "I've got it!" The driver smiles with relief. "Mate, you're a genius!" he exclaims. "Not really," replies the ana-lyst. "They included the unprotected key in the computer program. All I did was look."

Take four.

. . . "What's on there?" asks the driver. "It's encrypted," responds the analyst. "Can you break the code?" asks the driver. The analyst wrestles with the keypad while mysterious symbols dance across the screen, purses his lips, and slowly exhales. "They're using AES encryption," he says. "But can you crack it?" fires back the driver, as a timer on the screen hurtles second by second toward zero hour. The analyst grimaces and clatters his fingers over the keypad once more. "Looks like the key is generated from a password. Just give me a moment." Ticktock, ticktock, ticktock . . . The driver decides to take a shortcut and makes a sudden right turn, finding the way blocked by a garbage truck. The car screeches to a halt, and the driver sighs with despair as the timer enters the final seconds of countdown. The analyst gasps, "I've got it! Wannabe bad guys always use a password like 'Javier Bardem'."[30]

It's the Key Management, Stupid!

Good algorithm—check. Sound protocol—check. Careful implementation—check. Side channel masking—check. Good to go?

We're not quite done yet. Cryptography, as you know well by now, relies on keys. Indeed, assuming that the algorithms are designed and implemented correctly, cryptography translates the problem of protecting data into the (slightly easier) problem of safeguarding keys. If cryptography is going to do the job we intend it to do, then we need to take great care of our keys.[31]

One way of thinking about keys is to regard them as living objects. Keys are born, live their lives, and then die. Throughout this *key life cycle*, it is vital to nurture the key. The key life cycle includes a number of important stages. First keys are *generated* (created). Keys are then *distributed* to wherever they are needed in a cryptographic system. Then they are typically *stored*, awaiting use. In some systems, keys must be regularly *changed*. Ultimately, they are no longer required and need to be *destroyed*.

All these different stages in the life cycle of a cryptographic key need to be managed carefully, since a cryptographic system can fail if just one of these stages is handled inadequately. It's just the same for your front-door key. An overly simplistic front-door key will allow anyone with a metal hook to wiggle open the lock. A crooked real-estate agent could give a copy of your front-door key to a criminal gang. If you leave your front-door key under a flowerpot by the gate, then it's possible someone else will chance upon it. If a burglar breaks into your home and you subsequently fail to change the locks, the burglar may well return to steal all the replacement items you purchased with your home insurance payout.

Two core problems can arise if cryptographic keys are not managed properly. First, a key intended to be secret (such as a symmetric encryption key or an asymmetric private decryption or signature key) could become known. The three ways the world was (really) saved in our fictional scenario all resulted from a secret key becoming known through key management failures at different stages in the key life cycle. One was poor key generation (using a weak password). Another was poor key storage (including the key in software). A third was failure to change the key (keeping a factory default key rather than changing to a freshly generated personal key).[32] Failure to keep secret keys secret at any stage in the key life cycle can be disastrous (or save the planet, depending on whose side you're on). The need to protect secret keys is intuitive, since the same is true of physical keys.

The second core problem is that a cryptographic key's purpose might not be what you think it is. For example, a cryptographic key might not belong to whomever you think it does. This problem does not map so readily onto physical keys. Let's try.

Suppose you're a fugitive on the run and you meet up with an acquaintance, who offers you shelter for the night. The acquaintance gives you their address and a front-door key. You locate the house, open the door, and find yourself at the reception desk of the local police station. Unbeknownst to you, your acquaintance is an undercover cop! Hmm . . . Why is this scenario unlikely?

Apart from your failure to see the friendly "Police Station" sign on the building and notice all the brightly colored emergency vehicles parked around it, this scenario is unlikely because physical keys need to be physically transferred, and the context provides some assurance of the purpose of the keys. When a car salesperson hands over the keys to your newly purchased car and points you to a shiny BMW in the lot, there are many reasons to believe that these must be the keys to the car. Yes, it could turn out that the keys don't seem to open the BMW, while meanwhile, a rusty van parked next to it flashes its light in a welcoming manner and the salesman can be seen legging it down the road. That *could* happen. But it tends not to.

Cryptographic keys, being cyber things, lack physical context. When you connect to a remote website and the web server offers you its public encryption key in order to commence the building of a secure communication channel, how do you *know* that this public encryption key really belongs to the website?[33] When a friend emails you their public encryption key so that you can send them an encrypted message, how do you *know* that an attacker has not intercepted their email and replaced your friend's key with the attacker's key? When you buy a cheap cryptographic gizmo from a company in Ruritania, how do you *know* that its cryptographic keys are not also stored in a Ruritanian government database?

The main goals of key management are to keep secret keys secret, and to make sure we're using the right keys for the right things. Key management is arguably the hardest aspect of making cryptography work in real systems, because it's the interface between the cryptographic technology itself and the organizations and people who need to use it.

Good Key, Bad Key

Key generation is perhaps the most sensitive key management process. Since it differs slightly between symmetric and asymmetric cryptography, I will consider these cases separately.

The security of a symmetric cryptographic algorithm is based on the assumption that symmetric keys have been generated randomly. There are two problems with this idea.

First, generating keys in a random manner is difficult. In fact, the very idea of "true randomness" tends to send philosophers and physicists into frenzied debate, which I will steer well clear of in this book.[34] Genuinely random numbers, known as *nondeterminis-*

tic random numbers, typically require a "natural" physical source. One of the most obvious ways to generate nondeterministic randomness is to flip a coin. Assuming that the coin and the coin flipper are unbiased, each coin flip is an independent physical event equally likely to result in heads or tails. This is a great way to generate a random key, since, say, a head can be encoded by a 1 and a tail by a 0, resulting in a cryptographic key in which every bit is independent of those chosen before and after it.[35] It's also a completely impractical way of doing so for most applications of cryptography. *Would you like to buy something from my website? Could you first flip a coin 128 times in order to generate an AES key, please?*

Fortunately, nondeterministic random numbers can be generated from physical sources in various ways without human intervention. These include taking measurements from sources such as white noise, the atmosphere, physical oscillations, and radioactive decay, and then converting these into 1's and 0's.[36] These techniques are all effective, if slightly cumbersome. If you have access to such a physical device and can extract true randomness from it, then fine. But what happens if you don't?

There is another drawback to generating nondeterministic keys. You can't use this type of technique to generate two identical random keys in two different places. Indeed, the whole point of nondeterministic random number generation is that this should *not* happen. The reason coin flipping is such a good way of generating randomness is that the outcome is unpredictable. However, generating two identical keys in two different places is precisely what we *do* want for many applications of symmetric cryptography. When you make a phone call, your phone and your mobile-network operator both have immediate need of a key that you both know, in order to encrypt your call.

When the going gets tough, what do the tough do? They cheat, of course. As discussed on several previous occasions, the output of a good cryptographic algorithm should seem "random," so

cryptography itself is a potential source of "randomness." When
you make a mobile phone call, your phone and the mobile-network
operator both use a specific cryptographic algorithm to generate a
new "random" symmetric key that can be used to encrypt your call.
Both the phone and the operator already share a long-term symmetric key stored on your SIM card (which may well have been generated nondeterministically). This long-term key is used as input into
the cryptographic algorithm, which then outputs a new shared key.
The phone and the network operator use the same input and the
same deterministic algorithm to generate the same key. Because
this generation process is deterministic and thus repeatable in two
different places, it's not real randomness. Instead, it's fake randomness, or *pseudorandomness*.

The randomness might be fake, but pseudorandomly generated
keys are good enough for most applications of cryptography. A key
generated by a *pseudorandom number generator* (the cryptographic
algorithm used to create it) has the potential to be just as difficult
for an attacker to guess as is a key generated by coin flips. But only
the *potential* to be that difficult.

Over the years, use of poor pseudorandom number generators
has been a point of weakness in cryptosystems. This vulnerability
is probably down to oversight. It's common to see security products
advertising their use of "state-of-the-art AES 128-bit encryption,"
but rare to see them boasting proudly about how the keys are generated. A bad pseudorandom number generator will not generate
(seemingly) random keys. An attacker who analyzes such a generator may discover that some keys are never generated at all, or that
some are generated more commonly than others. This is extremely
useful knowledge if you're an attacker considering exhaustively
searching for an unknown secret key.[37]

As noted earlier, since large random numbers are not easily mem-
orized, one technique sometimes used for pseudorandomly generating a key is to derive it from a password. You enter the password,

and then a pseudorandom number generator is used to convert this password into a cryptographic key. If this is not done extremely carefully, all sorts of problems can arise. For example, keys derived from common passwords might be generated more commonly than others, while keys derived from highly unusual passwords might never be generated. The solution, as always, is to use the best tools available. In this case, cryptographers have designed special *key-derivation functions*, which are algorithms designed especially to generate keys from the likes of passwords.[38]

Key generation for asymmetric cryptography is even more complicated because asymmetric keys are not "simply" random numbers. The specification of every asymmetric algorithm includes information about how to generate the necessary keys. If this advice is adhered to, then all should be well. But alas, humans are notoriously poor at following advice, especially when it looks complicated. Investigations have shown that, in many cases, developers have simply not followed these instructions—the result being poor key generation. For example, studies have shown that vast numbers of RSA public keys on the internet share certain properties (more precisely, they share prime factors) that render them insecure.[39] This overlap cannot be a coincidence, and it strongly suggests that the key-generation processes used were flawed.

These days, most people don't design their own cryptographic algorithms (this message seems to have finally been heard by the majority of developers). Only the wise, however, resist the temptation to draw up their own key-generation methods on the back of an envelope.

Getting the Right Keys to the Right Places

Key distribution is one of the most critical stages of key management, and I've discussed it at some length. Key distribution is about getting the right keys securely to the right places.

Getting the right keys to the wrong places would clearly be a bad thing. Hence, considerable effort tends to be invested in key distribution, and there are many different techniques. As already noted, for many applications keys are distributed during manufacture, since keys come preinstalled on devices (mobile SIM cards, car key fobs, etc.). In other cases, key distribution is straightforward because devices that need to share keys are physically close to one another (for example, you read the key on the back of your Wi-Fi router and type it into devices permitted to connect to your Wi-Fi network). In centrally managed systems, keys can be distributed securely by means of closely governed processes and controls. Banks have highly secure processes for distributing keys used in the hardware of ATMs, customers' bank cards, and so on.

Once one key has been distributed to two parties, the hassle of further key distribution can often be avoided by the use of a key-derivation function to pseudorandomly derive new keys from the original key. Your mobile-network operator distributed a key to you embedded on the SIM card that you purchased with your call plan. Each time you make a phone call, the call is encrypted with an entirely new key. This new key is derived from the key on your SIM card. Since both you and the mobile-network operator know the original key, you can both individually derive the same new key from it; nothing further needs to be distributed. This new key is used to encrypt the call and is then discarded. The next time you make a call, yet another new key is derived from the original key on your SIM card.[40]

Key distribution is more challenging when the communicating parties are in open systems such as the internet. By this I mean that the parties are potentially located far from one another and have no prior business relationship during which keys could have been distributed. This is typically the case when, for example, you buy something from an online store, or exchange a WhatsApp message with a new contact. As noted previously, this is precisely the type of situation that motivates the use of asymmetric encryption. Hybrid encryption provides a means of distributing symmetric keys under the protection of asymmetric encryption. Another well-known technique for distributing keys in this scenario is *Diffie-Hellman key agreement*, which provides a means whereby two parties can each send the other a public key and then, from these, each derive a common secret key.[41]

Stopping the right keys from going to the wrong places addresses only half of the key-distribution problem. Just as problematic is stopping the wrong keys from going to the right places. I flagged this issue when I discussed the problems of asymmetric encryption, noting how important it is to make sure a public key is correctly associated with the identity of its owner. Without this linkage, a criminal might be able to create a convincing copy of a legitimate website, supply you with the criminal's public key instead of the legitimate website's public key, and then steal your bank card details when you, in good faith, tried to pay for something. What you need is some means of making sure that the public key supplied by a website belongs to the website you believe it does.

The standard tool for linking a public key to its owner is a *public-key certificate*. At its heart, a public-key certificate is a simple statement, much like all those other certificates you might have hanging on your wall at home. In my house we have the following:

This is to certify Kyla has passed her Grade 2 Guitar with Merit.
This is to certify Finlay won a Class Prize for his super listening.
This is to certify Ramon completed his Adult Dog Training Class.

A public-key certificate essentially states: *This is to certify the public key of* www.reallycheapwidgets.com *is X*, where X is a valid public key of such enormity that I won't write it out in full.[42]

Certificates make grand claims, but the question behind them is: "Who says so?" For the first of our wall certificates, it's the Chief

Executive of the Associated Board of the Royal School of Music; for the second, it's the Head Teacher, St. Cuthbert's Primary; for the third, Sarah Hickmott BSc (Hons) of Pet Necessities Professional Training. Who says so? Someone important. Someone who should know. All of these parties share a degree of authority and respect in their field.

Likewise, a public-key certificate needs to be created by someone trusted to vouch for the correctness of the linkage between a public key and its owner. In cyberspace, this role is played by a *certificate authority*, which could be an official body (for example, the government) or a commercial provider of such certification services.[43] Anyone relying on the public key needs to be able to trust the certificate authority. If you don't trust the certificate authority to have done its job, then you shouldn't trust the information in the certificate. It's that simple.

One common mistake is to read too much into the existence of a certificate. A certificate vouches only for precisely what it states, and nothing more. Finlay might well be a super listener at school, but does this make him a super listener at home? Ramon attended the dog training class, but did he actually learn anything? (Only that he loves cheese.) The simple fact that the public key of www.reallycheapwidgets.com is X does not automatically imply that the key is valid beyond a certain date or can be used to encrypt financial data, or anything else. Public-key certificates tend to include other related data to cover some of these issues. However, even a more detailed public-key certificate is just a set of facts relating to the public key. It doesn't provide assurance about deeper issues, such as whether the public key was generated securely in the first place.[44]

Ultimately, a certificate is only as good as the integrity mechanisms used to protect the information contained in it. Kyla's certificate has a watermark, is printed on regal parchment, and is adorned by various official logos. (The other two paper certificates feature colorful drawings of wax seals.) A public-key certificate, being a cyber object, needs a cryptographic data integrity solution. The certificate authority seals all the information in the public-key certificate by digitally signing it. Anyone relying on the information in the public-key certificate needs to verify this digital signature to confirm the integrity of the contents. To do so, they need the public verification key used to verify digital signatures created by the certificate authority. Since they need to be sure that this public key is *really* the public key associated with the certificate authority, this public key also needs to be linked to the certificate authority by means of a public-key certificate. So, who signs this one?

When you buy something online from the likes of Really Cheap Widgets, the matter of public-key certificates is largely handled for you by your web browser software. Before becoming an online trader, Really Cheap Widgets will have been required to obtain a public-key certificate from a recognized certificate authority. This certificate authority's public key will itself have been certified by a higher certificate authority. Ultimately, a *root* certificate authority will have had its public-key certificate verified and installed in your web browser software.[45] When Really Cheap Widgets sends its public-key certificate to your web browser, the browser software verifies all the relevant certificates. If everything is fine, then your transaction proceeds without incident. If one of the verifications fails, then your browser might issue a warning message, asking you whether you wish to continue. This message essentially informs you that the browser cannot guarantee that it is communicating with the genuine www.reallycheapwidgets.com. Whether or not you proceed is up to you. Prudence suggests you should terminate the connection.[46]

Hopefully, this discussion has strayed far enough into public-key management to demonstrate the general idea of using public-key certificates to vouch for the true owner of a public key. Enough, also, to show that public-key certification is a tricky business with plenty of management processes to conduct. I have not talked about *how* a certificate authority might identify the owner of a public key. Nor have I discussed what happens if the information contained in a public-key certificate needs to be changed. Supporting public-key certificates requires an entire infrastructure surrounding them to address those issues.[47]

Key distribution has its challenges, but there are many different solutions. We use cryptography every day because, when carefully chosen and implemented, these different solutions all work.

Beyond Cryptography

Recall what happens to data during the encryption process: Data . . . data . . . <encryption—kapow!>   encrypted   data . . . encrypted data . . . <decryption—kapow!> data . . . data . . . In other words, between the first kapow and the second, data is protected by encryption. But before the first, and after the second, it's not.

How obvious is this? Data is not encrypted when it's not encrypted. What an earth-shattering observation! Except that, a not uncommon failure of cryptographic protection is not to recognize when, and where, data might exist in unencrypted form.

A good illustration of the importance of *endpoint security* is the use of the TLS protocol for securing web connections. If you're buying a product from an online store, you will almost certainly use TLS to encrypt the transaction details when you check out. The TLS protocol encrypts data, such as your payment card details, between your web browser and the web server of the store. It does not encrypt this data from the point at which you enter it in your keypad. Here, the data might exist in temporary memory, or indeed it might be stored somewhere on your computer. The data could be obtained by anyone standing behind you, watching as you type. It is potentially available to anyone else who has access to your computer or can run a program on your computer. The data might also be available to anyone who has installed a keylogger on your keyboard to record your keystrokes. At the web server end, goodness knows who has access. Some websites store card details in a database, meaning, potentially, that anyone with access to the database could obtain them. While online retailers should protect such data with great care (using cryptography, of course), you can never be sure.[48]

Digital forensic investigators coming across encrypted data don't simply give up and go home. They know all too well that data often lies around, sometimes in surprising places, both before encryption and after decryption. A naive person trying to hide some data on a laptop might encrypt a file and then delete the original, leaving only an apparently encrypted file in their directory. However, deleting a file does not necessarily destroy it; it merely breaks the digital association between the file itself and the label the laptop uses to locate it. Someone who knows what they're doing can rummage around on the laptop and retrieve the unlabeled "deleted" file.[49]

As observed during take three of the scene in which an intelligence agent is working frantically against the clock to save the world, another piece of information that could be carelessly lying around at an endpoint is a cryptographic key. The best way of storing a cryptographic key is in secure hardware. Smartcards such as bank cards and SIM cards are lightweight examples. More heavyweight technologies for storing keys are *hardware security modules*, which are dedicated pieces of equipment for storing and managing keys.[50] Extracting a key from a secure hardware device is difficult. However, if an application has taken the lazier, and far cheaper, option of storing keys in software, then a detailed analysis of the endpoint might find them and unlock encryption.

Computer security expert Gene Spafford famously observed: "Using encryption on the Internet is the equivalent of arranging an armored car to deliver credit card information from someone living in a cardboard box to someone living on a park bench."[51]

Encryption works, but for much of what you do in cyberspace, you are on the park bench.

Carbon-Based Security

Cybersecurity experts have been known, perhaps too often, to claim that humans are the "weakest link" in any security system, including cryptosystems.[52] This claim seems to imply that most security incidents arise from the carelessness or stupidity of the human beings who use the system. You choose the best encryption algorithm in the business, implement it to perfection, manage the keys to the highest standards, and then what happens? Some idiotic human being writes the key on a Post-it note and sticks it on their screen.

Alas, this can happen. However, the claim that humans are the greatest point of vulnerability in a cryptosystem raises some pretty big questions. Who is serving whom in this scenario? Setting aside scary visions of the future, at least for now, most technology is designed for the benefit of human beings. Suggesting that humans are letting the technology down almost suggests that the tail is wagging the dog. Much more fundamentally, if it is, in fact, true that the points of interaction between humans and the rest of a cryptosystem are the places where things are most likely to go awry, then surely the system should be designed to counter this weakness. The human interaction part should be managed, not bemoaned.

What kind of cryptographic calamities could be induced by the human users at the endpoint of a cryptosystem? Users could encrypt a file on the secure system and then save an unencrypted copy on a memory stick, which they could then take home and lose on the bus. They could fail to encrypt sensitive material, or inadvertently turn encryption off. They could write down passwords for the derivation of cryptographic keys. They could lend smartcards containing cryptographic keys (bank cards, employee cards, identity cards) to friends. They could encrypt the data on their laptop and then lose the key. They could go to lunch, leaving their unattended cryptographically enabled device logged on and available for anyone passing by to use. Silly, silly humans. What to do?

Mistakes and incompetence are a fact of life. By far the best way of handling such risks is to deploy cryptography in such a way that there's no human interaction at all. Mobile phone call security is a good example. You enter the number and the line connects. When did the cryptography happen? Well, it just did, without your involvement. The same is true for many of our other everyday technologies, such as internet messaging services. Cryptography happens, by default, without human intervention.

One slight risk with making cryptography so seamless is that bypassing the human prevents a level of interaction between person and machine that might be *desirable* from a security perspective. For example, the invisible cryptography that is in operation between the key and door of your car does not demand anything of you other than having the car key in your pocket. This leaves little room for bumbling human misuse of cryptography and allows for flexibility, since you can permit a family member to borrow the car by simply lending them the key. However, it also means that anyone who steals your car key has everything they need to open your car door and drive away.

You probably don't want quite the same personal disengagement from the process when accessing your online bank account. This is why enabling the cryptographic services that support online banking typically requires human interaction, often through the presentation of PINs, passwords, biometrics, access codes delivered by mobile phone, and the like. These pieces of information strengthen security by linking the use of cryptography to a human being, rather than to simple possession of a security token such as a smartcard or authenticator. By involving a human, however, they also introduce a new point of vulnerability in the system: someone who can lose things, forget things, poorly choose things, or give things away.

Automatically applying cryptography also introduces some less obvious problems. For example, suppose an organization moves from a policy of permitting employees to optionally encrypt their own laptops, to enforcing laptop encryption through a centralized system. Such enforcement appears to solve the problem of information leaking from an unencrypted laptop. However, it introduces a potentially more serious vulnerability; namely, if the organization decides to use a single master key to encrypt each laptop's encryption key, then the information on *all* laptops will potentially be at risk if this master key is exposed.[53]

As another example, using an automatically encrypted messaging service might encourage a user to be less careful about the information they send over it. Should their phone be seized as part of an investigation, the unencrypted data might be recovered from the phone itself. Ironically, default application of encryption might result in *less* information remaining confidential than would otherwise have been the case.

Sometimes, however, we have no choice but to involve humans in the cryptographic process. You probably don't encrypt every attachment you send by email. Occasionally, however, you might want to send a confidential attachment. In this case, you'll need to activate encryption in some way, either through an extension to your email software or by means of a dedicated encryption tool on your computer. Such activation requires you, the human, to do something. Sadly, encryption products can be difficult for people with little understanding or experience of computers or cryptography to use.[54] Users have been known to abandon attempts to encrypt data, lost amid jargon and mystifying instructions. Humans should not be regarded as the weakest link, but a confused human has every chance of becoming so.

Cryptography serves humans, not the other way around. In a secure cryptosystem, the interaction between the cryptographic mechanisms and the human users of the technology should be carefully factored into the design, either by minimization of the need for user interaction, or by clear explanation and motivation for the relevant steps.[55] The real weakest link in a cryptosystem is failure to take into account how humans will interact with the system.

Making Cryptography Work

You could be forgiven for concluding that it's impossible to make cryptography work in practice, given the catalog of potential failures just presented. It's informative to have absorbed this message, but that verdict is not entirely fair. It might not be easy to get cryptography right, but with care, cryptography can be made to work.

It's certainly worth trying to do so. Some people argue that no cryptography is better than bad cryptography, since a poor cryptosystem, wherever its points of failure are, can lead to a dangerously false sense of security.[56] In many contexts this argument is hard to refute. However, although cryptography is hard to get right, the case for trying to do so is surely stronger than the case for giving up before you start. After all, even the Caesar cipher will keep your secrets secret from most people you know.

There's plenty of room for optimism. We, as a society, have become more skilled at designing cryptographic algorithms and protocols. We've improved our techniques for security design and implementation. We've developed standards for securely managing cryptographic keys. We've also become much more experienced at deploying cryptography, and we've learned many useful lessons from past mistakes. By and large, we know *how* to make cryptography work; what we need to do is practice what we already know.

Making cryptography work requires full consideration of the wider cryptosystem that surrounds the cryptographic algorithms and keys. We need to get every single part of this system right. Nothing made this clearer than Edward Snowden's 2013 revelations about various ways in which our use of cryptography in cyberspace was *not* working. Whatever your views are on the ethics of what Snowden did, his revelations served as a useful reminder that anyone trying to subvert the protection offered by cryptography only has to find a weak point *somewhere* in the cryptosystem. There are many potential "somewheres," and these are rarely the cryptography itself.

8

The Cryptography Dilemma

O f all the security mechanisms provided by cryptography, encryption is the most politically charged because it protects the confidentiality of information. Not only do we all wish to have secrets, but we all harbor a desire, at least to some extent, to learn what others want to keep secret. However, what should or should not be confidential is neither objective nor stable over time. We might all agree that personal financial data should generally be kept confidential. But should the financial data of a corporation accused of massive tax evasion be kept secret? This type of conflict creates social dilemmas, which continue to cause political storms over the use of encryption.

Naughty Crypto

Cryptography, I hope you'll agree, is immensely useful. By providing the basis for security, it enables us to do amazing things in cyberspace. But cryptography is not always benign. Here are six potentially unwelcome scenarios.

1. You are wise to the dangers of unprotected data, so you encrypt all the data on your laptop just before you go on vacation. You return after three weeks in the sun, rested and refreshed. Unfortunately, your mind is so refreshed that you can't recall the passphrase used to derive the key to decrypt the data. No passphrase, no key, no data.

2. You switch on your home computer, to be greeted by this message: *Oops, your files have been encrypted! Many of your documents, photos, videos, databases, and other files are no longer accessible. Do not waste time looking for your files. Nobody can recover them without our decryption service. You have three days to submit payment in bitcoin only, after which you won't be able to recover your files—forever.* Disaster! You've been infected by *ransomware*, a nasty computer program that has encrypted all your files, and now someone is demanding payment in exchange for the decryption key required to recover them.[1]

3. You are a network manager who has configured some rules governing the type of internet traffic that is allowed to enter your network. You have a blacklist of web addresses, keywords, and malware. Any connections from outside are inspected to see whether they relate to anything on the blacklist and, if so, are prevented from connecting. Alas, one day you discover that a known piece of malware is infecting many users on your system. How did it get past your checks? Apparently, it was encrypted, which made its true nature so hard to identify that it slipped through your protective net.

4. You are a detective, investigating a suspect accused of murder. You have seized the suspect's phone, on which you believe are a number of incriminating photographs. Unfortunately, the images stored on the phone are inaccessible, because the suspect has encrypted them. You are sure these images are critical to proving the case, but you just can't see them.[2]

5. You are a police investigator who has seized a web server that hosts indecent images of children. You can see from the logs that this server has a large number of visitors every day, whom you want to bring to justice. Unfortunately, the visitors are all using the cryptographic software Tor, designed to make it hard to trace their origin. Who are they? Where are they?[3]

6. You are an intelligence officer monitoring a cell of suspected terrorists. You have managed to obtain access to the communications to and from the mobile phone of one of the targets. The suspect is communicating by using an internet messaging service renowned for its strong cryptographic security. You can see that the suspect is in regular contact with another of the cell members, but you cannot access the details of their conversations.[4]

As you can see from these six scenarios, really only two functions of cryptography are problematic: Confidentiality allows everyone to hide their data, but "everyone" includes blackmailers, murderers, and terrorists. Anonymity allows everyone to be untraceable in cyberspace, but "everyone" includes child abusers. When cryptography hits the news, it tends not to be about hash functions, MACs, digital signatures, or perfect passwords. Instead, when debates rage about cryptography, they invariably concern the use of encryption, since encryption not only protects secrets but can be used to build technologies that provide anonymity such as Tor.

A Dilemma

Let's unpack the issues behind our six examples of instances when encryption causes problems. There is a big difference between the first three and the last three.

The first scenario is the only one relating to an accident, rather than a deliberate act. You forgot the password necessary to decrypt your disk. Such a lapse could be disastrous, but is cryptography at fault? I don't think so; it was your mistake. Encrypting your disk does more good than harm, but it does come with the caveat that you will need to be able to recall the key in order to retrieve your data. This key is so important that you must put in place a process for making sure you don't lose it. If you are prone to forgetting passwords, then this password should probably be stored securely on a separate device, or written down and stored somewhere physically secure. This scenario is not a problem with cryptography itself.[5] We don't often blame cars when we have accidents; it's the driver who tends to be at fault.

Ransomware, the culprit in the second scenario, is a problem created by cryptography. If there were no cryptography, there would be no ransomware. Analogously, if there were no electricity, there would be no electrocutions. The value of electricity far exceeds the element of danger presented by the widespread use of electricity. Likewise, I would argue, the benefits of encryption far exceed the problems created by ransomware. Besides, there are things that can be done about ransomware. Just as for other types of malware, controls such as having backups, keeping systems up to date, installing and maintaining antivirus software, and educating users not to click on unsolicited links and attachments all go a long way to reducing the risk of a ransomware infection. While cryptography can be used against you, you can also take simple steps to prevent bad things from happening.

Cryptography can sometimes pose difficulties for network security. A possible precaution, in the third scenario, would be to inspect any incoming data that appeared to be encrypted, treating it with the same level of suspicion that you treat other blacklisted items.[6] Legitimate uses of cryptography could then be identified, and allowed to pass through. Let's face it, it is very hard to defend a network from all the ills of cyberspace. Even highly secure networks that are not connected to the internet can become infected if someone manually introduces malware on the likes of a memory stick.[7] Networks should be managed in ways to ensure that the use of cryptography is a defense, not a threat.

The last three scenarios concerning problematic cryptography are quite different. They all feature (suspected) "bad" people using cryptography. However, they are using encryption for the same kinds of things you do.

The suspected murderer encrypted the photos on their phone, just like you probably do (most modern phones encrypt all stored data by default, which protects your privacy if your phone is stolen).

The child abusers connected to the image server using Tor to preserve their anonymity. There are many different reasons why you might, quite legitimately, wish to use Tor. Perhaps you are not a privacy advocate yourself and can only imagine that anyone desiring anonymity in cyberspace must be up to no good. But what if you were an investigative journalist or a whistle-blower, or you worked for law enforcement, or you were simply a regular citizen living in an oppressive regime?

The suspected terrorists used encrypted messaging so that nobody could learn the details of their conversation. What about you? Are you happy that anyone (not just the government, but potentially all your friends) could potentially read every conversation you have by using a messaging service? Today, messaging services increasingly encrypt all conversations by default, using state-of-the-art encryption algorithms. You now have to make an effort *not* to encrypt your messages.

The problem is that encryption works, regardless of the nature of the data it's applied to. These "bad" users of encryption are all doing things that you might quite legitimately want to do. Use of encryption thus presents society with a dilemma. If society allows widespread use of encryption, then cryptography will be used to protect data relating to illegitimate activities. If, on the other hand, society somehow tries to restrict the use of encryption, then attempts by honest citizens to protect data relating to legitimate activities might be thwarted.[8]

Should Something Be Done?

Should society do anything to control the use of encryption? Well, there are many disparate views, and I suspect there always will be.

The case for taking action to control the use of cryptography has been argued with passion by certain figures of authority. Speaking to law enforcement officers in 2014, Sir Bernard Hogan-Howe, former head of London's Metropolitan Police (the largest police force in the UK), warned: "The levels of encryption and protection that we are seeing in the devices and methods used to communicate are frustrating the efforts of police and intelligence agencies to keep people safe. . . . The Internet is becoming a dark and ungoverned space where images of child abuse are exchanged, murders are planned, and terrorist plots are progressed. . . . In a democracy we cannot accept any space—virtual or not—to become anarchic where crime can be committed without fear."[9]

In 2015, James Comey, then director of the FBI, raised similar concerns: "As all of our lives become digital, the logic of encryption is all of our lives will be covered by strong encryption, and therefore all of our lives—including the lives of criminals and terrorists and spies—will be in a place that is utterly unavailable to court-ordered process. And that, I think, to a democracy should be very, very concerning."[10]

US senator Tom Cotton was even more forceful in expressing a need for action against unfettered use of encryption: "The problem of end-to-end encryption isn't just a terrorism issue. It is also a drug-trafficking, kidnapping, and child pornography issue."[11]

In contrast, others have been outspoken on the need for widespread access to encryption technology. Speaking in response to widely expressed concerns about the use of strong encryption, Zeid Ra'ad Al Hussein, high commissioner for human rights at the United Nations, warned: "Encryption and anonymity are needed as enablers of both freedom of expression and opinion, and the right to privacy. Without encryption tools, lives may be endangered."[12]

Writing in a previous era of heated debate about the use of encryption, Esther Dyson, US journalist and businesswoman, argued in 1994: "Encryption . . . is a powerful defensive weapon for free people. It offers a technical guarantee of privacy, regardless of who is running the government. . . . It's hard to think of a more powerful, less dangerous tool for liberty."[13]

Computer science professor and cryptographer Matt Blaze has expressed an opinion shared by many academic researchers: "It may be true that encryption makes certain investigations of crime more difficult. It can close down certain investigative techniques or make it harder to get access to certain kinds of electronic evidence. But it also prevents crime by making our computers, our infrastructure, our medical records, our financial records, more robust against criminals. It prevents crime."[14] This viewpoint has been expressed more succinctly by Edward Snowden: "We need to think about encryption not as this sort of arcane, black art. It's a basic protection."[15]

Eating Cryptocake

A huge question is whether we can all benefit from the security protection provided by encryption but still have a means to, in specific circumstances, remove this protection. In other words, can we have our cryptocake and eat it too?

Some figures of authority believe we can. This argument is often made in terms of a need to balance competing goals. For example, the security of general users of a messaging service such as WhatsApp or Signal needs to be balanced against the privacy that the provider offers to customers who are using its services to support undesirable activities. Former UK home secretary Amber Rudd argued for the need to "balance encryption and counter-terrorism."[16] Former GCHQ director Sir David Omand has commented that he feels the UK is getting the balance between (national) security and privacy about right: "2017 is the year of reconciliation, in which we recognize as a mature democracy, it is possible to have sufficient security and sufficient privacy."[17]

The idea of there being such a "balance" may well be alluring, and those who call for it most surely have good intentions. But what does *balancing* the use of encryption mean? What is the unit of measurement? How do we know when a state of balance has been achieved? Who decides? And perhaps most importantly of all, is such balance even technically feasible?

Considering this issue from another angle, encryption has long been regarded as a *dual-use* technology. This term recognizes that certain technologies have both civilian and military applications and, broadly speaking, can be used to do good as well as execute harm. Cryptography joins an illustrious list that includes various nuclear materials, chemical processes, biological agents, thermal imaging, night vision cameras, lasers, and drones—all technologies that bring society a complex mix of gain and pain. Dual-use technologies are often subject to various government controls.[18]

The *dual-use* label is rather general and, I think, unhelpful when it comes to consideration of cryptography. It suggests that this technology is safe in the hands of government scientists but everything should be done to prevent it from being acquired by terrorists. This might be true of highly enriched plutonium, but what about encryption? Once upon a time, this argument had some validity, when cryptography was a technology mainly of the military domain. But today, when cryptography underpins everyone's security in cyberspace, is it appropriate to be so concerned about who is capable of protecting their data by using strong encryption?

To me, cryptography has more in common with a seat belt than with a bomb. A terrorist driving to conduct an attack might wear a seat belt, just like the rest of us. Seat belts thus save terrorists' lives, yet few would argue we shouldn't continue to strive to make seat belts more effective. The benefits of cryptography to the many far exceed the drawbacks of its use by the few.

Cryptography may well be used much more today than ever before, but it's not a new technology. Likewise, the debate concerning the use of encryption has raged ever since cryptography became more widely available.[19] It's worth reflecting on how the dilemma presented by encryption has been historically addressed. Such review reveals not just that all attempts to "balance" the use of encryption are at best temporary fixes, eventually swept aside by technological advances, but that most techniques to do so are, inevitably, problematic.[20]

Breakable Unbreakable Cryptosystems

When authorities call for some way to circumvent the cryptographic protection of data, let's be very clear about what they're asking for. The cryptosystem should, under normal circumstances, be secure enough to protect data. In other words, for all practical intents and purposes, the cryptosystem should be unbreakable. However, in special situations there should be some means of accessing data that has been encrypted using the cryptosystem. This requirement effectively demands a known means by which the cryptosystem can be "broken."[21] The design challenge is problematic from the outset. What is required is a "breakable unbreakable" cryptosystem.

Recall that there are many different ways of breaking a cryptosystem. An "attacker," who in this case let's assume is a legitimate authority (which I will loosely refer to as the *state*), could break a cryptosystem by exploiting any aspect of it. Aspects that could be exploited are the underlying cryptographic algorithm, implementation, key management, or security of the endpoints. In fact, as we will see shortly, all of these approaches have been used in the past.

In most circumstances it seems paradoxical that a normally unbreakable cryptosystem could be breakable. However, this idea is at least conceivable if there exists a significant imbalance between the capabilities of the state and those of "normal users"[22] of a cryptosystem. This imbalance could be in terms of knowledge (of cryptography or system design), computing power, or the ability to enforce behavior. If the state can do something nobody else can, then breakable unbreakable cryptosystems are at least a possibility.

Suppose that the state is believed to have such an advantage over everyone else, and a cryptosystem is designed that can be broken by exploitation of this advantage. Regardless of how it works, let's refer to this ability to break an unbreakable cryptosystem as the *magic wand*. Users of this cryptosystem can protect their data using encryption, believed to be strong enough to provide confidentiality against all potential attackers. However, should a user become the legitimate target of investigation, the state can wave the magic wand and—presto!—plaintext is revealed.

This magic wand scenario raises many issues. Let's set aside all the thorny political questions, including those of cross-border jurisdictions, and assume that we accept the state's need to have a magic wand. Let's also ignore the myriad procedural and implementation concerns, and trust the state to wave the wand responsibly. By far the most significant remaining question is this: Given that the magic wand exists, can we be sure nobody else can wield it? After all, a breakable unbreakable cryptosystem is *breakable*, so is it really safe to assume that its breakability will ever be exploitable only by the state? Keep this question in mind as some candidate magic wands are reviewed.

The Tradesman's Entrance

The Second World War provides a benchmark in our consideration of breakable unbreakable cryptography. Up until the end of the war, the only significant users of encryption were states, particularly the military, deploying their own encryption algorithms for their own private use. Since the use of encryption was restricted to top secret communications within tightly managed organizations, it made perfect sense for these encryption algorithms to be kept secret. Nobody else used them or even needed to know how they worked.

After the war, advances in communications led to an increased interest in encryption technology around the world, particularly from governments. Expertise in cryptography, however, was extremely limited, with only a few organizations able to build encryption machines. Demand for cryptography outstripped supply, and cryptography became a marketable product, albeit a highly specialized and sensitive one.[23]

Consider now a hypothetical scenario from, say, the late 1950s. The technologically advanced state of Freedonia manufactures and sells encryption devices. The Freedonians receive a request from the government of the less technologically advanced Ruritania for a set of encryption devices to protect Ruritanian diplomatic communications. Freedonia and Ruritania are not at war, but they have a combative relationship, and Ruritania tends to be less politically stable than Freedonia would like. Should Freedonia sell Ruritania some of its state-of-the-art encryption devices? It's a chance to make some money, sure, but it would also be a blow to Freedonian intelligence gathering.

Spot the capability imbalance here. Freedonia has knowledge and technology that Ruritania does not. Thus there's a potential opportunity for Freedonia to make some minor alterations to its normally unbreakable encryption technology, converting its encryption devices into breakable unbreakable devices. In other words, the devices will encrypt and decrypt as expected, but there is an additional magic wand trick, known only to Freedonia, that provides a means of decrypting ciphertext generated by the devices. Such a trick is sometimes referred to as a *backdoor*, because it provides a means of accessing the plaintext that is not apparent to most users of the cryptosystem.

The most natural place to establish a backdoor is in the encryption algorithm itself. For example, a very crude backdoor would be to reset the encryption key to a fixed value before encrypting the plaintext. The Ruritanians would think they were using different keys to encrypt, without realizing that the algorithm always resets the key to this fixed value. The Freedonians would know this fixed value and thus be able to decrypt Ruritanian communications.

We'd like to think such a backdoor would quickly be discovered by the Ruritanians. However, the Ruritanians know very little about cryptography, so they are probably not even aware of the possibility that the device will not function as intended. Even if they harbor suspicions, the Ruritanians probably lack the skills they would need to disassemble this device and determine how it works.

How can these Freedonians act so immorally! Well, security tends to be something that states take very seriously. In this case, Freedonia's concerns about its own security have edged any ethical concerns about revealing exactly how its export encryption devices function. Most importantly, Freedonia is confident it won't get caught. Freedonia wants to continue selling encryption devices around the world. Freedonia has rigged its exported encryption devices because . . . it can.[24]

Backdoors Become Front Doors

There are two very strong reasons why placing backdoors in cryptographic algorithms was an option for Freedonia in the 1950s but is not viable today as a means of addressing the dilemma created by the use of encryption.

First, cryptography is far too important today for the components at the heart of any cryptosystem, the cryptographic algorithms, to be "dodgy." If there is any justification for creating a breakable unbreakable cryptosystem, algorithms are the wrong part of any cryptosystem in which to introduce a backdoor. Imagine the situation today if the Ruritanian government were unwittingly sold an encryption algorithm with a backdoor. While Freedonia might have been intending to exploit the backdoor for acquiring diplomatic intelligence, with today's much more widespread use of cryptography, what would happen if the Ruritanians decided to use this same algorithm to protect the medical records of its citizens? Freedonia's intention was to gain a diplomatic edge, not risk the security of the sensitive personal data of the entire Ruritanian population.

Perhaps more fundamentally, while the Freedonians would quite possibly get away with "backdooring" an algorithm in the 1950s, they probably wouldn't be able to do so today. The knowledge about cryptography and the design of cryptographic algorithms is much greater now than it was then. There are more experts, all over the world, who can evaluate algorithms. Indeed, we have come to expect the details of cryptographic algorithms to be published, scrutinized, and approved for public use.[25] Even when algorithms are sold in hardware devices, they can often be inspected and tested. If an algorithm contains a backdoor, then experts will call foul and nobody will want to use the algorithm. More worryingly, anyone already using the algorithm will be put at risk.

Perhaps the most infamous attempt to place a backdoor in a twenty-first-century cryptographic algorithm is *Dual_EC_DRBG*. This is not an encryption algorithm, but rather a pseudorandom number generator that can be used to generate cryptographic keys. The algorithm was shepherded into an international standard by representatives of the US National Security Agency (NSA), but quickly questioned by cryptographers.[26] There was, it was pointed out, a means by which someone could foresee output from this generator. Consequently, keys that it generated could be predicted, and subsequent ciphertext could be decrypted. In the end, and after significant furor, Dual_EC_DRBG was withdrawn from the standards.[27]

Placing a backdoor in a modern cryptographic algorithm is a reckless act, with a high danger of unforeseen and undesirable consequences. The imbalance in knowledge about cryptographic algorithm design that existed in the 1950s no longer exists. Today, hidden backdoors readily become blatantly obvious front doors,[28] thereby defeating the purpose of using encryption in the first place.

Deploying the Long Arm of the Law

There is one area where the state tends to hold an advantage over others: its ability to make and enforce regulations. One approach to addressing the "problem" created by cryptography is to regulate its use.

Once upon a time, there was a technology that helped people exchange ideas in a new way. This technology soon came to the attention of authorities of the state, who regulated it through licensing and applying import and export controls. Some states simply banned it. The subsequent period was one of struggle against restrictions on its use. States argued for the need to control the technology to maintain order. Both users and suppliers of the technology called for an end to regulations in the name of political freedom and human rights.

This was the story of the printing press, which was invented in the mid-fifteenth century and was a political hot potato for well over three centuries.[29] A combination of social pressure and technological evolution eventually forced a relaxation of controls on the printing industry throughout most of the world, although some countries, such as Japan, have only relatively recently done so. Without changing a word, however, this story could have been about cryptography since the Second World War.

The crudest regulatory response to an unwelcome technology is an outright ban. Some states, such as Russia and the Ottoman Empire, were so fearful of the spread of ideas in books that they opted to ban the printing press. In similar fashion, some states today, such as Morocco and Pakistan, decree it illegal to use or sell encryption technology without prior approval by the government.[30] It's very hard to justify, or indeed enforce, contemporary bans on encryption. Cryptography is too widespread and useful to suppress.

A more common approach to controlling encryption is to regulate the export and import of encryption technology, as was done with the printing press. This approach makes the most sense in a world of limited providers of encryption technology—a world that no longer exists. An importer, such as Ruritania, could control who uses encryption by overseeing the entry of encryption technology into the country. An exporter, such as Freedonia, could control who buys its encryption technology. Export controls also enable a state to manage the strength of encryption permitted to enter or leave the country. In the early 1990s, an infamous US export policy permitted a maximum key length of only 40 bits on exported symmetric encryption technology. It is safe to assume that the NSA deemed an exhaustive search for a 40-bit key feasible. The early Netscape web browsers, for example, permitted strong 128-bit encryption on the internal US version of the software, but the international export version controversially provided only 40-bit security.[31]

Export and import controls are a viable means of governing the distribution of tangible objects, since these can be inspected at borders. Up until the 1970s, encryption happened only in objects that either were too heavy to lift or would at least hurt your foot if you dropped them. Restrictions on the movement of encryption around the world could thus, at least in theory, be enforced at borders.

This situation radically changed toward the end of the twentieth century, when encryption became more readily available in software. Since software consists of just a series of instructions for a computer to perform, its movement around the world is almost impossible to control. As a protest against US export controls, software for RSA encryption was documented in a book and even printed on T-shirts, instantly converting them from innocent items of clothing into illegal export-restricted munitions.[32] Nowadays, software is transferred around the world at the mere click of a mouse or press of a button.

The use of export and import controls as a means of addressing the state's concerns about the use of cryptography has considerably weakened over time, leading to almost farcical situations. In the late 1990s, I was working on a multipartner European project that developed a piece of software to show how cryptography could support making small payments on a mobile phone. The software ran on a standard personal computer and was implemented by a partner in southern Germany. The European Commission required that the software be demonstrated at an event in Como, in northern Italy. For the Germans, this should have been a short, four-hour hop south through Switzerland. However, Switzerland at this time had strict regulations on the export of cryptography, which would have required the acquisition of a special license to permit movement of the software across its border. My German colleagues thus embarked on an epic, although admittedly highly scenic, twelve-hour detour through the Austrian Alps in order to circumnavigate the Swiss border. What a waste of time and energy, all because of a somewhat archaic solution to the "problem" of cryptography.

Toward a Cryptopia

In the search for balance between national security and privacy, the 1990s was an awkward decade to be a state controller of cryptography. Export controls had served their purpose well, but things were changing. The problem wasn't that strong cryptography, including asymmetric encryption, had entered the public domain. This knowledge had been out there for almost two decades. What radically changed in the 1990s is that people sat up and took notice.

Advancements in computers and the networks connecting them led some people to imagine very different futures, enabled by the power of connected machines. Some simply spotted commercial opportunities. Others, however, dreamt of a new society, freed from the shackles of conventional governance.

States determined to maintain control of encryption could probably strike deals with aspiring businesspeople. However, a much more powerful force to counter is social change. The internet and nascent World Wide Web opened many people's eyes to an entirely new universe where amazing things could be done: ideas could be shared with like-minded strangers anywhere in the world; items could be traded globally without a sales counter; virtual societies could be established among people who could never physically meet.

Behind the more extreme end of these visions were enthusiasts who realized that these new activities could happen without conventional societal constraints. New rules could be established, set by "We the People" in cyberspace. This wasn't conventional anarchism, since its aim wasn't the elimination of central state governance. Rather, it imagined cyberspace as a parallel existence within which certain aspects of state rule could be bypassed.

What all these visions fundamentally relied on was an emerging cyberspace where secrets could be kept. These future worlds required encryption, not just for confidentiality but also for its ability to facilitate anonymity. Somewhat surprisingly, cryptography suddenly found itself to be the flag around which proponents of these ideas rallied. Groups such as *cypherpunks* and *crypto-anarchists* published manifestos declaring how important cryptography was to achieving their visions of a different society.[33] For example, Timothy May, in his "Crypto Anarchist Manifesto," referred to asymmetric encryption (presumably with RSA in mind) as a "seemingly minor discovery out of an arcane branch of mathematics" that will "come to be the wire clippers which dismantle the barbed wire around intellectual property."[34] Powerful stuff!

Such utopian views of how cryptography could transform the world arose, in part, from a deep distrust of the state. However, concerns about existing controls on cryptography did not come from only the fringes of mainstream society. Many technologists could see just how important cryptography would be in the future. They were concerned that state restrictions on cryptography would hamper the development of security in cyberspace.

States were nervous, and rightly so. Widespread access to encryption and anonymity technologies threatened the effectiveness of several aspects of current state governance, including intelligence gathering and dealing with crime. Export controls on encryption technology now seemed like a weak dam wall, close to bursting point, and the champions of a less inhibited access to cryptography could see the cracks forming. A perhaps unlikely alliance of freethinkers, technologists, corporations, and civil libertarians began to argue vocally for the relaxation of controls over cryptography. They released free cryptographic software, such as Phil Zimmermann's Pretty Good Privacy (PGP).[35] They issued legal challenges, such as *Bernstein v. United States*.[36] They even declared war.

Crypto War

The so-called *crypto war* began in the 1990s and continues to this day (some would argue the war is much older). War is, of course, too strong a term, since barely a shot has been fired in anger, but the arguments about control of cryptography have been heated, and occasionally framed in terms of life and death.

The center of the crypto war has been, and remains, the US, although it is a global conflict. Many attribute the start of the crypto war to President Bill Clinton's administration, who sought to control the use of cryptography in a time of rapid technological change. The essential idea was simple, in both description and sophistication: Want to use cryptography? Use as much as you want, for whatever you like; just make sure you slip us a copy of the decryption key. Ouch! Really?

According to this proposal, officially termed *key escrow*, users of encryption would need to use approved algorithms and hand over a copy of the decryption key to the government. This decryption key would be accessed by the state only if a legal warrant to do so had been granted by the courts.

Well, you can just imagine how well key escrow went down as an idea for controlling the use of cryptography! There were the security concerns: Can the state really be trusted to look after decryption keys? There were the logistical concerns: How would key escrow systems be built and integrated into business processes? There were the cost concerns: Who is paying for key escrow?[37] Most fundamentally, however, was this question: What problem did key escrow really solve?

If the ultimate goal was to enable the state to access data that had been encrypted by targets of an investigation, why would a potential target use an escrowed cryptosystem in the first place? By the 1990s, encryption software was widely available, so anyone really wishing to hide their data could do so without using an approved algorithm and escrowing the key. Would using non-escrowed encryption now become a crime? As the cypherpunks paraphrased it: "If crypto is outlawed, only outlaws will have crypto."[38]

Key escrow was not adopted. Export controls on cryptography were slackened. As the century turned, we entered an era of apparent pragmatism with respect to control of cryptography. States such as the UK, unable to license and escrow cryptography, instead passed laws requiring suspects who possessed encrypted data to release decryption keys under warrant. This is quite a cumbersome type of control to apply from the state's perspective. First there are legal technicalities to be followed. Then the suspect has to be persuaded to cooperate. Finally, the suspect has to actually find their decryption key and make it available, and not "forget" it, "lose" it, or simply not know how to begin going about finding it.[39]

Meanwhile, use of cryptography increased rapidly. Encryption software became widely available. Cryptography was embedded into our daily technologies. Devices containing strong cryptography were traded around much of the world without legal obstruction.

One day, not long after key escrow had faded as an initiative, I sat in the office of a wise colleague, a cryptography pioneer. "There's no going back, is there?" I observed. "Cryptography is out there, and you can't stop anyone from using it. The crypto war has been won." I was expressing a commonly held sentiment among those who had been following the struggles over key escrow. My colleague leaned back in his chair, eyes smiling at my naivete, and chuckled. "It will all be back; you'll see."

What he knew then, we all know now. The crypto war continues, and it will never have a victor.

The Age of Mass Encryption

The first decade of the twenty-first century saw few public skirmishes in the crypto war. Not because the war was over, but because one side was much too distracted by playing with all the cryptography it had fought so hard to liberate from state control. The other side, however, was far from idle.

In an age of widespread knowledge and mass use of cryptography, where anyone can invent their own strong encryption algorithm and freely use it, it might be tempting to believe the state has no advantage when it comes to tackling cryptography. It's probably true that in terms of cryptographic algorithm expertise, the state no longer has the significant edge it once enjoyed. Nor, it seems, does the state have an advantage with respect to raw computation ability, since the most powerful supercomputer in the world can't do much to counter AES encryption.

However, the state retains several significant advantages that can be used against cryptography. One is that the state tends to be in control of the critical physical infrastructure, such as backbone network technology, that cyberspace depends on. Another is that the state has an ability to influence and regulate the organizations whose products and services provide the means by which we engage with cyberspace, such as internet service providers. The state also has extensive resources, both computing and human, to devote to tackling the "cryptography problem." But perhaps the state's greatest advantage is its unique capability to see the big picture concerning how and where data flows and rests as it journeys through the networks connecting cyberspace. The state sees the whole forest, while we, at best, see trees.

It is often claimed that *complexity is the enemy of security*.[40] We have created an incredibly complex cyberspace, and we continue to develop it further. We use cryptography in many sophisticated ways, to secure the things we do there. This cryptography needs to be carefully implemented and integrated. The keys need to be managed. Attention needs to be paid to where unprotected data resides before encryption and after decryption. Remember, there are many ways to break a cryptosystem, and few of them these days have anything to do with breaking cryptographic algorithms.

The crypto war resumed, full tilt, in 2013. Like some of the most sordid conflicts in history, it was triggered by an attempted assassination.

Kiss and Tell

When discussing Edward Snowden, it's important to disentangle the ethical questions around what he did from the issues concerning what he revealed. Snowden, a contractor with the NSA, publicly released extensive sensitive information about, among other things, methods by which the NSA had been dealing with the surveillance challenge provided by encryption. It was a devastating series of leaks, which exposed many of the NSA's tools, techniques, and tactics, and forced Snowden into exile.[41]

Whether you believe that Snowden deserves a pedestal and plinth, or handcuffs and a dungeon, is a discussion for another day (or book). What is indisputable is that we now have an indication of how certain states (in particular, the US and the UK) reacted following the failure to establish key escrow. The state could have done many things to combat the use of cryptography. What we learned from Edward Snowden is that the state did *all* of them.

Of course, we don't know *exactly* what has been going on. Snowden released a substantial number of documents and presentations,[42] but much of the information lacks detail and is hard to confirm. The overall picture, however, is clear. For intelligence purposes, the state has been doing everything it can to try to overcome cryptography.

Rather than focusing on particular allegations, which may or may not be true, it is perhaps more informative to consider the wide range of things that a state *could* do. Let's imagine what might be well within the capabilities of a state, particularly one with some influence over many of the most powerful technology companies. Some of the following techniques do appear among the Snowden revelations.

A state with extensive funds, reach, and facilities could store as much of the data whizzing around in cyberspace as possible, encrypted or not. This data could include copies of all communications as they arrive at a major entry hub of the state's national computer networks (in the UK, for example, many of the international communications flow in via undersea cables, which reach land at a few remote locations). The state could then attempt to analyze this data in order to build a comprehensive picture of a target individual's engagement with cyberspace. Even if messages and phone calls are encrypted, linking information like who was communicating with whom (and when) to data such as web browsing history could yield a very detailed picture of a suspect's life.

A state could come to an agreement with a company providing internet access and email services to millions of citizens. Suppose this company uses encryption to protect email and connections to the servers where client email is stored. The company could give the state access to all the metadata associated with its customers' activities, decrypt email on behalf of the state, or provide the state with the necessary decryption keys.

A state could employ some of its cybersecurity experts to hack into a company's networks and try to obtain data surreptitiously—for example, by seeking plaintext on unprotected internal networks.

A state could fool a computer network switch into encrypting traffic using a public encryption key belonging to the state instead of the public encryption key belonging to the intended recipient. The state could then decrypt the traffic using its private decryption key, take a copy of the plaintext, and then re-encrypt the plaintext by using the intended recipient's public encryption key. The recipient would receive correctly encrypted traffic and be none the wiser.

A state could influence encryption standardization processes in order to have a cryptographic algorithm with a backdoor approved for widespread use.

A state could develop, or purchase, cyberattack techniques that the wider world is not yet aware of and thus has no defenses against (sometimes referred to as *zero-day exploits*). The state could fool a suspect using encryption into clicking on a web link or opening an attachment that launched an attack on the suspect's smartphone. Such an attack might, for example, read data before it was encrypted, steal decryption keys, or switch on the smartphone's microphone to record the content of encrypted calls.[43]

Frankly, Snowden's revelations haven't left much to our imagination.

Life after Snowden

Whether the world is a more secure place as a result of the Snowden revelations depends on your point of view. Michael Hayden, former director of the NSA, described Snowden's action as "the greatest hemorrhaging of legitimate American secrets in the history of my nation."[44] Strictly from an intelligence perspective, Hayden may well be correct, but I would argue that, from the point of view of our security in cyberspace, we are possibly better off because wider society is now able to better appreciate and debate the relevant issues.

Perhaps most fundamentally, the revelations are a spectacular, and timely, reminder of how full of vulnerabilities cyberspace is. The internet is not a carefully designed network with strong built-in security features. The cyberspace we interact with today has evolved in a somewhat disorganized, piecemeal manner, with security often provided (if at all) as an afterthought. As an overall system, cyberspace is full of security gaps, created by weaknesses in technology, poor integration of different technologies, process failures, and bad governance. Even when we encrypt data, these gaps provide myriad opportunities for anyone trying to learn something about the data we have encrypted. I think most cybersecurity professionals were well aware of these vulnerabilities before the Snowden revelations. But like many hidden truths, not enough is done about it until a light is shone on what is really going on.[45]

Snowden's revelations have had many consequences. From a cryptographic perspective, the most significant has been the increased adoption of *end-to-end* encryption by many technology providers, including the likes of Apple for its messaging service. All encryption has "ends," in the sense that data is encrypted from only one point to another. However, *end-to-end encryption* is a term used to indicate that the endpoints for an encrypted communication should be devices under the control of the communicating parties, and not a server in between. In particular, it should mean that the provider of the service (such as Apple in the case of its messaging service) is unable to decrypt the communications.

Much to the frustration of some state authorities, end-to-end encryption eliminates some of the routes to obtaining plaintext, such as doing a deal with (or compelling) the corporate provider of the service to cooperate. During the 2016 dispute between Apple and the FBI over access to an encrypted iPhone, supporters of the FBI claimed that Apple had chosen to "protect a dead ISIS terrorist's privacy over the security of the American people,"[46] whereas Apple's Tim Cook claimed that giving in to the FBI's demands would be like creating the "software equivalent of cancer."[47]

At a more basic level, the revelations have at least resulted in soci-

ety discussing the issue of encryption and its impact on state governance. Commenting on the challenge of accessing encrypted data,
former Australian prime minister Malcolm Turnbull announced,
somewhat bravely, that "the laws of mathematics are very com-
mendable, but the only law that applies in Australia is the law of
Australia."[48]

The very fact that so many prominent people have spoken out
about encryption, whether in favor of or against the control of its
use, has to be a good thing. Some states, such as Australia, the UK,
and the US, have been revising relevant legislation. Many users of
technology have been made aware of encryption, thus creating a
demand for services deploying it. The Tor network, for example, has
more than quadrupled in size since 2010.[49] Many influential companies have reacted by enhancing their cryptographic security.[50]

Only time will tell whether we will see substantial changes
to the way cryptography is implemented and used in the light of
Snowden's revelations. They have certainly given society plenty
to contemplate regarding the data we generate, the digital surveillance of that data, and the dilemma arising from the use of
encryption. While simply talking about these issues doesn't solve
anything, being ignorant of them is far worse.

Cryptopolitik

In one sense, the crypto war has been well and truly won by proponents of the unrestricted use of cryptography. Today, we all use
strong cryptography, and there is no going back to an era in which
states can control precisely what strength of cryptography is used,
and for what purpose. Many governments openly recognize cryptography as being vital to establishing a secure digital society.[51]

Yet, the dreams of those who regarded cryptography as the facilitating technology for a new world remain unfulfilled. Cryptography creates genuine difficulties for states, who will always, perhaps

justifiably, seek means of addressing them. Backdoors in cryptographic algorithms and export controls on cryptographic devices are no longer regarded as appropriate ways of dealing with the cryptography dilemma. However, some of the breakable unbreakable cryptosystems that we use today seem, at least to me, to be far *too* breakable. The complexity of cyberspace leaves too many points of vulnerability, which are not just routes to plaintext for state authorities but also potential attack points for others. By embracing cryptography without building into it an ability to apply state control, we have forced states to adopt approaches to tackling encryption that are not widely acknowledged, are at times disproportionate, and potentially place our computer systems at risk.[52]

I'm sure you are hoping for an optimistic close to this discussion. Perhaps a proposal for a crypto war peace accord? I wish I had an elegant suggestion for a way forward, but I don't, and I'm not sure anyone else does either. I'll at least offer some thoughts on what the future could look like, but they are certainly not proposals for a full cessation of hostilities.

Perhaps the biggest obstruction to resolving the crypto war is a combination of the behavior and nature of the two sides in the argument. Each uses inflammatory and ambiguous dialogue, and arguably fails to acknowledge the very genuine concerns that the other holds about the use of cryptography, both now and in the future. This sort of entrenchment is dangerous since, as former US president Barack Obama observed when considering regulatory change in the US, "If everybody goes to their respective corners, and the tech community says 'either we have strong perfect encryption or else it's Big Brother and an Orwellian world,' what you'll find is that after something really bad happens, the politics of this will swing and it will become sloppy and rushed and it will go through Congress in ways that are dangerous and not thought through."[53] This is kind of where we are right now.

Addressing this lack of mutual understanding requires the

development of shared trust and an ongoing series of very clear conversations. The problem in the case of cryptography tends to be that one of the two sides, the intelligence community, is traditionally somewhat unknowable and reluctant to be transparent. This issue needs to be overcome, at least to some extent, if we are going to make real progress.

Another reason we find ourselves in such a predicament regarding encryption is that the architecture of cyberspace, particularly the internet, is a complete mess. This messiness can be bad for security, and it also creates opportunities for exploiting weaknesses in cryptographic infrastructure. It would surely be preferable to have a tidier, more transparent architecture, but this is not something that can easily be retrofitted. If provision were made, somehow, within any redesigned architecture for lawful access to plaintext, then it is at least vaguely conceivable that the processes and risks involved could be understood, debated, and agreed.[54] Maybe.

There's also a disproportionate percentage of technology and services under the control of just a few states. Is it any surprise that the United States, home of the internet and the most influential companies in cyberspace, exploits this advantage when encryption gets in the way of other matters? Will it ever be possible to develop a more geopolitically fair and democratic cyberspace?

We are, quite rightly, employing cryptography to defend ourselves in cyberspace. I don't think we should stop doing this, but it could be argued that, just occasionally, perhaps, we are using *too much* cryptography.

Think about mobile phones for a moment. Your mobile calls are encrypted between your phone and the nearest base station, in order to prevent the call from being intercepted over the air by anyone with a simple receiver. After this point, traditionally the data has been decrypted and has entered the standard telephone network.[55] It is re-encrypted only for the final part of its journey back over the air between a base station close to the recipient and their mobile phone. In other words, for most of this journey the call is not encrypted. It doesn't need to be, because the standard telephone network is relatively hard to break into. We don't ever hear the state complaining that we are using mobile phones to make calls. This is because, if the state really needs to, and follows due legal process, it can intercept a mobile call after the call has been decrypted. Nor, indeed, do we hear many people complaining that the state can do this. We seem to accept that the state will apply this capability responsibly, which hopefully it does.

Now consider sending a message from your mobile phone using a secure messaging app. If you use an app that supports end-to-end encryption, then your message is encrypted for the entire journey from phone to phone. This is stronger confidentiality protection than you get when you make a phone call, send an email, or even mail a letter. In one sense, this is a wonderful thing. But, is this level of confidentiality *really* necessary? If we were to negotiate a new relationship between the state and the individual with respect to the use of cryptography, might the users of encryption be willing to make some concessions with respect to the strength of cryptographic security they enjoy today?[56]

There is past precedent for restraining the use of cryptography. During the Cold War, as part of the second round of Strategic Arms Limitation Talks (SALT II), the United States and the Soviet Union agreed not to use encryption during particular types of weapons testing so that the other side could gather intelligence on the function and capability of the armaments.[57] Relaxing their use of cryptography might appear to be a backward step in terms of data security, but it reassured each side about the other's capability in order to help relieve tensions. Phone messaging and weapons testing are clearly very different applications, but the point is that sometimes security can be weakened for justifiable reasons.

Don't get me wrong; I'm all in favor of end-to-end encryption. While cyberspace remains a messy space, with states indiscriminately capturing data, and infrastructure companies exploiting user data in less-than-transparent ways, end-to-end encryption seems the safest way to ensure that data on the move is adequately protected. I'm just proposing that in a future cyberspace, it might be possible to reimagine what is strictly necessary.

One possibility, which is more a reframing of the cryptography dilemma than a resolution, is for cyberspace to become more partitioned than it is today. Cyber "subspaces" might form that would be deemed "safer" than the rest of cyberspace. Users could join these virtual gated communities and gain a level of protection by doing so. If sufficient trust were established in the design and governance of these safe spaces, then users might accept a level of state capability to access encrypted traffic within them, as long as this government access took place openly and within the terms of the law. Outside of safe spaces, in the badlands, the crypto war would rage uncontrolled.

Elements of this partitioning concept have already emerged. Apple, for example, has created a somewhat restricted space for users of its devices, where only certain approved software can be installed. Some people criticize Apple for being overly controlling, while others embrace Apple technology because they believe it to be more secure as a result.

Restricting software downloads is one thing, but providing the capability to access encrypted traffic is quite another. Is it, in fact, even possible to engineer a system in which such access capability is guaranteed to remain under the control of the relevant authorities? It's far from clear whether this type of system could be built. And, of course, most of the people the authorities are really concerned about would probably never use such a system.

The crypto war will cease only if we engage in careful and constructive debate about the type of cyberspace we wish to inhabit in the future. Daniel Moore and Thomas Rid offer the following argument:

The future design of cryptosystems should be informed by hard-nosed political and technical considerations. A principled, yet realistic, assessment of encryption and technology more broadly is needed, informed by empirical facts, by actual user behavior and by shrewd statecraft—not by cypherpunk cults, an ideology of technical purity and dreams of artificial utopias. Pragmatism in political decision-making has long been known as realpolitik. Too often, technology policy has been the exception. It is high time for cryptopolitik.[58]

Cyberspace certainly has its dangers, but most of us, taking moderate precautions, muddle through. Even those of us who know we are potentially exposed to state surveillance programs simply press Return and carry on. When we choose to deploy cryptography, I think it would be better to know precisely what security we're getting for our efforts, and not be left to wonder what's going on behind the scenes. We should accept that using encryption creates a dilemma, but the state's response to this dilemma should be transparent and acceptable to us. What's wrong with dreaming?

9

Our Cryptographic Future

Today, we have excellent cryptographic tools available to support the security of the many things we do in cyberspace. Sure, the use of encryption gives rise to social dilemmas, but cryptography is far too useful for these dilemmas to stifle future deployment. Cryptography is here to stay. But what does the future hold for cryptography and its usage?

The Future Is Already Here

Suppose you possess a letter whose contents need to remain confidential well into the future. You keep the letter in a security box, protected by a state-of-the-art lock, and sleep soundly until the day, a decade on, when you read in the paper that thieves have found a way of breaking into this model of security box. So, you buy a new security box, with a stronger locking mechanism, and transfer the letter to the new box. Several years later the same thing happens, so you buy another box, and so on. In other words, as attacks on security boxes become more sophisticated, so, too, does your defense against the evolving threat.

This strategy works fine for security boxes, but it doesn't work for encryption. Encryption works more like this. You possess a confidential letter, of which you make multiple copies and place each copy in its own security box protected by a state-of-the-art lock. You give one of these security boxes to each of your worst enemies. Ten years later you learn that this model of security box can be broken into, so you buy a bunch of new security boxes and ask your enemies to give you back the old boxes so that you can upgrade them.[1] Um, that's not going to end well, is it?

The problem is simply that digital information is so readily copied and stored that we must assume encrypted data will be forever accessible to an attacker. In the event of future breakthroughs in attacks on cryptography, it's not realistic to rely on simply upgrading the encryption algorithm in order to protect existing data. You can re-encrypt old plaintext with this stronger encryption algorithm, but you cannot guarantee that copies of the original ciphertext will not still be available for an attacker to break.[2]

The biggest challenge for designers of cryptographic algorithms is that the cryptography of today *will* be attacked tomorrow. If a deployed algorithm is rendered insecure by a future attack, the time and cost involved in replacing the algorithm is potentially substantial.[3] When the block cipher DES was deemed insecure in the 1990s, it was so embedded in the banking infrastructure that replacing it was almost unthinkable. As a result, we still use DES today, albeit in the more secure form of Triple DES.

Consequently, modern cryptographic algorithms are designed very conservatively, with highly demanding security requirements and as much proofing against the future as possible. Designers try to anticipate how computers will evolve in the future, particularly with respect to improvements in processing power, and then add a significant margin for error. Recall that the fastest computer in the world today takes 50 million billion years to search for a 128-bit AES key. This sounds like excessive protection, but we want to encrypt data today that will still be confidential in, say, twenty-five years (in some cases, much longer). How good will the fastest computer be then? The cautious design of AES even supports longer key lengths, of 192 and 256 bits, which can either be used today for data needing extremely high levels of protection, or can be more cost-effectively switched to in the future.

As far as cryptography is concerned, the future must concern us today. It doesn't matter precisely how the future eventually unfolds; what matters is that we anticipate it and prepare for it.

The "Q" Word

The word *quantum* seems to exert an almost mesmeric effect on people. It conjures up fascinating, sometimes alarming, notions of complex future technology beyond our intuition and comprehension.[4] We shake our heads bemusedly and think: "Better leave that to the experts." (For you, hopefully, the word *cryptography* no longer has the same impact.)

You must not back away, however, from the importance of the adjective *quantum* with respect to cryptography. It arises in at least three different contexts that, although fundamentally different, are often confused. The first relates to existing technologies of varying degrees of practicality. The second concerns important technology not yet existing but of high relevance today. The third concerns technologies neither existing today nor likely to be relevant in the near future.

Two potentially useful quantum technologies relating to cryptography already exist. Both of these concern different aspects of key management. The first is *quantum random number generation*. As we've seen, random numbers are extremely important in cryptography, particularly for key generation, and nondeterministic random number generators based on natural physical sources are top of the range. Some of the best of these are based on quantum mechanics.[5] The second technology addresses the problem of establishing a common secret key in two different locations. *Quantum key distribution* is a means of transferring a randomly generated key from one location to another over a special quantum channel.

A revolution is coming in computing technology. *Quantum computers* will, apparently, be able to perform some tasks much more speedily than today's computers do.[6] Quantum computers will have a significant impact on cryptography because some tasks relating to cryptography that are currently computationally infeasible on a conventional computer will become computationally feasible. Only a few fledgling quantum computers exist today, and their extremely limited capability makes a pocket calculator seem like a supercomputer. But quantum computers will only improve, so we need to take quantum computing seriously and prepare for its arrival.

Quantum computers will be capable of breaking some of the cryptographic algorithms that we use today. It is tempting to turn to the capabilities of quantum computers for a solution to this problem. After all, if quantum computers can break existing cryptography, why don't we design new quantum cryptographic algorithms that run on quantum computers? There's nothing wrong with this idea, but in terms of securing cyberspace, it should be a fairly low priority.

We don't have serious quantum computers today, nor are we likely to have them soon. Time will pass. Eventually, probably, quantum computers will be developed by a few technologically advanced organizations. Only they will have the capability of using quantum cryptographic algorithms. Much more importantly, the rest of us will need cryptography that runs on conventional computers to protect us from the few quantum computers in existence. More time will pass. Eventually, maybe, quantum computers will become a bit more mainstream. Only *then* might quantum cryptographic algorithms possibly become useful. Eventually, maybe, might, possibly . . . I suspect this is more of an issue for our children (or perhaps their children) than for you or me.

Beware of anyone talking more generally about *quantum cryptography*. This ill-defined notion is often used to capture any, or all, of the three contexts I described at the start of this section. Quantum cryptography can thus exist today or not exist, be revolutionary or speculative, be practical or impractical. This is why *quantum cryptography* is a term I'll avoid. We must not, however, avoid quantum computers. While they cannot yet hurl an angry bird at a pig,[7] they have the potential to be devastating for modern cryptography.

Weapons of Mass Decryption

Here's what we *do* know about quantum computers. They work in a fundamentally different way than the computers we use today. The data they process is represented in a form different from the binary encoding used by conventional computers. Through an ability to conduct some types of operations in parallel, they will be able to perform certain tasks much more efficiently than classical computers do.

Here's what we *don't* know about quantum computers. We don't know when a practical quantum computer will be built. We don't know whether quantum computers will be able to achieve in practice all that they promise in theory. We don't know who will build the first practical quantum computers. We don't know what the eventual rollout of quantum computers will look like. We don't know whether quantum computers will ever become a mainstream consumer technology. In terms of cryptographic planning for the future, however, *none of this matters*. What matters is that future quantum computers are possible, and we need to develop the capability of defending against them today.[8]

It is true that quantum computers will have a significant impact on modern cryptography, but they won't break *all* the cryptography that we use today. While some of the cryptographic algorithms in current use offer little protection against a quantum computer, others remain highly effective. It's important to understand these different prognoses and their implications.

The main area of concern is asymmetric encryption and related digital-signature schemes. Almost all the asymmetric encryption and digital-signature schemes that we use today are based on the perceived difficulty of two mathematical problems: factoring and finding discrete logarithms. It is known that a sufficiently powerful quantum computer could, unfortunately, both factor and find discrete logarithms efficiently.[9] In other words, a quantum computer would render all our current asymmetric encryption and digital-signature schemes ineffective. Not good.

The problem with the asymmetric encryption algorithms in use today is that their security is based on specific computational problems that are believed to be hard on conventional computers. If a quantum computer does not find these computational problems difficult, then we're in trouble if such a machine ever becomes a reality.

For this reason, researchers are currently developing and analyzing new asymmetric encryption algorithms based on alternative computational problems not believed to be efficiently solvable by a quantum computer. These *postquantum* asymmetric encryption algorithms will replace the asymmetric encryption algorithms that we use today.[10] A similar process is under way for developing new postquantum digital-signature schemes. Importantly, these postquantum cryptographic algorithms need to be capable of running on conventional computers; they do not themselves use quantum techniques, but they are designed to secure information against a future attacker with access to a quantum computer.

There is better news for some other cryptographic tools. Symmetric encryption algorithms tend not to rely on any one specific computational problem for their security. They rely more on intelligent engineering than just on mathematics, placing such a complex computational obstacle course between plaintext and ciphertext that the best option for an attacker is to simply search for the correct key rather than try to break the algorithm itself.

It is currently believed that the best a quantum computer can do is reduce the time it takes to perform an exhaustive key search by a margin that is substantial, but not so significant that all the symmetric encryption algorithms we use today would be ineffective. More specifically, it is believed that symmetric-key lengths need to double in order to protect against an attacker with a quantum computer.[11]

The symmetric encryption algorithm most widely deployed today is AES, typically with a key length of 128 bits. However, AES also supports a key length of 256 bits, so anyone fearing a quantum computer could simply switch to this key-length setting. That said, some ubiquitous applications do not use AES. Most card payment networks currently rely on Triple DES, which has shorter keys, so these networks will need to change the symmetric encryption algorithm they use in order to become secure against a quantum computer.

Quantum computers present a genuine threat to the cryptography we use today. We are taking urgent action now to address this threat, and I am quietly confident that we will develop a suite of cryptographic algorithms suitable for protecting against quantum computers long before quantum computers themselves become practical reality. Until we do so, however, there remains a risk that data encrypted today could be broken in the future by a quantum computer.

Magic Channels

What is a reality today is technology providing quantum key distribution (QKD). This is neither an encryption algorithm nor anything requiring a quantum computer. Rather, QKD is precisely what it's called: a method of using quantum mechanics to distribute a symmetric key.

Let's go back to basics on the key-distribution problem. Two users wish to exchange an encrypted message using their favorite symmetric encryption algorithm. To facilitate the exchange, they each somehow need to obtain a copy of the same secret symmetric key. One option is for the sender to generate a random key and then transfer this key to the receiver. But how?

In the absence of telepathy, we have a real problem here to solve. The sender cannot simply send the key to the receiver over an unprotected communication channel, since an attacker could be watching the channel and would thus learn the key. Right?

As it turns out, this isn't quite true. If the communication channel is a standard one, such as a mobile telecommunications network, Wi-Fi, or the internet, then the argument is valid. Suppose, however, that the channel is instead a "magic" communication channel, with the special property that if any attacker intercepts information being exchanged over it, the recipient is made aware of this interception (an alarm bell rings, if you like). The sender could then simply transfer the key over the magic channel to the receiver. If no alarm bell rang, the users would know that nobody else had seen the key. If the alarm bell did ring, then the sender and receiver would throw the key away and try again.

The process of QKD works precisely in this way, where the "magic" channel is a quantum optical channel, instantiated through the likes of either line-of-sight aligned lasers or optical fibers. The key is encoded as quantum states, and a special property of quantum mechanics means that anyone attempting to read data on the channel will inadvertently alter these states in a way that can later be detected by the receiver.[12] There is no doubt that QKD is an extremely clever application of quantum mechanics. Various experimental networks have been set up using QKD, and QKD has been used to distribute a key in space via satellites.[13] You can buy commercial QKD systems today, although they are not cheap.

Just because a technology is exciting and innovative, however, does not mean we really need it. Hovercraft, the Concorde, and Sony's MiniDisc were all brilliant inventions addressing real problems, but they never made it into the mainstream, for a variety of reasons. Although QKD may well find niche applications, it seems likely it will join this list of technologies more hyped than deployed. Here's why.

First, QKD is an expensive solution for a problem that can be solved more cheaply. QKD distributes a symmetric key for use with any symmetric encryption algorithm. This is great, but we already have many ways of solving this particular problem, including pre-installing long-term keys and deriving encryption keys from them when needed, as is done for your mobile phone, Wi-Fi network, bank card, and other devices.

It is argued that QKD might keep us safe from attackers with quantum computers, since QKD could be used to distribute keys for a special symmetric encryption algorithm known as the *one-time pad*. This algorithm is as theoretically secure as it is possible to make any symmetric encryption algorithm, since it encrypts every single bit of the plaintext individually by using a random key.[14] Unfortunately, the one-time pad is an expensive algorithm to use because it requires random keys that are as long as the plaintext. For most of us, why go to all the hassle of distributing one-time pad keys when, as previously noted, AES, with a relatively short (256-bit) key, is also secure against an attacker with a quantum computer?

Second, with respect to the emergence of quantum computers, QKD addresses the wrong problem. To use QKD requires having a fixed network of known devices, each using special technology to establish connections. This is precisely the kind of setting where symmetric cryptography is sufficient to secure the network.

But symmetric encryption is not what will be severely compromised if practical quantum computers are ever built. The cryptographic emergency arising from quantum computers appears to be the need for new forms of asymmetric encryption. We need new asymmetric encryption algorithms in order to secure connections in open environments, such as the World Wide Web, where there is no preestablished relationship between communicating parties. Connections in open environments cannot be secured by the use of QKD. This is why the development of postquantum asymmetric encryption algorithms is far more important to our future security than QKD is.

Cryptography Everywhere!

Hopefully you are now more than aware of your personal dependency on cryptography for securing your activities on the internet, making phone calls, purchasing items with bank cards, and so on. Most of these clearly need cryptography, because they are activities that necessarily occur in some aspect of what we would traditionally regard as cyberspace.

One trend we are witnessing is a blurring of the separation between objects we readily associate with cyberspace, such as computers, tablets, and phones, and other everyday items. We are becoming used to the idea that televisions, gaming consoles, watches, and cars are also increasingly connected to cyberspace. Perhaps we can (almost) see the case for those being joined by the likes of thermostats, ovens, window blinds, and washing machines. But do we really need internet-enabled salt shakers, mirrors, toasters, and trash cans, all of which have appeared on the retail market?[15]

This phenomenon of increased connectivity is sometimes referred to as the *Internet of Things* (*IoT*) and is being driven partially by the development of minute, low-cost sensing technologies, capable of being embedded in everyday objects. Since almost anything could be connected to cyberspace, and most cyber-enabled things need some degree of security, as the IoT expands we're going to be using even more cryptography in the future, and in surprising places.[16]

One environment ripe for IoT innovation is your home. You can buy technology today that will connect your home appliances, making it easier to control electrical devices such as lighting and heating, and improving energy efficiency. You might not consider your domestic appliances in need of much security, but think again. Much of the data on a smart home network is sensitive. The times that your lights and heating go on and off, when you watch television, when you cook, and when you run the shower all provide a template of your typical day. This might not make exciting reading for everyone, but it could be priceless for someone intending to break into your home.

You want all this data to be correct in order to obtain an accurate energy bill. And you clearly don't want just anyone having access to this network; otherwise, a mischief maker might condemn you to living in a haunted house where lights flick on and off mysteriously, the oven heats up in the middle of the night, and your heating is turned off on the coldest night of the year. Fortunately, your cyber home could be made safe and secure with the appropriate deployment of cryptography. Let's hope that those developing all this connected technology are paying attention.[17]

One advantage of smart ovens, internet-enabled light switches, and cyber heaters is that they are all large enough "things" to potentially support the same type of cryptography that we use in our phones, bank cards, and car locks. The same is not true, however, for some of the other devices that we're connecting to the internet. Tiny devices such as RFID (radio-frequency identification) tags (which can be used to label products) and miniature wireless sensors (which have all sorts of intriguing applications, like crop monitoring and wildlife tracking) are constrained in their ability to store and process data. They tend to have limited memory and a need to conserve power in order to prolong their battery life.

To secure such devices using cryptography, researchers are developing special lightweight cryptographic algorithms, and in the future even lighter algorithms may be needed.[18] These lightweight algorithms typically sacrifice some security in order to make substantial performance gains over conventional cryptographic algorithms. This is arguably an acceptable compromise, since data gathered by such devices may not need to remain confidential for a long period of time. And, certainly, using lightweight cryptography is better than no cryptography at all.

One notable implication of the way we use cryptography today is that, from the perspective of many systems you interact with in cyberspace, *you are your cryptographic key*. An ATM will dispense money only if the system is convinced that the chip on the presented card contains the cryptographic key it believes belongs to you. You will be charged for any phone call made using the cryptographic key stored on the SIM card linked to your name. Your car door will open for anyone who is able to use the cryptographic key associated with your car key fob.

In the future, however, this embodiment of the cryptographic key is likely to be taken one step further. You won't just be represented by cryptographic keys; your body will contain cryptographic keys, possibly many of them. A major area that is likely to benefit from IoT technologies is the arena of medical science and health care. The types of things connected to cyberspace in the future will include medical implants such as pacemakers and other wearable or ingestible monitoring devices. These technologies may well communicate data to health-related apps running on your mobile phone, or possibly report directly to your doctor's office. This *Internet of Me* isn't speculation; it's already happening. It most definitely requires security, and hence cryptography.[19]

In 2012, the US TV series *Homeland* featured an episode in

which Vice President Walden is assassinated by a remote attacker who connects to and accelerates his pacemaker. This episode must have been very uncomfortable viewing for the thousands of pacemaker patients around the world. Yet, just as for all IoT applications of the future, if we design and deploy cryptography appropriately, their hearts needn't flutter. Medical databases can be kept confidential, and pacemakers can be designed to communicate only with authorized medical experts and to restrict acceptable settings to safe values. The challenge for society is to ensure that such fictional attacks remain so.

Cloudy, with Sunny Cryptographic Intervals

Once upon a time, the world worked like this: You generated data (documents, photos, emails, whatever) and stored it on your personal computer under your control. If you worried about the security of your data, then it was your responsibility to protect it, using cryptography, of course. This arrangement applied just as much to situations in which "you" related to an organization as to "you" the individual.

Nowadays, the world often works more like this: You generate data and store it somewhere (goodness knows where) under someone else's (goodness knows whose) control. You can access your data anytime from anywhere, and you can generate much more data than you have the ability to store locally. This is how the likes of Gmail for email, Dropbox for file sharing, Spotify for music streaming, and Flickr for photo curation all work. More significantly, many organizations are increasingly entrusting their entire data sets to similar data-hosting services because it's easier, cheaper, and much more convenient than managing their own systems. This general idea is rather loosely refer to as the *cloud*. Of course, there isn't just one cloud—there are many—but the fundamental principle behind them all remains the same.

Handing your data over to someone else is not without obvious risks.[20] That said, a decent cloud service provider should take cybersecurity seriously. Indeed, it's even possible that data in the cloud is safer than data stored locally, since data owners are not always good at basic security measures such as backing up. However, in some situations—for example, when outsourcing a medical database—we do not want a cloud service provider to view the data they store on our behalf. In these cases the obvious solution is to encrypt the data before we submit it to the cloud.

Alas, an encrypted medical database in the cloud presents a significant problem. Suppose we want to identify patients with a particular condition, or rearrange database entries by date of birth, or compute the average age of patients who have a specific medical profile. Since conventional encryption schemes are designed to produce unintelligible ciphertext with no apparent relationship to the plaintext it represents, we cannot conduct these operations directly on the ciphertext. We must thus download the encrypted database from the cloud, decrypt the data, and then analyze it locally. This process is both inefficient and inconvenient, since the primary motivation for using the cloud in the first place was to avoid having all this data stored on our own computers.

The need for cryptography seems to erode some of the benefits of cloud computing. In fact, however, something more interesting has happened: the need for cloud computing has driven a wave of innovation in cryptography. Special types of cryptographic algorithms are being designed precisely for the types of scenarios just discussed.[21] For example, *searchable encryption schemes* enable data owners to search data while it remains encrypted, while *homomorphic encryption* enables data owners to perform a range of different types of computation (such as addition and multiplication) on encrypted data without first decrypting it. Encrypting data by using such schemes allows encrypted data to be processed while still being stored securely in the cloud.

A searchable encryption scheme allows the encrypted database to be searched, items matching the search to be identified, and only those matching items then to be returned to the data owner, who decrypts them locally. Homomorphic encryption schemes allow a data owner to compute the average value of some encrypted numerical database items by first computing the average ciphertext value (in the normal way), which are returned to the data owner, who then decrypts this value locally to obtain the average plaintext value. This capability paves the way for more complex computations, such as running data analytics on encrypted data.

This sort of functionality is very much a work in progress, since many of these new cryptographic schemes are not yet efficient enough to see wide-scale deployment.[22] Nonetheless, it shows how far cryptography has advanced since the early 1970s, when the cryptographic tool kit really consisted of only symmetric encryption. As new cyberspace applications emerge, with specific security requirements, we can expect even more cryptographic tools to be designed to secure them. The future is not just wider use of cryptography; it's more cryptography itself.

The Rise and Rise of the Machines

The day is not far off, we are told, when computers may become more intelligent than humans. Nobody knows when this *technological singularity* will occur (some say the 2030s, others the 2040s).[23] Nor does anyone know whether these ultraintelligent computers will be technologies like the computers of today, or whether they will be digital cyborgs, arising from the convergence between computer networks and the human brain. It's not even clear exactly what *more intelligent* means, or whether we'll even be aware that the technological singularity has taken place.

These issues are details. What is beyond dispute is that computers are becoming more and more capable of conducting tasks previously associated with humans. Today, computers can do things that only humans could have done a few decades ago, such as interpreting human speech and driving cars. Advances in artificial intelligence are expected to push this process further and further. It's possible to imagine the development of robots capable of providing medical diagnoses, binoculars able to identify all objects in their view, and vehicular systems that operate fully automatically. Unnervingly, artificial intelligence will undoubtedly deliver many things we cannot yet imagine, some of which could end up being beyond our full control.[24]

We are fueling this progress by the sheer volume of data being generated. In 2018, users posted about 50,000 photos to Instagram, created 500,000 tweets, and sent 13 million text messages—*every minute of the day*.[25] This creation of vast amounts of data, and improvements in the algorithms used to process and make deductions from it, are helping computers to perform analytical tasks well beyond the capabilities of humans.[26]

What does all this mean for the future of cryptography? Whatever their form and function, the computers of the future will certainly need cryptography to protect their data. It's quite possible that these computers will be better at using cryptography than we are, capable of making sure that appropriate cryptographic protection has been applied.

The more fascinating question to consider, however, is: What impact might artificial intelligence have on cryptography itself?[27] Could a computer of the future become so smart that it could break all known cryptography, just like the machine in Dan Brown's *Digital Fortress*?

I doubt it. Cryptography is threatened when there is a capability gap of some sort between users and attackers of cryptography. As illustration, it's worth reflecting on which capability gaps were exploited by past governments to control the use of encryption. In the 1950s and 1960s, the capability gap was superior knowledge of how to design cryptography. In the 1970s and 1980s, it was the ability to legally restrict the strength and movement of cryptographic technology. More recently, the Snowden revelations suggest it was a superior ability both to have a systemic view of how cryptography was used, and to politically influence some of the main technology providers. If we fail to develop quantum-resistant asymmetric encryption algorithms, then a future capability gap could be represented by possession of a quantum computer.

I can certainly imagine advances in automated reasoning and artificial intelligence threatening today's cryptography. A highly sophisticated computer program might well be able to conduct a more thorough security analysis of a cryptosystem than we can carry out today. It might find subtle flaws, discoverable only by sophisticated investigation. It might be able to find unobvious patterns in encrypted data. But for advances in artificial intelligence to lead to a capability gap, it is necessary to imagine an advanced attack machine being capable of doing things the rest of us are totally unaware of. I can't completely rule this out, but I think the advancement of modern science unfolds in a sufficiently open and collaborative environment that it's unlikely anyone can keep this type of capability a secret for very long.

Once we know about it, we can do something about it. If intelligent computers make a leap forward in their ability to *attack* cryptography, I believe this intelligence will almost certainly permit the more intelligent *design* of cryptography. Today's cryptography is designed by humans, with computers used to model and test its security. Future computers may well be better at this design process than we are, creating stronger cryptography that has been more thoroughly scrutinized. They will probably also be smarter than we are at analyzing entire computer systems, determining what cryptography to apply, and then making sure it is implemented correctly.

Cryptographic progress is sometimes framed as a "race" between attackers and designers. When attack techniques improve, so, too, must cryptographic designs in order to counter them. Overall, I think the designers generally stay ahead in this game, as long as they pay attention to the way attack techniques develop. If cryptographic design heeds the progress of artificial intelligence, I believe the cryptography used to support our future computing needs will be sufficient. However, nobody alive today has any idea how our artificially intelligent future is really going to pan out.

Trusting Cryptography

One thing that will need to change in our cryptographic future concerns the notion of *trust*.[28] Cryptography is closely linked to trust, and our future security ultimately relies on this connection becoming even tighter. It's important to understand why.

Trust is the "firm belief in the reliability, truth, or ability of someone or something."[29] This is precisely what cryptography facilitates in cyberspace. We need to know who knows what. We need to know which information is correct. We need to know who is communicating with whom. Because of the nature of cyberspace, trust is impossible to build *without* cryptography.

Cryptography also *relies* on trust. For cryptography to work, we need to trust that certain mathematical computations are hard to perform on a computer. We need to trust that an attacker's computing power does not exceed anticipated levels. We need to trust that users of cryptography will behave in expected ways and not, for example, share their cryptographic keys on their social media accounts.

Ultimately, however, cryptography itself must be trusted. The 2013 Snowden revelations significantly dented many people's trust in cryptography.[30] As previously discussed, the design process for cryptographic algorithms cannot always be trusted. Nor can the implementation of cryptography on the technologies we use today, or the ways in which keys are managed. If there is no belief in the reliability of cryptography, what hope is there of establishing meaningful trust in cyberspace?

Establishing trust in cryptography is challenging. A significant barrier is the sheer complexity of what we need to trust in order to trust cryptography. It's not just about algorithms; it's necessary to trust the entire system in which cryptography is used, including the manufacturers of the technologies and the operators of the networks on which cryptography is deployed. All this is made yet more complex by the fact that different people trust and mistrust different sets of things.[31]

Nonetheless, some positive trends suggest that we're moving in the right direction.

The first relates to choice. Parliamentary democracy is a system of government whose popularity arises, in part, because citizens can choose their representatives. We don't always trust our politicians, but we probably trust them more than if they'd been imposed on us. In the mid-1970s, cryptography didn't offer much choice. If you wanted to use symmetric encryption, then DES was almost your only option. Today, there are dozens of symmetric encryption algorithms to choose from. Choice doesn't imply greater security, but it can help to build trust.

The cryptography used to protect 4G and 5G telecommunications networks supports a choice of cryptographic algorithms, including special algorithms developed in China, for use in China. The Chinese don't appear to trust cryptographic algorithms developed by others (and no doubt, some other people don't trust Chinese algorithms), but having their own algorithms included in the specifications means that the Chinese have greater trust in telecommunications security. Similarly, you can configure the TLS security settings in your web browser so that, from the choice of cryptographic algorithms offered there, only algorithms you trust can be used to secure connections to a web server.

A second trend has been an increased interest, in both the academic and practitioner communities, in deploying cryptography securely in real technologies. In the past, the security of cryptography was evaluated independently from the operating environments in which it was used. Now, we are evaluating algorithms not just in isolation, but mindful of the wider cryptosystem within which they are used. For example, a cryptographic protocol such as TLS is evaluated to determine not just that it's logically correct and achieves its stated security goals, but also that these qualities remain true after implementation in a real environment where auxiliary information such as error messages could be exploited by a clever attacker. While there are several smaller annual gatherings of cryptographic experts to discuss the theory of cryptography, one of the biggest meetings is now the *Real World Crypto Symposium*, where hundreds of researchers and developers together advance their collective knowledge about how to foster greater trust in the cryptography used to secure technologies in widespread use today.[32]

Most fundamentally, I believe—post-Snowden—users tend to be less complacent about security. This shift includes a greater awareness of the need to have cryptography that we can trust. The arguments between governments and technology providers about end-to-end encryption are just one example. The fact that you are reading this book is perhaps another.

Do you trust cryptography to provide adequate security for your needs? I have given you plenty of indication that you should, with some caveats. If we work toward having not just secure cryptographic algorithms but also secure cryptographic systems that run secure implementations of cryptography, then in the future it should be possible to trust cryptography even more. I certainly hope so.

Cryptography and You

What about your personal cryptographic future? It's good to know how, and why, cryptography underpins cybersecurity. Should you now just carry on with your future activities in cyberspace as before, safe in the knowledge that cryptography is out there "doing its job" to keep you secure?

For one thing, I hope demystifying cryptography has removed some of the fear of the unknown when you consider cybersecurity. It's not something that only computer whiz kids have any hope of understanding. Cryptography provides the basic tools from which security technologies are built. By appreciating how cryptography works, you already have some of the fundamental knowledge about how security is constructed in cyberspace.

I also hope that knowing about cryptography will change the way you think about security in cyberspace. Regarding cybersecurity through a cryptographic lens can be very useful. When your bank issues you a gadget to use when accessing your account online, you now know that it's really giving you an algorithm and a unique cryptographic key. As long as you keep the device under your personal control, you have a much securer way of logging in than if, say, you are asked for a six-digit PIN and your mother's maiden name.

Thinking cryptographically can also help you make sense of current affairs. When you read in the media that the security of a particular technology you use has been "broken," where does the problem actually lie? Is there a problem with the cryptographic algorithms used, is there a flaw in the ways the keys are generated, or have the keys been stolen from a central server? Do you, personally, need to take any action as a result? Should you wait for the technology provider to fix the problem, should you just change your password, or should you abandon the technology in favor of another?

Knowing the basics of cryptography should also give you the confidence you need to evaluate your current cybersecurity practices. How is data protected on your current devices? Are your network connections to websites cryptographically protected? How easy would it be for someone else to "become you" in cyberspace? You might even decide to take proactive action. If you have really sensitive data on your laptop, perhaps you should encrypt it. If you regularly put confidential data onto memory sticks, perhaps you should upgrade to using those with cryptographic protection.

Just as importantly, you can utilize your cryptographic knowledge when deciding which technologies or services you engage with in the future. Ask yourself awkward questions. What security is provided? What algorithms are used? Who generates the keys, and where are they stored? It's not always easy to have these questions answered, but providers are getting better about releasing the details because they're increasingly realizing that security doesn't just make products safer; security sells. Make cryptography part of the way you evaluate what to use, and what to do, in cyberspace.

Appreciating the role that cryptography plays in underpinning cybersecurity should also help you contribute to the wider societal debates concerning its use. I encourage you to have your say about how society should juggle desires for security and privacy in cyberspace. This doesn't mean you have to become a politician. Big issues are best addressed by a combination of high-level policy and action on the ground. The response to global warming, for example, requires a combination of global political leadership and day-to-day changes by every individual. The two are intertwined, since individual actions can influence policy, and policy can change personal behaviors. Thus you, too, can contribute to the debates about security and privacy, including control of the use of cryptography, through your individual actions. You do so when you decide what information to share online, when you choose which technologies to interact with, and when you react to news stories or relevant events. Have your say, and don't let others decide the future for you.

Be aware of cryptography and what it can do for you. Today, our security relies on cryptography. Our future security will depend on it even more.

Acknowledgments

The inspiration for this book came from three unwitting sources.

The first was my father. I thought somewhat optimistically that my original (more academic) book about cryptography would be accessible to an informed general reader. My father's polite indication that he had only managed to dip in and out of the text was a clear signal that a broader audience would require a very different approach to writing. I believe this book has passed the "Dad test." The second was Edward Snowden. His 2013 revelations launched a public debate about the use of cryptography, and, during the subsequent analysis, I was struck by the discomfort shown by many journalists and politicians concerning cryptography. The third was the anonymous literary agent who, on the basis of articles I wrote for *The Conversation*, suggested I write a popular science book about cyber security. Be careful what you wish for!

I am fortunate to have worked with Peter Tallack from The Science Factory, who believed in this project from the outset and introduced me to the world of publishing beyond the academic sphere. Thomas Rid told me that Norton would be an outstanding publisher to work with, and he was right. Many thanks to my editor, Quynh Do, for her constant enthusiasm and support, and to Drew

Weitman for shepherding the process along so efficiently. I also owe a great debt to Stephanie Hiebert for doling out the punishment I have administered to countless graduate students by "red-penning" the original manuscript so insightfully.

Crucially, a book needs readers. I am extremely grateful for the feedback I received from Sue Barwick, Nicola Bate, Liqun Chen, Jason Crampton, Anne Craw, Ben Curtis, Maurice Elphick, Steven Galbraith, Wen-Ai Jackson, Angus Henderson, Thalia Laing, Henry Martin, Ian McKinnon, Kenny Paterson, Maura Paterson, and Nick Robinson. I'd particularly like to thank Colleen McKenna for her close scrutiny of my wordcraft, and Fred Piper for the eagle eye he cast over my cryptography. Your joint approval gave me the confidence that the balance between the two might be just about right.

Lastly, my special thanks to Ramon the dachshund for loyally sitting by my side as these words were painfully, slowly ground onto the laptop screen, to Kyla and Finlay for suitably distracting me throughout the process, and to Anita for always loving and believing, despite it all.

Notes

Introduction

1 Dami Lee, "Apple Says There Are 1.4 Billion Active Apple Devices," *Verge*, January 29, 2019, https://www.theverge.com/2019/1/29/18202736/apple-devices-ios-earnings-q1-2019.

2 As of April 2018, there were 7.1 billion global bank cards enabled with EMV (Europay, Mastercard, and Visa) "chip and PIN" technology: "EMVCo Reports over Half of Cards Issued Globally Are EMV®-Enabled," EMVCo, April 19, 2018, https://www.emvco.com/wp-content/uploads/2018/04/Global-Circulation-Figures_FINAL.pdf.

3 This is WhatsApp's own figure from mid-2017, but even if slightly exaggerated, it is most likely of the correct order of magnitude: WhatsApp, "Connecting One Billion Users Every Day," *WhatsApp Blog*, July 26, 2017, https://blog.whatsapp.com/10000631/Connecting-One-Billion-Users-Every-Day.

4 Mozilla reported that the percentage of web pages loaded by Firefox browsers using https (encrypted) as opposed to http (not encrypted) passed the 75 percent mark in 2018: "Let's Encrypt Stats," Let's Encrypt, accessed June 10, 2019, https://letsencrypt.org/stats.

5 *Enigma* (directed by Michael Apted, Jagged Films, 2001) is a fictional account of cryptographers working at Bletchley Park, England, during the Second World War and their efforts to decrypt traffic encrypted by Nazi Enigma machines. In *Skyfall* (directed by Sam Mendes, Columbia

Pictures, 2012), James Bond and his master technician, Q, engage in some impressive (and somewhat implausible) analysis of encrypted data. *Sneakers* (directed by Phil Alden Robinson, Universal Studios, 1992) was arguably a film ahead of its time, featuring two students who hack into computer networks and eventually end up embroiled in the world of intelligence gathering and devices capable of breaking cryptography.

6 *CSI: Cyber* (Jerry Bruckheimer Television, 2015–16) is an American drama series involving FBI agents investigating cybercrimes. It features some unusual cryptographic practices, including the storage of encryption keys as body tattoos! *Spooks* (Kudos, 2002–11), also known as *MI-5*, is a British television series about fictional intelligence officers. Several of the episodes feature agents having to make sense of encrypted data, often demonstrating extraordinary abilities to overcome encryption in real time!

7 Dan Brown has featured cryptography in several of his books, most notably *Digital Fortress* (St. Martin's Press, 1998), which is based around surveillance and a machine capable of breaking all known encryption techniques. Interestingly, Brown's most famous novel, *The Da Vinci Code* (Doubleday, 2003), stars a cryptologist but does not, itself, feature any cryptography per se.

8 My colleague Robert Carolina argues that cyberspace is not a place but rather a medium of communication. He draws a comparison between *cyberspace* and *televisionland*, which was a term used at the advent of television to describe the abstract connection between people and a new technology. Just as "Good morning, everyone in televisionland!" (the opening phrase of the *Apollo 7* crew's first broadcast from space in 1968) seems a preposterous greeting to us today, so Carolina expects the concept of something being "in cyberspace" to eventually fade from use. I tend to agree.

9 Cyberspace is an extremely hard concept to define. The novelist William Gibson is widely credited with first using the term, but modern definitions tend to be based on abstract descriptions of computer networks and the data that resides on them. Dr. Cian Murphy (University of Bristol), speaking at *Crypto Wars 2.0* (the third inter-CDT cybersecurity workshop, University of Oxford, May 2017), suggested a more concise definition: "I don't like the word *cyberspace*—I prefer *electronic stuff*."

10 According to Internet World Stats (Miniwatts Marketing Group), accessed July 14, 2019, https://www.internetworldstats.com/stats.htm, just over half of the world population is now online.

11 "2017 Norton Cyber Security Insights Report Global Results," Norton
    by Symantec, 2018, https://www.symantec.com/content/dam/symantec/
    docs/about/2017-ncsir-global-results-en.pdf.

12 Almost half of all organizations claim to have suffered from fraud and
    economic crime, of which 31 percent is attributed to cybercrime: "Pull-
    ing Fraud Out of the Shadows: Global Economic Crime and Fraud Sur-
    vey 2018," PwC, 2018, https://www.pwc.com/gx/en/services/advisory/
    forensics/economic-crime-survey.html.

13 These are wild estimates of an unmeasurable quantity. However, they
    capture the idea that as we do more things in cyberspace, so, too, can we
    expect to be defrauded more in cyberspace. This particular estimate is
    from "2017 Cybercrime Report," Cybersecurity Ventures, 2017, https://
    cybersecurityventures.com/2015-wp/wp-content/uploads/2017/10/2017
    -Cybercrime-Report.pdf.

14 The computer malware Stuxnet was used to attack the Natanz uranium
    enrichment plant in Iran, which was noticed to be failing in early 2010.
    This was arguably the first globally reported example of a significant
    industrial facility falling victim to an attack from cyberspace. In addi-
    tion to stirring up emotions around this incident with respect to inter-
    national politics and nuclear danger, Stuxnet has served as a wake-up
    call to everyone that critical national infrastructure is increasingly con-
    nected to cyberspace. The attack on Natanz did not come directly from
    the internet, but is believed to have originated from infected USB mem-
    ory sticks. Much has been written on Stuxnet and Natanz—for exam-
    ple, Kim Zitter, *Countdown to Zero Day: Stuxnet, and the Launch of the
    World's First Digital Weapon* (Broadway, 2015).

15 In November 2014, Sony Pictures Studios was subjected to a raft of
    cyberattacks, resulting in the release of confidential employee informa-
    tion and deletion of data. The attackers demanded that Sony stop the
    release of an upcoming comedy film about North Korea. See, for exam-
    ple, Andrea Peterson, "The Sony Pictures Hack, Explained," *Washing-
    ton Post*, December 18, 2014, https://www.washingtonpost.com/news/the
    -switch/wp/2014/12/18/the-sony-pictures-hack-explained/?utm_term=
    .b25b19d65b8d.

16 Widely reported *key reinstallation* attacks affected the WPA2 proto-
    col, which is a security protocol used to cryptographically protect Wi-
    Fi networks: Mathy Vanhoef, "Key Reinstallation Attacks—Breaking
    WPA2 by Forcing Nonce Reuse," last updated October 2018, https://www
    .krackattacks.com.

17 The *ROCA* attack exploits a vulnerability in the generation of RSA keys in a cryptographic software library used by smartcards, security tokens, and other secure hardware chips manufactured by Infineon Technologies, which results in private decryption keys becoming recoverable: Petr Svenda, "ROCA: Vulnerable RSA Generation (CVE-2017-15361)," release date October 16, 2017, https://crocs.fi.muni.cz/public/papers/rsa_ccs17.

18 The *Meltdown* and *Spectre* bugs exploited weaknesses in commonly deployed computer chips and were reported in January 2018 to affect billions of devices around the world, including iPads, iPhones, and Macs: "Meltdown and Spectre: All Macs, iPhones and iPads affected," BBC, January 5, 2018, http://www.bbc.co.uk/news/technology-42575033.

19 The *WannaCry* cyberattack crippled many older computers in the UK's National Health Service (and elsewhere) by installing ransomware that encrypted the disks of affected computers and then demanded a ransom to unlock the trapped data. The National Audit Office later published a detailed investigation into the incident and how it could have been prevented: Amyas Morse, "Investigation: WannaCry Cyber Attack and the NHS," National Audit Office, April 25, 2018, https://www.nao.org.uk/report/investigation-wannacry-cyber-attack-and-the-nhs.

20 Comey became somewhat of a legend in cybersecurity circles for various quotes regarding his anxieties over how the use of cryptography hampers law enforcement. In one such statement from September 2014, he was said to be worried about the strengthening of encryption services on various mobile devices: Ryan Reilly, "FBI Director James Comey 'Very Concerned' about New Apple, Google Privacy Features," *Huffington Post*, September 26, 2014, http://www.huffingtonpost.co.uk/entry/james-comey-apple-encryption_n_5882874. In a May 2015 announcement, Comey was reported to be even more upset: Lorenzo Franceschi-Bicchierai, "Encryption Is 'Depressing,' the FBI Says," *Vice Motherboard*, May 25, 2015, https://motherboard.vice.com/en_us/article/qkv577/encryption-is-depressing-the-fbi-says.

21 Like him or loathe him, Snowden's revelations have been highly influential, and I will discuss them in much greater detail when I later consider the dilemma created by the use of cryptography.

22 Cameron's answer to his own question was: "No, we must not." This remark was widely interpreted as proposing a ban on encryption technology: James Ball, "Cameron Wants to Ban Encryption—He Can Say Goodbye to Digital Britain," *Guardian*, January 13, 2015, https://www

.theguardian.com/commentisfree/2015/jan/13/cameron-ban-encryption -digital-britain-online-shopping-banking-messaging-terror.

23 Brandis made this announcement ahead of a meeting of a *Five Eyes* intelligence alliance meeting: Chris Duckett, "Australia Will Lead Five Eyes Discussions to 'Thwart' Terrorist Encryption: Brandis," ZDNet, June 26, 2017, https://www.zdnet.com/article/australia-will-lead-five -eyes-discussions-to-thwart-terrorist-encryption-brandis.

24 Kieren McCarthy, "Look Who's Joined the Anti-encryption Posse: Germany, Come On Down," *Register*, June 15, 2017, https://www.theregister .co.uk/2017/06/15/germany_joins_antiencryption_posse.

25 "Attorney General Sessions Delivers Remarks to the Association of State Criminal Investigative Agencies 2018 Spring Conference," US Department of Justice, May 7, 2018, https://www.justice.gov/opa/speech/ attorney-general-sessions-delivers-remarks-association-state-criminal -investigative.

26 Zeid stated: "Encryption tools are widely used around the world, including by human rights defenders, civil society, journalists, whistle-blowers and political dissidents facing persecution and harassment. Encryption and anonymity are needed as enablers of both freedom of expression and opinion, and the right to privacy. It is neither fanciful nor an exaggeration to say that, without encryption tools, lives may be endangered. In the worst cases, a Government's ability to break into its citizens' phones may lead to the persecution of individuals who are simply exercising their fundamental human rights.": "Apple-FBI Case Could Have Serious Global Ramifications for Human Rights: Zeid," UN Human Rights Office of the High Commissioner, March 4, 2016, http://www.ohchr.org/ EN/NewsEvents/Pages/DisplayNews.aspx?NewsID=17138.

27 "The Historical Background to Media Regulation," University of Leicester Open Educational Resources, accessed June 10, 2019, https://www.le .ac.uk/oerresources/media/ms7501/mod2unit11/page_02.htm.

28 Former UK home secretary Amber Rudd was quite open about this issue in October 2017 when she stated: "I don't need to understand how encryption works to understand how it's helping—end-to-end encryption—the criminals.": Brian Wheeler, "Amber Rudd Accuses Tech Giants of 'Sneering' at Politicians," BBC, October 2, 2017, http://www.bbc.co.uk/news/uk -politics-41463401.

29 There are numerous books about the rich and fascinating history of cryptography. Simon Singh, *The Code Book* (Fourth Estate, 1999), is one of the most accessible. The benchmark history of cryptography

remains David Kahn, *The Codebreakers* (Scribner, 1997); but other titles include Charles River Editors, *World War II Cryptography* (CreateSpace, 2016); Craig P. Bauer, *Unsolved!* (Princeton University Press, 2017); Alexander D'Agapeyeff, *Codes and Ciphers—A History of Cryptography* (Hesperides, 2015); and Stephen Pincock, *Codebreaker: The History of Codes and Ciphers* (Walker, 2006). Mark Frary, *Decipher: The Greatest Codes Ever Invented and How to Break Them* (Modern Books, 2017) chronologically surveys a number of historical codes and ciphers. Steven Levy's superb book *Crypto: Secrecy and Privacy in the New Cold War* (Penguin, 2000) documents the political events in the US relating to cryptography during the latter decades of the twentieth century.

30 There are various books about cryptographic puzzles. Examples include *The GCHQ Puzzle Book* (GCHQ, 2016); Bud Johnson, *Break the Code* (Dover, 2013); and Laurence D. Smith, *Cryptography: The Science of Secret Writing* (Dover, 1998).

Chapter 1: Security in Cyberspace

1 Many national mints provide detail of currency security features in order to assist with fraud detection. These relate to both the feel of currency, as well as its look. You can learn more about security features of the UK pound coin in "The New 12-Sided £1 Coin," Royal Mint, accessed June 10, 2019, https://www.royalmint.com/new-pound-coin; of UK banknotes in "Take a Closer Look—Your Easy to Follow Guide to Checking Banknotes," Bank of England, accessed June 10, 2019, https://www.bankofengland.co.uk/-/media/boe/files/banknotes/take-a-closer-look.pdf; and of US dollar bills in "Dollars in Detail—Your Guide to U.S. Currency," U.S. Currency Education Program, accessed June 10, 2019, https://www.uscurrency.gov/sites/default/files/downloadable-materials/files/CEP_Dollars_In_Detail_Brochure_0.pdf.

2 The UK General Pharmaceutical Council sets standards for pharmacy professionals. Standard 6 is "Pharmacy professionals must behave in a professional manner," which includes being polite and considerate, showing empathy and compassion, and treating people with respect and safeguarding their dignity: "Standards for Pharmacy Professionals," General Pharmaceutical Council, May 2017, https://www.pharmacyregulation.org/sites/default/files/standards_for_pharmacy_professionals_may_2017_0.pdf.

3 These are not always accurate, since many dangers, such as commercial air accidents, tend to be overestimated in peoples' minds, while others, such as air pollution, are severely underestimated.

4 Financial fraud across payment cards, remote banking, and checks in the UK totaled £768.8 million in 2016: "Fraud: The Facts, 2017," Financial Fraud Action UK, 2017, https://www.financialfraudaction.org.uk/fraudfacts17/assets/fraud_the_facts.pdf.

5 Stefanie Hoehl et al., "Itsy Bitsy Spider . . . : Infants React with Increased Arousal to Spiders and Snakes," *Frontiers in Psychology* 8 (2017): 1710.

6 "9/11 Commission Staff Statement No. 16," 9/11 Commission, June 16, 2004, https://www.9-11commission.gov/staff_statements/staff_statement_16.pdf.

7 The kingdom of Ruritania is a fictional country in central Europe that forms the setting for Anthony Hope's 1894 novel *The Prisoner of Zenda*. I am taking the liberty of using Ruritania to represent a generic state to avoid treading on any diplomatic toes. This use is (shamelessly) inspired by my colleague Robert Carolina's adoption of Ruritania during his cyberlaw classes.

8 There is an increasing amount of advice for customers on how to detect fraudulent electronic communications. See, for example: "Protecting Yourself," Get Safe Online, accessed June 10, 2019, https://www.getsafeonline.org/protecting-yourself.

9 Software written to gather and utilize information relating to an unsuspecting computer user is often referred to as *spyware*. This type of software ranges from relatively benign tracking software designed to target advertising at the user based on their computer activity, to monitoring software that reports all activity, including keystrokes, to a third party.

10 The general lack of understanding of how cyberspace works creates problems for individuals, but it is perhaps even more chronically an issue for societies. A UK government report highlights the economic costs of a broad lack of digital skills, identifying the need to significantly improve digital skills training in schools, higher education, and on-the-job training: "Digital Skills Crisis," UK House of Commons Science and Technology Committee, June 7, 2016, https://publications.parliament.uk/pa/cm201617/cmselect/cmsctech/270/270.pdf.

11 In 2010, a Dutch website called Please Rob Me caused a controversy by combining social media feeds and those of a mobile location app to produce addresses of potentially empty homes. The stated intention

was user awareness, but the initiative was condemned by many as irresponsible. Although the *PleaseRobMe* tool no longer exists, since 2010 the number of location-based apps, as well as the capability and effectiveness of combining data sources to determine this type of information, has significantly increased: Jennifer van Grove, "Are We All Asking to Be Robbed?" Mashable, February 17, 2010, https://mashable .com/2010/02/17/pleaserobme.

12 As just one example, in 2016 a platform known as *Avalanche* was taken down by an international consortium of law enforcement agencies. Based in eastern Europe, Avalanche operated a network of compromised computer systems from which a variety of cybercrimes could be conducted, including phishing, spam, ransomware, and denial-of-service attacks. It was estimated that, at its peak, about half a million computers were controlled by Avalanche: Warwick Ashford, "UK Helps Dismantle Avalanche Global Cyber Network," *Computer Weekly*, December 2, 2016, http://www.computerweekly.com/news/450404018/UK-helps-dismantle -Avalanche-global-cyber-network.

13 The most infamous example of such a network was the one set up by the Ministry for State Security (*Stasi*) in East Germany between 1950 and 1990. The Stasi engaged over a quarter of a million East German citizens in an espionage network designed to monitor the entire population for signs of dissident activity.

14 Just pause, for a moment, to reflect on how much each of your mobile phone, search engine, and social media providers might know about your daily activities from the data you generate when interacting with them. Now imagine how much more they would all know if they shared this information. Less hypothetically, type "employee monitoring" into your favorite search engine (adding slightly to what they already know about you). The results might disturb you.

15 Cryptography underpins all forms of financial transactions, including those made using ATMs, debit and credit cards, and the global SWIFT (Society for Worldwide Interbank Financial Telecommunication) network. An annual Financial Cryptography and Data Security conference has run since 1997, dedicated to the theory and practice of using cryptography to protect financial transactions and creating new forms of digital money: International Financial Cryptography Association, accessed June 10, 2019, https://ifca.ai.

Chapter 2: Keys and Algorithms

1 Physical letters of introduction are, admittedly, relatively rare these days. However, we still rely heavily on written references for the likes of job applications. Indeed, more intangibly, much of our security in the physical world revolves around what other trusted sources believe about situations. For example, a previously unknown person might be introduced to us by a friend; this is, in some sense, a spoken "letter of introduction."

2 "Open sesame" comes from the story of "Ali Baba and the Forty Thieves," in *One Thousand and One (Arabian) Nights*, a compendium of folk tales possibly dating back to the eighth century.

3 Note, perhaps confusingly, that the keyboard character "9" is labeled in ASCII as the fifty-seventh keyboard character, so it is represented as the binary equivalent of 57, not the binary equivalent of the decimal number 9.

4 Key length is sometimes referred to as *key size*. I will treat these terms as synonymous.

5 There are over 5 billion global mobile phone subscribers: "The Mobile Economy 2019," GSM Association, 2019, https://www.gsma.com/mobileeconomy.

6 This example is based on a lore figure of about 10^{22} stars in our universe. Star counting is not a precise science, since the number can only be approximated from what we have been able to observe through existing telescopes. Recent estimates place this number at closer to 10^{24} stars, and many experts suspect this figure is also too low. See, for example, Elizabeth Howell, "How Many Stars Are in the Universe?" *Science & Astronomy*, May 18, 2017, https://www.space.com/26078-how-many-stars-are-there.html. Counting numbers of cryptographic keys is a much more accurate process!

7 The term *personal identification number* (*PIN*) tends to be used for a password that is short and consists of numerical digits. The term dates back to the introduction of automatic teller machines (ATMs) in the late 1960s. For our purposes, passwords and PINs are really examples of the same thing—a string of secret characters.

8 In fact, this process often does involve cryptography, because most computers do not store copies of your password, but instead store a value computed from your password using a special type of cryptographic function.

9   When we submit a PIN to an ATM, we are inherently trusting that the ATM will not misuse it. However, there have been many attacks known as *ATM skimming*, in which criminals modify an ATM in order to capture card and PIN data (the latter can be captured via the overlaying of a fake keypad).

10 One method of doing this is to use the function *PBKDF2*, which is specified in "PKCS #5: Password-Based Cryptography Specification Version 2.1," Request for Comments: 8018, Internet Engineering Task Force, January 2017, https://tools.ietf.org/html/rfc8018.

11 *The Oxford English Dictionary*, Oxford Dictionaries, accessed June 10, 2019, https://languages.oup.com/oed.

12 An excellent introduction is Deborah J. Bennett, *Randomness* (Harvard University Press, 1998).

13 Indeed, one of the most common methods of randomly generating keys for use in a cryptographic algorithm is to generate them using a (different) cryptographic algorithm.

14 A typical formal requirement for a good cryptographic algorithm is that it be impossible to tell the difference between outputs of the cryptographic algorithm and those of a random number generator.

15 Security products based on home-cooked cryptographic algorithms fall into the category that some cryptographers call *snake oil*: Bruce Schneier, "Snake Oil," *Crypto-Gram*, February 15, 1999, https://www.schneier.com/crypto-gram/archives/1999/0215.html#snakeoil.

16 This isn't strictly true for applications not in the public domain. It would be perfectly reasonable for a government agency to choose to design a secret algorithm for its own internal use, as long as that agency had access to sufficient cryptographic expertise.

17 For supporting public technologies, there has been a noticeable shift from secret to open cryptographic algorithm design over the last few decades, assisted by the development of open cryptographic standards.

18 There are plenty of examples of secret algorithms in public technologies that have been successfully reverse engineered. The encryption algorithm A5/1 used in the GSM (Global System for Mobile Communications) standard is one such case.

19 Auguste Kerckhoffs, "La cryptographie militaire," *Journal des sciences militaires* 9 (January 1883): 5–83; and (February 1883): 161–91. English translation of the principles can be found in Fabien Petitcolas, "Kerckhoffs' Principles from 'La cryptographie militaire,'" Information Hiding Homepage, accessed June 10, 2019, http://petitcolas.net/kerckhoffs.

20 The encryption algorithms used to protect telecommunications were secret in the GSM standard of the 1990s, but in more recent iterations, such as the 2008 LTE (Long-Term Evolution) standard, these are publicly specified.

21 Merchandise 7X appears to remain a secret, despite claims otherwise over the years: William Poundstone, *Big Secrets* (William Morrow, 1985).

Chapter 3: Keeping Secrets

1 Everyone needs confidentiality because everyone has something to hide. There is an oft-repeated mantra that if you have nothing to hide, then you should not worry about government surveillance programs. The fallacy of this argument is explored in detail in Daniel J. Solove, *Nothing to Hide* (Yale University Press, 2011); and David Lyon, *Surveillance Studies: An Overview* (Polity Press, 2007).

2 Eric Hughes, "A Cypherpunk's Manifesto," March 9, 1993, https://www .activism.net/cypherpunk/manifesto.html.

3 I use the phrase "should not fully trust" to instill a degree of caution about trusting devices and networks rather than to induce paranoia about rampant insecurity. The bottom line is that we can never be sure that our devices and networks have not been compromised in some way (such as through installation of malware), and it is thus prudent to be wary about trusting them completely.

4 This argument is certainly contestable. The metadata relating to calling patterns can be very useful to investigators who do not have access to call content. Indeed, the utility of such metadata was made apparent through one of Edward Snowden's revelations concerning the NSA's collection of metadata from the US telecom provider Verizon: Glenn Greenwald, "NSA Collecting Phone Records of Millions of Verizon Customers Daily," *Guardian*, June 6, 2013, https://www.theguardian.com/ world/2013/jun/06/nsa-phone-records-verizon-court-order.

5 A good introduction to steganography is Peter Wayner, *Disappearing Cryptography: Information Hiding: Steganography & Watermarking* (MK/Morgan Kaufmann, 2009).

6 For some real examples of steganography being used as a tool for attacking computers, see Ben Rossi, "How Cyber Criminals Are Using Hidden Messages in Image Files to Infect Your Computer," *Information Age*, July 27, 2015, http://www.information-age.com/how-cyber-criminals-are -using-hidden-messages-image-files-infect-your-computer-123459881.

7   Although this type of application is often discussed, and advice for how to deploy it can easily be found on the internet (for example, Krintoxi, "Using Steganography and Cryptography to Bypass Censorship in Third World Countries," *Cybrary*, September 5, 2015, https://www.cybrary .it/0p3n/steganography-and-cryptography-to-bypass-censorship-in-third -world-countries), there is not much evidence that it is widely deployed. The reasons are probably similar to those outlined by critics of post-9/11 claims that steganography was heavily used by terrorists: Robert J. Bag- nall, "Reversing the Steganography Myth in Terrorist Operations: The Asymmetrical Threat of Simple Intelligence Dissemination Techniques Using Common Tools," SANS Institute, 2002, https://www.sans.org/ reading-room/whitepapers/stenganography/reversing-steganography -myth-terrorist-operations-asymmetrical-threat-simple-intellig-556. In fact, since Bagnall's 2002 comments, and particularly since Edward Snowden's 2013 revelations, the range of methods of secure communi- cations available to anyone wishing to avoid government surveillance has expanded.

8   The Atbash cipher is an ancient Hebrew means of scrambling letters (indeed, the name *Atbash* derives from the first and last pairs of letters of the Hebrew alphabet). Some commentators believe that the biblical book of Jeremiah deploys the Atbash in several places: Paul Y. Hoskis- son, "Jeremiah's Game," *Insight* 30, no. 1 (2010): 3–4, https://publications .mi.byu.edu/publications/insights/30/1/S00001-30-1.pdf.

9   For a brief history and specification of Morse code, see *Encyclopae- dia Britannica*, s.v. "Morse Code," accessed July 21, 2019, https://www .britannica.com/topic/Morse-Code.

10   For the history of deciphering Egyptian hieroglyphs, see Andrew Rob- inson, *Cracking the Egyptian Code: The Revolutionary Life of Jean- François Champollion* (Thames and Hudson, 2012).

11   Dan Brown, *The Da Vinci Code* (Doubleday, 2003).

12   Most modern uses of encryption are also accompanied by a separate cryp- tographic check that enables the receiver to detect whether the cipher- text has been modified in any way. Increasingly, these two processes are being combined through the use of special *authenticated-encryption* algorithms that provide both cryptographic services.

13   My cryptographic colleague Steven Galbraith completely disagrees. He argues that Turing was sufficiently smart that if someone had suggested the idea of asymmetric encryption to him, Turing would have probably responded with: "Yes, of course!"

14 Named after Blaise de Vigenère, this encryption algorithm was invented by Giovan Battista Bellaso in 1553. Widely believed at the time to be "unbreakable," the Vigenère cipher is relatively easily decrypted, once the length of the key is determined—a process that can be conducted by statistical analysis of the ciphertext. A good explanation of both the algorithm and how to break it can be found in Simon Singh, *The Code Book* (Fourth Estate, 1999).

15 For more details about the history and breaking of Enigma machines, see, for example, Hugh Sebag-Montefiore, *Enigma: The Battle for the Code* (Weidenfeld & Nicolson, 2004).

16 "Data Encryption Standard (DES)," Federal Information Processing Standards, FIPS Publication 46, January 1977. This standard was subsequently revised several times and ultimately withdrawn in 2005. The last revised version, FIPS Publication 46-3, is archived at https://csrc.nist.gov/csrc/media/publications/fips/46/3/archive/1999-10-25/documents/fips46-3.pdf.

17 Triple DES encryption essentially uses DES to encrypt the data with one key, decrypt it with a second key, and then encrypt the result with a third key (Triple DES decryption is the reverse process). Initially a quick fix for DES, Triple DES is still used by many applications, particularly in the financial sector. Details and recommendations for deployment of Triple DES can be found in Elaine Barker and Nicky Mouha, "Recommendation for the Triple Data Encryption Standard (TDEA) Block Cipher," National Institute of Standards and Technology, NIST Special Publication 800-67, rev. 2, November 2017, https://doi.org/10.6028/NIST.SP.800-67r2.

18 "Specification for the Advanced Encryption Standard (AES)," Federal Information Processing Standards, FIPS Publication 197, November 26, 2001, https://nvlpubs.nist.gov/nistpubs/fips/nist.fips.197.pdf.

19 A historical overview of the AES process, including relevant documentation, can be found in "AES Development," NIST Computer Security Resource Center, updated October 10, 2018, https://csrc.nist.gov/projects/cryptographic-standards-and-guidelines/archived-crypto-projects/aes-development.

20 All the AES operations are conducted on a square of bytes—it is no coincidence that the original encryption algorithm from which the AES was developed was called *Square*.

21 The AES design process lasted almost four years, with fifteen candidate designs eventually whittled down to one, following an intense evaluation

process that included three dedicated conferences. The precise details behind the design of AES are documented in Joan Daemen and Vincent Rijmen, *The Design of Rijndael* (Springer, 2002).

22 The block ciphers indirectly referred to here include *BEAR*, *Blowfish*, *Cobra*, *Crab*, *FROG*, *Grand Cru*, *LION*, *LOKI*, *Red Pike*, *Serpent*, *SHARK*, *Skipjack*, *Twofish*, and *Threefish*.

23 NIST provides a list of some recommended modes of operation, including those for confidentiality only (CBC, CFB, ECB, OFB), authentication only (CMAC), authenticated encryption (CCM, GCM), disk encryption (XTS), and protection of cryptographic keys (KW, KWP): "Block Cipher Techniques—Current Modes," NIST Computer Security Resource Center, updated May 17, 2019, https://csrc.nist.gov/Projects/Block-Cipher -Techniques/BCM/Current-Modes.

24 It's not quite the chicken-or-the-egg dilemma, because using encryption is not the only conceivable means by which a secret key can be distributed to someone. It's just the most obvious means, and one that is often used in practice.

25 The security of Wi-Fi networks has a somewhat checkered history. The main security standards are covered in the IEEE 802.11 series. These standards effectively restrict access to authorized devices and enable communications on a Wi-Fi network to be encrypted. Other related standards, such as WPS (Wi-Fi Protected Setup), are designed to make it easier to initialize keys on a Wi-Fi network.

Chapter 4: Sharing Secrets with Strangers

1 "Total Number of Websites," Internet Live Stats, accessed June 10, 2019, http://www.internetlivestats.com/total-number-of-websites.

2 The trusted-center scenario for key distribution can work very well in environments that are centralized and have obvious trust points. For example, the network authentication system Kerberos works this way: "Kerberos: The Network Authentication Protocol," MIT Kerberos, updated January 9, 2019, https://web.mit.edu/kerberos.

3 There are many good online videos of the subsequent process for using padlocks to exchange a secret—for example: Chris Bishop, "Key Exchange," YouTube, June 9, 2009, https://www.youtube.com/watch ?v=U62S8SchxX4.

4 A function suitable for asymmetric encryption is sometimes called a *trapdoor one-way function.* "One-way" refers to the fact it must be easy

to compute but hard to reverse, while "trapdoor" indicates there must be a way for the genuine recipient to reverse the process (knowledge of the private decryption key being the trapdoor).

5 *Computational complexity theory* is concerned with classifying computational problems according to their difficulty. A good textbook focusing on the relationship between computational complexity and cryptography is John Talbot and Dominic Welsh, *Complexity and Cryptography: An Introduction* (Cambridge University Press, 2006).

6 The history of the study of primes and why they are so significant both to mathematics and to other fields of study is discussed in Marcus du Sautoy, *The Music of the Primes: Why an Unsolved Problem in Mathematics Matters* (HarperPerennial, 2004).

7 Ron Rivest, Adi Shamir, and Len Adleman, "A Method for Obtaining Digital Signatures and Public-Key Cryptosystems," *Communications of the ACM* 21, no. 2 (1978): 120–26.

8 A list of the world's fastest supercomputers is periodically updated at "TOP500 Lists," TOP500.org, accessed July 21, 2019, https://www.top500.org/lists/top500.

9 23,189 is the 2,587th prime. If you are unconvinced and don't want to check this, I recommend you visit Andrew Booker, "The Nth Prime Page," accessed June 10, 2019, https://primes.utm.edu/nthprime.

10 The NIST recommendations for data that needs protection up until the year 2030 suggest using a product of two primes that is more than 3,000 bits long (see "Recommendation for Key Management," National Institute of Standards and Technology, NIST Special Publication 800-57, Part 1, rev. 4, 2016). Such a number is more than 900 decimal digits long, and RSA uses primes of roughly equal size, making each of the two primes more than 450 decimal digits long.

11 The mathematical knowledge required to appreciate how RSA works is a basic understanding of modular arithmetic and the Fermat-Euler theorem, both of which should be familiar to anyone who has studied an introduction to number theory. Many introductory cryptography textbooks also explain the minimum mathematics required, including Keith M. Martin, *Everyday Cryptography*, 2nd ed. (Oxford University Press, 2017).

12 This remark is a combination of fact and slightly facetious speculation. The fact relates to the time required to factor a number of this size on conventional computers. It is believed that this factoring would take approximately the same time as a search for a 128-bit key, which

is something I later argue would need about 50 million billion years. The speculation is, of course, that *Homo sapiens* may not stick around for that length of time. It is believed that *Homo sapiens* has existed for about 300,000 years, so projecting this far into the future is guesswork. A range of possible futures for our species is discussed in Jolene Creighton, "How Long Will [It] Take Humans to Evolve? What Will We Evolve Into?" *Futurism*, December 12, 2013, https://futurism.com/how-long-will-take-humans-to-evolve-what-will-we-evolve-into.

13 A table that sorts block ciphers into categories relating to their frequency of use (common, less common, and other) can be found at the bottom of Wikipedia, s.v. "Block Cipher," accessed June 10, 2019, https://en.wikipedia.org/wiki/Block_cipher.

14 The threat presented by quantum computers, which I discuss later, has spurred a major international effort to find new asymmetric encryption algorithms based on new hard problems: "Post-quantum Cryptography," NIST Computer Security Resource Center, updated June 3, 2019, https://csrc.nist.gov/Projects/Post-Quantum-Cryptography. However, even this process involves only a handful of fundamentally different problems around which candidate algorithms are based.

15 The history of the development of asymmetric (public-key) encryption is fascinating. The earliest discovery is now attributed to researchers at GCHQ, who were seeking a solution to the problem of distributing secret keys around a network. The conceptual idea behind asymmetric encryption was set out by James Ellis in a 1969 document, although not instantiated until Clifford Cocks proposed a real scheme in 1973. Only in 1997, however, did these discoveries come to public light. In the meantime, a similar process occurred in the public space, with Whitfield Diffie and Martin Hellman conceptualizing the idea in 1976 and with a number of researchers later proposing instantiations, including the RSA algorithm formulated by Rivest, Shamir, and Adleman in 1977. For more information, see James Ellis, "The History of Non-secret Encryption," *Cryptologia* 23, no. 3 (1999): 267–73; Whitfield Diffie and Martin Hellman, "New Directions in Cryptography," *IEEE Transactions on Information Theory* 22, no. 6 (1976): 644–54; and Steven Levy, *Crypto: Secrecy and Privacy in the New Cold War* (Penguin, 2000).

16 While factoring and finding discrete logarithms over modular numbers are broadly believed to be equally difficult, the advantage of basing an asymmetric encryption algorithm on elliptic curves is that finding discrete logarithms over elliptic curves is believed to be a magnitude more

difficult, which allows the keys used for elliptic-curve-based encryption to be shorter than those for RSA. The mathematics behind elliptic curves is straightforward for those with a numerical background, but it is otherwise not for the fainthearted. Most mathematical introductions to cryptography explain all you need to know; for example, see Douglas R. Stinson and Maura B. Paterson, *Cryptography: Theory and Practice*, 4th ed. (CRC Press, 2018).

17 A well-documented example of this problem concerns an attack in which 300,000 Iranian citizens believed they were communicating, by computer, with Google Gmail servers, when in fact they had been presented with alternative public keys that connected them to an attack site, which was then used to monitor their communications. This attack happened because a company called DigiNotar, which issued certified public keys, was itself hacked in order to create the public keys that fooled the Iranian Gmail users. See, for example, Gregg Keizer, "Hackers Spied on 300,000 Iranians Using Fake Google Certificate," *Computerworld*, September 6, 2011, https://www.computerworld.com/article/2510951/cybercrime-hacking/hackers-spied-on-300-000-iranians-using-fake-google-certificate.html.

18 Laurie Lee's iconic novel *Cider with Rosie* (Hogarth Press, 1959) is based on his childhood in the 1920s, describing life in a small English village before the arrival of transformational technology such as the motor car. It represents an apparently lost rural idyll, free from the pressures of time and connectivity to the outside world.

19 Examples of important internet standards that all use hybrid encryption include *Transport Layer Security* (*TLS*) for secure web connections, *Internet Protocol Security* (*IPSec*) for establishing virtual private networks to enable activities such as working from home, *Secure Shell* (*SSH*) for secure file transfer, and *Secure Multipurpose Internet Mail Extensions* (*S/MIME*) for secure email.

20 The research and advisory company Gartner is associated with a simple methodology known as the *Gartner Hype Cycle* for tracking expectations concerning new technologies (see "Gartner Hype Cycle," Gartner, accessed June 10, 2019, https://www.gartner.com/en/research/methodologies/gartner-hype-cycle). This cycle is characterized by an early peak of exaggerated and often poorly informed interest, then a rapid decline as the realities of implementation kick in, followed by a gentle rise as the true niches for the technology become understood. Asymmetric encryption has probably now journeyed to the "plateau of

productivity," where its advantages and disadvantages are understood well enough that it is deployed appropriately.

Chapter 5: Digital Canaries

1 Studies in cognitive psychology indicate that most people prefer to avoid losses rather than to acquire gains of an equivalent amount. This *loss aversion* is one of a number of cognitive biases brought to popular attention in Daniel Kahneman, *Thinking Fast and Slow* (Penguin, 2012).

2 Note that data integrity is only about detecting errors, not correcting them. Separate mathematical techniques known as *error-correcting codes* enable a degree of automatic correction of errors. These are not normally regarded as security techniques, and they are used in applications where errors are expected but we don't want to be made aware of their existence, such as when we're listening to digital music.

3 Until the mid-1980s, miners in the UK and other countries deployed caged canaries to detect the presence of toxic gases—a practice ultimately replaced by digital detectors: Kat Eschner, "The Story of the Real Canary in the Coal Mine," *Smithsonian*, December 30, 2016, https://www.smithsonianmag.com/smart-news/story-real-canary-coal-mine-180961570.

4 The term *fake news* is often associated with Donald Trump, who used the term to describe negative press coverage during his run for the presidency. However, the intentional spreading of information (accurate or otherwise) is an ancient craft. What is relevant to our discussion is that digital media make it easier and faster to distribute such information.

5 There is evidence that people have more trouble identifying fake news when it is spread via digital media: Simeon Yates, "'Fake News'—Why People Believe It and What Can Be Done to Counter It," *Conversation*, December 13, 2016, https://theconversation.com/fake-news-why-people-believe-it-and-what-can-be-done-to-counter-it-70013.

6 "Integrity," Lexico, accessed June 12, 2019, https://www.lexico.com/en/definition/integrity.

7 Notably, these trust links fade quickly. If you trust your friend Charlie, who in turn trusts his friend Diane, then to what extent do you trust Diane? Maybe you will trust her for some specific things, but you are unlikely to trust many of Diane's other friends; the links quickly become somewhat tenuous. This fading of trust as links become more and more distant has potential ramifications in cyberspace, where, for

example, enthusiastic users of social media can rapidly assemble legions of alleged "friends."

8 *MD5* is a cryptographic hash function invented by Ronald Rivest (the "R" of RSA) in 1991. The value it outputs is 128 bits long. MD5 is fully specified in "The MD5 Message-Digest Algorithm," Request for Comments: 1321, Internet Engineering Task Force, April 1992, https://tools .ietf.org/html/rfc1321. Note that serious weaknesses have subsequently been discovered in MD5; see "Updated Security Considerations for the MD5 Message-Digest and the HMAC-MD5 Algorithms," Request for Comments: 6151, Internet Engineering Task Force, March 2011, https:// tools.ietf.org/html/rfc6151.

9 The use of seals for this purpose is as old as civilization itself, with ancient stone seals used to make impressions in clay being a significant archaeological artifact for historians: Marta Ameri et al., *Seals and Sealing in the Ancient World* (Cambridge University Press, 2018).

10 First developed in 1970, a modern ISBN consists of thirteen digits, including identifiers for the country of origin and publisher of the book. You can submit an ISBN to obtain full details of the book at ISBN Search, accessed June 10, 2019, https://isbnsearch.org.

11 The majority of these examples use an algorithm named after Hans Peter Luhn, who patented it in 1960. The Luhn algorithm for computing a check digit is similar to, but different from, that used for the ISBN: Wikipedia, s.v. "Luhn Algorithm," accessed June 10, 2019, https://en .wikipedia.org/wiki/Luhn_algorithm.

12 Confusingly, the term *hash function* is used in the field of computer science for several different purposes. I will restrict my use of the term to what are sometimes known as *cryptographic hash functions*.

13 I previously mentioned the hash function MD5, which is often used for integrity checking of downloaded files. Other examples of practically deployed hash functions include *SHA-1*, the *SHA-2 family*, and the *SHA-3 family*, the latter of which was selected in 2015 as the winner of an international competition held by the US National Institute of Standards and Technology: "Hash Functions," NIST Computer Security Resource Center, updated May 3, 2019, https://csrc.nist.gov/Projects/Hash-Functions.

14 The problem is not the basic idea, but the way that many hash functions are designed. To put it crudely, it is common for a hash function to input some of the data, compress it, input a bit more, compress it, and so on. Therefore, appending the key to the end of the data means that the key will not be mixed in with the data as well as it could be.

15 "HMAC: Keyed-Hashing for Message Authentication," Request for Comments: 2104, Internet Engineering Task Force, February 1997, https://tools.ietf.org/html/rfc2104.

16 "The AES-CMAC Algorithm," Request for Comments: 4493, Internet Engineering Task Force, June 2006, https://tools.ietf.org/html/rfc4493.

17 There are many different reasons why authenticated encryption modes, which combine encryption and MAC computation, offer advantages over encrypting and adding a MAC separately. Some of these relate to efficiency, but the most compelling apply to security. In essence, certain things can go wrong with their integration when the two operations are conducted separately, and these problems can be avoided if an approved authenticated encryption mode is used. Examples of authenticated encryption modes include *CCM* ("Recommendation for Block Cipher Modes of Operation: The CCM Mode for Authentication and Confidentiality," NIST Special Publication 800-38C, July 20, 2007) and *GCM* ("Recommendation for Block Cipher Modes of Operation: Galois/Counter Mode [GCM] and GMAC," NIST Special Publication 800-38D, November 2007).

18 This argument assumes no auxiliary evidence, such as a secure network log entry demonstrably proving that the MAC was sent over a network whose origin was the sender's internet address.

19 Digital signatures would also be insecure. If you wanted to digitally sign a very long document, then it would need to be broken up into independent chunks of data, each signed separately. An attacker could intercept this string of separate chunks of data and their accompanying signatures and swap chunks around, along with their signatures. The result would appear to be a valid set of data chunks and signatures. In reality, however, the combined message would be incorrectly ordered.

20 In many ways, the longevity and ubiquity of handwritten signatures are surprising, and testament to their convenience. Even as we move toward increased use of digital documents, the handwritten signature seems to prevail through the widespread acceptance of digital scans of handwritten signatures. The digital scan of a handwritten signature is just a small image file that is easily extracted from a document; it is, in this regard, an even weaker mechanism than a handwritten signature.

21 Reporters Without Borders produces the *World Press Freedom Index*, which bases its results on analyses of media independence, self-censorship, legislation, transparency, and quality of media infrastructure. North Korea, which regards listening to or viewing media content

that originates outside of the country as a criminal offense, is consistently close to the bottom of the table: "North Korea," Reporters Without Borders, accessed June 10, 2019, https://rsf.org/en/north-korea.

22 This idea was brought to popular attention in Eli Pariser, *The Filter Bubble* (Penguin, 2012).

23 In my experience, the quality of information on Wikipedia concerning cryptography is pretty good. This reliability is probably indicative of both a strong interest in cryptography across the internet community, and perhaps a high correlation between people interested in cryptography and people with the will (and/or capability) to edit Wikipedia pages.

24 Money being moved elsewhere is, of course, precisely what happens when confidence is lost in a bank, such as during the 2007 collapse of the UK bank Northern Rock: Dominic O'Connell, "The Collapse of Northern Rock: Ten Years On," BBC, September 12, 2017, https://www.bbc.co.uk/news/business-41229513.

25 A plethora of information about Bitcoin is available. An excellent background on the need for (and use of) Bitcoin is Dominic Frisby, *Bitcoin: The Future of Money?* (Unbound, 2015). A readable introduction to the cryptography used in Bitcoin is Andreas M. Antonopoulos, *Mastering Bitcoin: Unlocking Digital Cryptocurrencies* (O'Reilly, 2014).

26 There have been many examples of attempts to facilitate certain aspects of digital cash through the centralized banking system. These include 1990s digital-wallet technologies such as Mondex and Proton, and more recently the likes of Apple Pay. While these all offer some of the convenience of cash, they remain linked to traditional bank accounts.

27 Banks pioneered the commercial use of cryptography in the 1970s. The motivation and success of the Data Encryption Standard (DES) was due largely to the need for digital security in the financial sector.

28 One of the many clever features of Bitcoin is that it has a parameter that can be adjusted to control the frequency of block creation.

29 Somewhat against the decentralization spirit behind Bitcoin, the profitability of bitcoin mining has led to the development of enormous processing centers dedicated solely to mining bitcoin. These are sometimes referred to as *bitcoin farms*: Julia Magas, "Top Five Biggest Crypto Mining Areas: Which Farms Are Pushing Forward the New Gold Rush?" Cointelegraph, June 23, 2018, https://cointelegraph.com/news/top-five-biggest-crypto-mining-areas-which-farms-are-pushing-forward-the-new-gold-rush.

30 This is often referred to as a *fork* in the blockchain.

31 For a full list of current cryptocurrencies, see "Cryptocurrency List," CoinLore, accessed June 10, 2019, https://www.coinlore.com/all_coins.

Chapter 6: Who's Out There?

1 See, for example, Michael Cavna, "'Nobody Knows You're a Dog': As Iconic Internet Cartoon Turns 20, Creator Peter Steiner Knows the Joke Rings as Relevant as Ever," *Washington Post*, July 31, 2013.

2 Facebook reported to the US Securities and Exchange Commission that it made $20.21 from each of its 1.4 billion users in 2017: Julia Glum, "This Is Exactly How Much Your Personal Information Is Worth to Facebook," *Money*, March 21, 2018, http://money.com/money/5207924/how -much-facebook-makes-off-you.

3 For a discussion about common threats to passports and the security techniques used to counter them, see "Passport Security Features: 2019 Report Anatomy of a Secure Travel Document," Gemalto, updated May 20, 2019, https://www.gemalto.com/govt/travel/passport-security-design.

4 This is why we use a variety of security mechanisms with our mobile phones. The mobile phone company uses security mechanisms on the SIM card to identify the account holder. The phone owner typically uses a PIN or password to control who can use the phone.

5 While it is technically possible to install software on a phone that could conduct bank fraud, more common attacks on mobile banking involve criminals stealing phone numbers or linking different mobile phone accounts to a target's bank account. See, for example, Miles Brignall, "Mobile Banking in the Spotlight as Fraudsters Pull £6,000 Sting," *Guardian*, April 2, 2016, https://www.theguardian.com/money/2016/ apr/02/mobile-banking-fraud-o2-nationwide; and Anna Tims, "'Sim Swap' Gives Fraudsters Access-All-Areas via Your Mobile Phone," *Guardian*, September 26, 2015, https://www.theguardian.com/money/2015/ sep/26/sim-swap-fraud-mobile-phone-vodafone-customer.

6 Alan Turing introduced the famous Turing test, which is designed to distinguish the behavior of a computer from that of a human: Alan M. Turing, "Computing Machinery and Intelligence," *Mind* 59, no. 236 (October 1950): 433–60.

7 This type of malware is often referred to as a *keylogger*. A good introduction to the topic is Nikolay Grebennikov, "Keyloggers: How They Work and How to Detect Them," SecureList, March 29, 2007, https://securelist .com/keyloggers-how-they-work-and-how-to-detect-them-part-1/36138.

8 Captchas are fairly unpopular because they waste time and are easy to get wrong, resulting in further delays. A discussion of some alternative approaches can be found in Matt Burgess, "Captcha Is Dying. This Is How It's Being Reinvented for the AI Age," *Wired*, October 26, 2017, https://www.wired.co.uk/article/captcha-automation-broken-history-fix.

9 A good introduction to biometrics is John R. Vacca, *Biometric Technologies and Verification Systems* (Butterworth-Heinemann, 2007).

10 A famous example of biometrics being "stolen" is the case of so-called *gummy fingers*, which are artificial fingers designed to fool fingerprint recognition systems: Tsutomu Matsumoto et al., "Impact of Artificial 'Gummy' Fingers on Fingerprint Systems," *Proceedings of SPIE* 4677 (2002), https://cryptome.org/gummy.htm.

11 Banks could be more thorough—for example, if every personal device had a card reader that could detect the physical card rather than just the embossed card data. Like all security measures, however, this is an issue of striking a balance between security, cost, and usability.

12 Levels of card-not-present fraud around the world are reviewed in "Card-Not-Present Fraud around the World," US Payments Forum, March 2017, https://www.uspaymentsforum.org/wp-content/uploads/2017/03/CNP-Fraud-Around-the-World-WP-FINAL-Mar-2017.pdf. For example, card-not-present fraud accounted for 69 percent of card fraud in the UK in 2014, and 76 percent of card fraud in Canada in 2015.

13 Authentication and authorization are related concepts and often confused. Authentication is primarily about establishing who is out there. Authorization concerns what someone is permitted to do. When you log on to your social media account, you are authenticating. The social media platform then uses the process of authorization to determine which data you are allowed to view. Although authorization often follows authentication, it does not necessarily require it. A supermarket assistant authorizes the sale of alcohol by determining the age of a shopper—either by looking at the person or by demanding age-verifying evidence—without requiring knowledge of who they are. Cryptography provides tools for authentication. While cryptography can be used to support it, authorization is commonly managed by other means (for example, through rules governing access to entries in a database).

14 This technique is no longer reliable, given the powerful digital editing software that is freely available.

15 Elizabeth Stobert, "The Agony of Passwords," in *CHI '14 Extended Abstracts on Human Factors in Computing Systems* (ACM, 2014), 975–80.

16 Advice on managing passwords is often contradictory because difficult trade-offs must be made. For example, regular password change reduces the impact of a compromise, but it also complicates life for password users and may push them toward unsafe practices, such as writing passwords down. For general guidance on password management, see, for example, "Password Administration for System Owners," National Cyber Security Centre, November 19, 2018, https://www.ncsc.gov.uk/collection/passwords.

17 Perhaps even worse than an individual breach, the results of such attacks appear to be aggregating in enormous repositories of stolen passwords and accompanying credentials: Mohit Kumar, "Collection of 1.4 Billion Plain-Text Leaked Passwords Found Circulating Online," *Hacker News*, December 12, 2017, https://thehackernews.com/2017/12/data-breach -password-list.html.

18 In 2019, Facebook acknowledged that a bug in its password manage-ment systems had resulted in hundreds of millions of user passwords being stored unencrypted on an internal platform: Lily Hay Newman, "Facebook Stored Millions of Passwords in Plaintext—Change Yours Now," *Wired*, March 21, 2019, https://www.wired.com/story/facebook -passwords-plaintext-change-yours.

19 There are many sources of advice about how to select strong passwords. One example is the guidelines from the National Institute of Standards and Technology, which are summarized in Mike Garcia, "Easy Ways to Build a Better P@$5w0rd," NIST, *Taking Measure* (blog), October 4, 2017, https://www.nist.gov/blogs/taking-measure/easy-ways-build-better -p5w0rd.

20 This attitude is not new. A colleague of mine was informed by a sys-tems engineer in the 1980s that "cryptography is nothing more than an expensive way of degrading performance."

21 Examples of key-stretching algorithms include *PBKDF2* and *Argon2*.

22 For a UK government perspective on the value of password managers, see Emma W., "What Does the NCSC Think of Password Managers?" National Cyber Security Centre, January 24, 2017, https://www.ncsc.gov .uk/blog-post/what-does-ncsc-think-password-managers.

23 The "2016 Data Breach Investigations Report" by Verizon claimed that 63 percent of confirmed data breaches exploited passwords that had

either been poorly generated, unchanged from default, or stolen. The latest Verizon report can be downloaded from Verizon at https://www.verizonenterprise.com/verizon-insights-lab/dbir.

24 A range of examples of phishing scams, as well as advice about how to detect phishing attacks and avoid falling for them, can be found at Phishing.org, accessed August 4, 2019, https://www.phishing.org.

25 A substantial body of evidence suggests that mandating regular password changes can be unproductive: Lorrie Craynor, "Time to Rethink Mandatory Password Changes," Federal Trade Commission, March 2, 2016, https://www.ftc.gov/news-events/blogs/techftc/2016/03/time-rethink-mandatory-password-changes.

26 While online-banking authentication tokens remain in widespread use, they are relatively expensive to implement. An alternative solution is to utilize devices capable of cryptographic computation that customers already possess, which is why banks are increasingly supporting the use of apps running on mobile phones for authentication. Another approach is to use *keys* that customers already possess, which is why some banks issue card readers capable of communicating with keys stored on the chip on the customer's bank card.

27 Predictive algorithms can be used to monitor the lag between an individual token and the master clock on which the system is based. When a customer attempts to authenticate, the bank uses the predictive algorithm to estimate the time that's on the token's clock, on the basis of past interactions with that token. The bank could also choose to consider any time within a small time window to be acceptable.

28 Numerous well-publicized attacks have targeted car key systems. Some of these have been possible because a car manufacturer didn't adopt "perfect passwords" and instead used default passwords common to all cars of a certain type. However, even those using perfect passwords have come unstuck through variants of *relay attacks*, in which an attacker with a special radio device positions themselves in the middle of an attacker-initiated conversation between a car (sitting on a driveway) and a key (hanging in the hallway of a house); see, for example, David Bisson, "Relay Attack against Keyless Vehicle Entry Systems Caught on Film," Tripwire, November 29, 2017, https://www.tripwire.com/state-of-security/security-awareness/relay-attack-keyless-vehicle-entry-systems-caught-film.

29 Not all boomerangs are designed to come back. In this hunting scenario, the boomerang is intended to fly behind the ducks and scare them into

flight toward the hunter; hence, the boomerang is not really required to return to the hunter's hand. Never mind—I only want an analogy! Boomerang purists are strongly encouraged to read Philip Jones, *Boomerang: Behind an Australian Icon* (Wakefield Press, 2010).

30 *Melaleuca quinquenervia* is a tree, native to Southeast Asia and Australia, that has been introduced throughout the world both as an ornamental tree and for draining wetlands. It has a strong-scented blossom whose fragrance is not always appreciated.

31 A similar principle lies behind *identification, friend or foe* (*IFF*) systems, first designed in the 1930s to address the problem of establishing whether an approaching aircraft was an ally or an enemy. For a historical review, see Lord Bowden, "The Story of IFF (Identification Friend or Foe)," *IEE Proceedings A (Physical Science, Measurement and Instrumentation, Management and Education, Reviews)* 132, no. 6 (October 1985): 435–37.

32 The most recent version of TLS is specified in "The Transport Layer Security (TLS) Protocol Version 1.3," Request for Comments: 8446, Internet Engineering Task Force, August 2018, https://tools.ietf.org/html/rfc8446.

33 The case for anonymity being regarded as a fundamental human right is made in Jillian C. York, "The Right to Anonymity Is a Matter of Privacy," Electronic Frontier Foundation, January 28, 2012, https://www.eff.org/deeplinks/2012/01/right-anonymity-matter-privacy.

34 An introduction to the different ways that human behavior appears to change in cyberspace is Mary Aiken, *The Cyber Effect* (John Murray, 2017).

35 A good resource for explanations about the threats that harassing behaviors present and how to address them is "Get Safe Online—Free Expert Advice," Get Safe Online, accessed June 10, 2019, https://www.getsafeonline.org.

36 The data we leave in our tracks as we conduct activities in cyberspace is sometimes known as our *digital footprint*. One of the best ways of understanding this concept is to appreciate how investigators attempt to reconstruct activities in cyberspace by using digital forensics. A good introduction is John Sammons, *The Basics of Digital Forensics* (Syngress, 2014).

37 Tor is free software that can be downloaded from https://www.tor project.org.

38 A fascinating investigation into some of the more sinister activities in cyberspace facilitated by anonymity is Jamie Bartlett, *The Dark Net* (Windmill, 2015).

39 Many of the original pioneers of the internet regarded cyberspace as a new world free from the constraints of established society. The ability to remain anonymous in cyberspace was key to realizing this vision, as documented in Thomas Rid, *Rise of the Machines* (W. W. Norton, 2016).

40 Andrew London, "Elon Musk's Neuralink—Everything You Need to Know," TechRadar, October 19, 2017, https://www.techradar.com/uk/news/neuralink.

Chapter 7: Breaking Cryptosystems

1 Even when nuts and bolts are blamed for the failure of a bridge, the reason is often that they were inappropriately used. For example, the failure of a 2016 bridge in Canada was blamed on the overloading of bolts, not on the bolts themselves: Emily Ashwell, "Overloaded Bolts Blamed for Bridge Bearing Failure," *New Civil Engineer*, September 28, 2016, https://www.newcivilengineer.com/world-view/overloaded-bolts-blamed-for-bridge-bearing-failure/10012078.article. As I will discuss later, inappropriate use of cryptographic algorithms is a potential reason for failure of a cryptosystem.

2 Caesar's use of encryption is described in C. Suetonius Tranquillus, "De vita Caesarum," 121. A translation is available from "The Lives of the Twelve Caesars, Complete by Suetonius," Project Gutenberg, accessed June 10, 2019, https://www.gutenberg.org/files/6400/6400-h/6400-h.htm (see Caius Julius Caesar Clause 56 for discussion of encryption).

3 For more information about Mary's ciphers and the Babington Plot to oust Elizabeth I, see "Mary, Queen of Scots (1542–1587)," National Archives (UK), accessed June 10, 2019, http://www.nationalarchives .gov.uk/spies/ciphers/mary. Mary's use of encryption is also discussed in Simon Singh, *The Code Book* (Fourth Estate, 1999).

4 Further details of Elizabeth I's sophisticated espionage agency can be found in Robert Hutchinson, *Elizabeth's Spy Master: Francis Walsingham and the Secret War That Saved England* (Weidenfeld & Nicolson, 2007).

5 For example, ISO/IEC 18033 is a multipart standard that specifies a range of encryption algorithms: "ISO/IEC 18033 Information

Technology—Security Techniques—Encryption Algorithms," International Organization for Standardization.

6 Bruce Schneier has, over the years, "outed" a long list of mis-sold substandard cryptographic products, which he refers to as cryptographic "snake oil," in the archives of his *Crypto-Gram* newsletter: Schneier on Security, accessed August 4, 2019, https://www.schneier.com/crypto-gram.

7 According to Donald Rumsfeld: "Reports that say that something hasn't happened are always interesting to me, because as we know, there are known knowns; there are things we know we know. We also know there are known unknowns; that is to say we know there are some things we do not know. But there are also unknown unknowns—the ones we don't know we don't know. And if one looks throughout the history of our country and other free countries, it is the latter category that tend to be the difficult ones." Full transcript available from Donald H. Rumsfeld, "DoD News Briefing—Secretary Rumsfeld and Gen. Myers," US Department of Defense, February 12, 2002, http://archive.defense.gov/Transcripts/Transcript.aspx?TranscriptID=2636.

8 While the NSA appeared to shorten the DES key length, it is believed that the agency strengthened the algorithm itself by optimizing it against an attack technique known as *differential cryptanalysis*, which was not discovered by the public research community until the 1980s. See, for example, Peter Bright, "The NSA's Work to Make Crypto Worse and Better," *Ars Technica*, June 9, 2013, https://arstechnica.com/information-technology/2013/09/the-nsas-work-to-make-crypto-worse-and-better; for more details, see Don Coppersmith, "The Data Encryption Standard (DES) and Its Strength against Attacks," *IBM Journal of Research and Development* 38, no. 3 (1994): 243–50.

9 This follows from the fact that the playing field is not level. The intelligence community employs many cryptographers and has access to everything the public community publishes. However, the intelligence community only rarely shares its knowledge. The intelligence community thus must know more about cryptography. The question is: Does it know anything significant that is not known by the public community? And how would we ever find out?

10 The most famous technique for predicting computing power is Moore's law. Intel's Gordon Moore proposed a rule of thumb that the number of components on an integrated circuit would approximately double every two years. While this estimate was believed to be fairly accurate

for several decades, it now looks unlikely to be the best gauge of future progress: M. Mitchell Waldrop, "The Chips Are Down for Moore's Law," *Nature*, February 9, 2016, https://www.nature.com/news/the-chips-are -down-for-moore-s-law-1.19338.

11 Xiaoyun Wang et al., "Collisions for Hash Functions MD4, MD5, HAVAL-128 and RIPEMD," Cryptology ePrint Archive 2004/199, rev. August 17, 2004, https://eprint.iacr.org/2004/199.pdf.

12 Intriguingly, a machine that can decrypt ciphertext without knowledge of the algorithm that was used features in Dan Brown's novel *Digital Fortress* (St. Martin's Press, 1998).

13 Exhaustive key searches are sometimes known as *brute force* attacks.

14 I based this crude calculation on an analysis similar to that provided in Mohit Arora, "How Secure Is AES against Brute Force Attacks?" *EE Times*, May 7, 2012, https://www.eetimes.com/document.asp?doc_ id=1279619.

15 This estimate is from Whitfield Diffie and Martin E. Hellman, "Exhaustive Cryptanalysis of the NBS Data Encryption Standard," *Computer* 10 (1977): 74–84.

16 The DESCHALL Project was the first winner of a set of challenges issued by the cybersecurity company RSA Security in 1997, winning a $10,000 prize for successfully conducting an exhaustive search for a DES key. The full story of the project is told in Matt Curtin, *Brute Force* (Copernicus, 2005).

17 See Sarah Giordano, "Napoleon's Guide to Improperly Using Cryptography," *Cryptography: The History and Mathematics of Codes and Code Breaking* (blog), accessed June 10, 2019, http://derekbruff.org/blogs/ fywscrypto.

18 Much has been written about the cryptanalysis of the Enigma machines. One of the most detailed and authoritative sources is Władysław Kozaczuk, *Enigma: How the German Machine Cipher Was Broken, and How It Was Read by the Allies in World War Two* (Praeger, 1984).

19 These techniques include encrypting each plaintext block along with a counter that increments after each encryption, and encrypting each plaintext block along with the previous ciphertext block (which is essentially a random number). For details, see "Block Cipher Techniques— Current Modes," NIST Computer Security Resource Center, updated May 17, 2019, https://csrc.nist.gov/Projects/Block-Cipher-Techniques/ BCM/Current-Modes.

20 You can see a copy of this message at "The Babington Plot," Secrets and Spies, National Archives (UK), accessed June 10, 2019, http://www .nationalarchives.gov.uk/spies/ciphers/mary/ma2.htm.

21 Indeed, some phishing attacks work this way by offering you an apparently secure web link to a website address that closely resembles a genuine one (such as your bank's address) but is, in fact, the attacker's website. By using a TLS connection, the attacker is now able to use cryptography to prevent any other attacker from viewing or modifying the data that you now mistakenly send to the attack website!

22 RC4 is no longer regarded as secure enough for most modern applications of cryptography: John Leyden, "Microsoft, Cisco: RC4 Encryption Considered Harmful, Avoid at All Costs," *Register*, November 14, 2013, https://www.theregister.co.uk/2013/11/14/ms_moves_off_rc4.

23 The details of cryptographic weaknesses in WEP are widely available. See, for example, Keith M. Martin, *Everyday Cryptography*, 2nd ed. (Oxford University Press, 2017), 488–95.

24 The WEP protocol for Wi-Fi security was first upgraded to a protocol called WPA (Wi-Fi Protected Access), then in 2004 to a securer version called WPA2, which became the default security protocol for Wi-Fi. In 2018 it was announced that WPA2 itself was to be upgraded to WPA3, although the rollout of this latest version is expected to take many years to complete, since, in many cases, the protocol will be upgraded only when equipment is replaced.

25 Bruce Schneier, "Why Cryptography Is Harder Than It Looks," *Information Security Bulletin*, 1997, Schneier on Security, https://www.schneier .com/essays/archives/1997/01/why_cryptography_is.html.

26 "Keynote by Mr. Thomas Dullien—CyCon 2018," NATO Cooperative Cyber Defence Centre of Excellence (CCDCOE), YouTube, June 20, 2018, https://www.youtube.com/watch?v=q98foLaAfX8.

27 Paul C. Kocher, "Announce: Timing cryptanalysis of RSA, DH, DSS," sci.crypt, December 11, 1995, https://groups.google.com/forum/#!msg/sci .crypt/OvUlewbjfa8/a1kP6WjW1lUJ.

28 Paul C. Kocher, "Timing Attacks on Implementations of Diffie-Hellman, RSA, DSS, and Other Systems," in *Proceedings of the 16th Annual International Cryptology Conference on Advances in Cryptology*, Lecture Notes in Computer Science 1109 (Springer, 1996), 104–13.

29 It turns out that the intelligence community was aware of some of the threats posed by side channels much earlier, as shown by a 1972 article that was declassified in 2007: "TEMPEST: A Signal Problem," *NSA*

Cryptologic Spectrum 2, no. 3 (Summer 1972): 26–30, https://www.nsa
.gov/news-features/declassified-documents/cryptologic-spectrum/assets/
files/tempest.pdf.

30 These sketches could easily come from a James Bond movie. Spanish
actor Javier Bardem played the villain in the 2012 Bond movie *Skyfall*
(directed by Sam Mendes, Columbia Pictures, 2012).

31 This is just the same as for physical keys. Looking after a front-door key
is easier than protecting an entire property. Safeguarding the key might
not be as strong a security measure as employing a team of guards and
vicious dogs, but it's a pragmatic substitute.

32 Use of default passwords is more common than many people realize:
"Risks of Default Passwords on the Internet," Department of Homeland
Security, June 24, 2013, https://www.us-cert.gov/ncas/alerts/TA13-175A.

33 The website does not explicitly offer *you* the public key, of course; this
happens in the background, and it's your web browser that receives the
offered key on your behalf. You can, however, choose to take a look at this
key by selecting appropriate browser settings.

34 You can have a lot of fun, and waste an enormous amount of time,
researching views on this topic. Just one example of many forums where
the question of the existence of true randomness has been posed is
Debate.org, where you can find the following discussion: "Philosophically
and Rationally, Does Randomness or Chance Truly Exist?" Debate.org,
accessed June 10, 2019, http://www.debate.org/opinions/philosophically
-and-rationally-does-randomness-or-chance-truly-exist.

35 Tossing a coin might not be as good a way of generating randomness
as some people think. A 2007 study showed that there tends to be a
slight bias toward a manually flipped coin landing the same way up as
it was before being tossed: Persi Diaconis, Susan Holmes, and Richard
Montgomery, "Dynamical Bias in the Coin Toss," *SIAM Review* 49, no. 2
(April 2007): 211–35.

36 An interesting website on the topic of randomness is Random.org,
accessed June 10, 2019, https://www.random.org. You can learn more
about the challenges involved in generating true randomness from physical sources, as well as generate your own true random numbers using a
generator based on atmospheric noise.

37 A well-publicized example in 2008 was the extremely poor pseudorandom number generator used in the Debian operating system for supporting an earlier version of the TLS protocol. This generator could generate
only a small fraction of the "random" numbers that were required for

the algorithms it supported: "Debian Security Advisory: DSA-1571-1 openssl—Predictable Random Number Generator," Debian, May 13, 2008, https://www.debian.org/security/2008/dsa-1571.

38 Wikipedia, s.v. "Key Derivation Function," accessed June 10, 2019, https://en.wikipedia.org/wiki/Key_derivation_function.

39 Arjen K. Lenstra et al., "Ron Was Wrong, Whit Is Right," Cryptology ePrint Archive, [February 12, 2012], https://eprint.iacr.org/2012/064.pdf.

40 This process is governed by a set of security standards for GSM, and for 3G and 4G security, that specify the cryptography used in mobile systems. See, for example, Jeffrey A. Cichonski, Joshua M. Franklin, and Michael J. Bartock, "Guide to LTE Security," NIST Special Publication 800-187, December 21, 2017, https://nvlpubs.nist.gov/nistpubs/specialpublications/nist.sp.800-187.pdf.

41 The Diffie-Hellman key agreement protocol is increasingly preferred over more classical hybrid encryption as a means of agreeing on a secret key. The primary reason is that it offers greater security in the event that a long-term private key is exposed (a property sometimes called *perfect forward secrecy*). Details of the Diffie-Hellman protocol can be found in almost any cryptographic textbook. The protocol first appeared in Whitfield Diffie and Martin E. Hellman, "New Directions in Cryptography," *IEEE Transactions on Information Theory* 22, no. 6 (1976): 644–54.

42 For example, a public key based on 256-bit elliptic curves is often represented by about 130 hexadecimal characters.

43 A certificate authority can be any organization that users trust enough to issue certificates. *Let's Encrypt* is an example of a noncommercial certificate authority established to encourage the widespread use of cryptography, particularly TLS, by issuing free certificates. For more information, see Let's Encrypt, accessed June 10, 2019, https://letsencrypt.org.

44 The aforementioned problems regarding poorly generated RSA keys cannot be solved by certification. Most of these poorly generated RSA keys were certified by CAs that were simply asserting who owned the keys, not vouching for the quality of the keys. The situation might be different when a certificate authority has extended responsibilities that include key generation. In this case, a certificate authority could develop a poor reputation from reported incidents involving bad practice and, as a result, become less trusted.

45 Web browser providers should maintain lists of root certificates that they have agreed to support within their software. The list of those supported

by Apple, for example, can be inspected at "Lists of Available Trusted Root Certificates in iOS," Apple, accessed June 10, 2019, https://support .apple.com/en-gb/HT204132.

46 You have almost certainly been in the situation when, during an attempt to access a web page, you received a certificate warning and just ignored it by clicking it away. We take a risk when we do this. While certificate warnings can arise through errors or failures to update certificates, they do also arise in situations where there is a more serious problem, such as when the web site is known to be untrustworthy.

47 A detailed exploration of the intricacies of managing public-key certificates can be found in Johannes A. Buchmann, Evangelos Karatsiolis, and Alexander Wiesmaier, *Introduction to Public Key Infrastructures* (Springer, 2013).

48 The seemingly endless reports of mass data breaches often concern databases that are insecurely maintained by organizations. The European Union *General Data Protection Regulation* (*GDPR*), which came into force in May 2018, is partly about trying to address incidents of this type.

49 For guidance on how to really get rid of data, see, for example, "Secure Sanitisation of Storage Media," National Cyber Security Centre, September 23, 2016, https://www.ncsc.gov.uk/guidance/secure-sanitisation -storage-media.

50 For an introduction to hardware security modules, see Jim Attridge, "An Overview of Hardware Security Modules," SANS Institute Information Security Reading Room, January 14, 2002, https://www.sans .org/reading-room/whitepapers/vpns/overview-hardware-security -modules-757.

51 The original quote is from G. Spafford, "Rants & Raves," *Wired*, November 25, 2002.

52 See, for example, Arun Vishwanath, "Cybersecurity's Weakest Link: Humans," *Conversation*, May 5, 2016, https://theconversation.com/ cybersecuritys-weakest-link-humans-57455.

53 Any organization protecting laptops in this way would, hopefully, use a hardware security module and serious security management procedures to protect the master key, so our disastrous scenario should not unfold.

54 A series of papers on the difficulty that users experience with encryption software began with Alma Whitton and J. D. Tygar, "Why Johnny Can't Encrypt: A Usability Evaluation of PGP 5.0," in *Proceedings of the Eighth USENIX Security Symposium (Security '99), August 23–26, 1999,*

Washington, D.C., USA (USENIX Association, 1999), 169–83. It was followed by Steve Sheng et al., "Why Johnny Still Can't Encrypt: Evaluating the Usability of Email Encryption Software," in *Proceedings of the Second Symposium on Usable Privacy and Security* (ACM, 2006); and then Scott Ruoti et al., "Why Johnny Still, Still Can't Encrypt: Evaluating the Usability of a Modern PGP Client," arXiv, January 13, 2016, https://arxiv.org/abs/1510.08555. You can see where this is going without even reading these articles.

55 Note that sending users on a training course does not necessarily solve this problem. A system that is difficult to use may suffer from ongoing problems even after users have attended a formal training program. Unless humans regularly perform a complex task, we are quite likely to forget the skills acquired during training.

56 The argument that bad cryptography is sometimes worse than no cryptography is made, for example, in Erez Metula, "When Crypto Goes Wrong," OWASP Foundation, accessed June 10, 2019, https://www.owasp.org/images/5/57/OWASPIL2011-ErezMetula-WhenCryptoGoesWrong.pdf.

Chapter 8: The Cryptography Dilemma

1 One of the most infamous ransomware attacks was WannaCry, which affected over 200,000 computers worldwide in May 2017. Defense measures against WannaCry were developed relatively quickly, limiting its damage. For an introduction to ransomware and how to deal with it, see, for example, Josh Fruhlinger, "What Is Ransomware? How These Attacks Work and How to Recover from Them," CSO, December 19, 2018, https://www.csoonline.com/article/3236183/ransomware/what-is -ransomware-how-it-works-and-how-to-remove-it.html.

2 For a list of real cases in which criminal investigators came up against encrypted devices, see Klaus Schmeh, "When Encryption Baffles the Police: A Collection of Cases," ScienceBlogs, accessed June 10, 2019, http://scienceblogs.de/klausis-krypto-kolumne/when-encryption-baffles -the-police-a-collection-of-cases.

3 There is some evidence that cyberattacks have been launched by law enforcement agencies against services using Tor. See, for example, Devin Coldewey, "How Anonymous? Tor Users Compromised in Child Porn Takedown," NBC News, August 5, 2013, https://www.nbcnews.com/technolog/how-anonymous-tor-users-compromised-child-porn-takedown -6C10848680.

4   The use of messaging services by terrorist groups has provoked some of
    the most contentious controversies over the use of encryption: Gordon
    Rayner, "WhatsApp Accused of Giving Terrorists 'a Secret Place to Hide'
    as It Refuses to Hand Over London Attacker's Messages," *Telegraph*,
    March 27, 2017, https://www.telegraph.co.uk/news/2017/03/26/home
    -secretary-amber-rudd-whatsapp-gives-terrorists-place-hide.

5   In fact, encrypting and throwing away the key is sometimes proposed
    as a deliberate means of permanently deleting data on a disk. There
    are, however, some strong arguments for why this might not be the
    best way of disposing of data: Samuel Peery, "Encryption Is NOT Data
    Sanitization—Avoid Risk Escalation by Mistaking Encryption for Data
    Sanitation," IAITAM, October 16, 2014, http://itak.iaitam.org/encryption
    -is-not-data-sanitization-avoid-risk-escalation-by-mistaking-encryption
    -for-data-sanitation.

6   The case for inspecting incoming encrypted traffic is made in, for exam-
    ple, Paul Nicholson, "Let's Encrypt—but Let's Also Decrypt and Inspect
    SSL Traffic for Threats," Network World, February 10, 2016, https://
    www.networkworld.com/article/3032153/security/let-s-encrypt-but-let-s
    -also-decrypt-and-inspect-ssl-traffic-for-threats.html.

7   This is almost certainly what happened in the case of the Stuxnet infec-
    tion of the Iranian Natanz uranium enrichment plant in 2010.

8   The Electronic Frontier Foundation provides guidance on tools that can
    be used to protect online privacy, most of which are based on the use of
    cryptography: "Surveillance Self-Defense," Electronic Frontier Founda-
    tion, accessed June 10, 2019, https://ssd.eff.org.

9   Tom Whitehead, "Internet Is Becoming a 'Dark and Ungoverned Space,'
    Says Met Chief," *Telegraph*, November 6, 2014, https://www.telegraph.co
    .uk/news/uknews/law-and-order/11214596/Internet-is-becoming-a-dark
    -and-ungoverned-space-says-Met-chief.html.

10 "Director Discusses Encryption, Patriot Act Provisions," *FBI News*, May
    20, 2015, https://www.fbi.gov/news/stories/director-discusses-encryption
    -patriot-act-provisions.

11 "Cotton Statement on Apple's Refusal to Obey a Judge's Order to
    Assist the FBI in a Terrorism Investigation," Tom Cotton, Arkansas
    Senator, February 17, 2016, https://www.cotton.senate.gov/?p=press_
    release&id=319.

12 "Apple-FBI Case Could Have Serious Global Ramifications for Human
    Rights: Zeid," UN Human Rights Office of the High Commissioner,

March 4, 2016, http://www.ohchr.org/EN/NewsEvents/Pages/DisplayNews
.aspx?NewsID=17138.

13 Esther Dyson, "Deluge of Opinions on the Information Highway," *Computerworld*, February 28, 1994, 35.

14 David Perera, "The Crypto Warrior," Politico, December 9, 2015, http://www.politico.com/agenda/story/2015/12/crypto-war-cyber-security-encryption-000334.

15 "Snowden at SXSW: 'The Constitution Was Being Violated on a Massive Scale,'" RT, March 10, 2014, https://www.rt.com/usa/snowden-soghoian-sxsw-interactive-914.

16 Amber Rudd, "Encryption and Counter-terrorism: Getting the Balance Right," *Telegraph*, July 31, 2017, https://www.gov.uk/government/speeches/encryption-and-counter-terrorism-getting-the-balance-right.

17 Omand was speaking about the passing of the UK Investigatory Powers Act 2016, which regulates aspects of interception of communications data. The quote is from Ruby Lott-Lavigna, "Can Governments Really Keep Us Safe from Terrorism without Invading Our Privacy?" *Wired*, October 20, 2016, https://www.wired.co.uk/article/david-omand-national-cyber-security.

18 Encryption ("cryptography for data confidentiality") mechanisms were classified as a dual-use technology under the 1996 Wassenaar Arrangement on Export Controls for Conventional Arms and Dual-Use Goods and Technologies: "The Wassenaar Arrangement," accessed June 10, 2019, https://www.wassenaar.org.

19 Even before cryptography entered mainstream use, the dilemma presented by the use of encryption existed because that dilemma is hardwired into the basic functionality of encryption. Encryption protects secrets. Mary, Queen of Scots, used encryption, which both protected her personal privacy and threatened the power of the state. Which of these mattered more is a question that depends on your point of view.

20 By *problematic* I am not suggesting that these techniques should not have been pursued, but arguing that there are underlying difficulties with the approach that are very hard to mitigate.

21 I am being deliberately provocative here. Nobody is asking for a cryptosystem to be made insecure. The state is asking for an alternative means of accessing the data protected by the cryptosystem. However, any such means, if deployed by the "wrong people" (such as criminals), would be regarded as a "break" of the cryptosystem.

22 *Normal users* refers to essentially everyone except the state itself. This is a highly simplified scenario, as I hope you already realized.

23 One of the first companies offering such a cryptographic product was Crypto AG, established in Switzerland in 1952 and still trading today: Crypto AG, accessed August 11, 2019, https://www.crypto.ch.

24 There have long been rumors, partially substantiated, that in the 1950s Crypto AG cooperated with the NSA concerning sales of its devices to certain countries: Gordon Corera, "How NSA and GCHQ Spied on the Cold War World," BBC, July 28, 2015, https://www.bbc.com/news/uk-33676028.

25 Some governments almost certainly design their own secret algorithms to protect their data, which is fine if they have the expertise. Today, however, it would be naive for the government of Ruritania to blindly trust the government of Freedonia to supply it with technology that uses a secret Freedonian algorithm. Ruritania would be better served if it purchased commercial equipment that used state-of-the-art published algorithms.

26 See, for example, Bruce Schneier, "Did NSA Put a Secret Backdoor in New Encryption Standard?" *Wired*, November 15, 2007, https://www.wired.com/2007/11/securitymatters-1115.

27 The removal of Dual_EC_DRBG was announced in "NIST Removes Cryptography Algorithm from Random Number Generator Recommendations," National Institute of Standards and Technology, April 21, 2014, https://www.nist.gov/news-events/news/2014/04/nist-removes-cryptography-algorithm-random-number-generator-recommendations. However, this action came nine years after Dual_EC_DRBG was approved as a standard for generating pseudorandom numbers. During this time it was adopted by several well-known security products, the manufacturers of some of which are alleged, controversially, to have cooperated with the NSA: Joseph Menn, "Exclusive: Secret Contract Tied NSA and Security Industry Pioneer," Reuters, December 20, 2013, https://www.reuters.com/article/us-usa-security-rsa/exclusive-secret-contract-tied-nsa-and-security-industry-pioneer-idUSBRE9BJ1C220131220.

28 Former NSA director Michael Hayden has suggested that some existing cryptosystems contain nobody-but-us (NOBUS) vulnerabilities, which are weaknesses known to the NSA that Hayden believes only the NSA could exploit. This is a very uncomfortable idea, requiring trust not just that the NSA's exploitation of NOBUS vulnerabilities is ethical, but also that these weaknesses are not discoverable and exploitable by other

parties: Andrea Peterson, "Why Everyone Is Left Less Secure When the NSA Doesn't Help Fix Security Flaws," *Washington Post*, October 4, 2013, https://www.washingtonpost.com/news/the-switch/wp/2013/10/04/why-everyone-is-left-less-secure-when-the-nsa-doesnt-help-fix-security-flaws.

29   See, for example: "The Historical Background to Media Regulation," University of Leicester Open Educational Resources, accessed June 10, 2019, https://www.le.ac.uk/oerresources/media/ms7501/mod2unit11/page_02.htm.

30   Global Partners Digital maintains a world map that identifies national restrictions and laws concerning the use of cryptography: "World Map of Encryption Laws and Policies," Global Partners Digital, accessed June 10, 2019, https://www.gp-digital.org/world-map-of-encryption.

31   For a wider discussion of the politics surrounding cryptography in the latter decades of the twentieth century, including the issues of export controls, see Steven Levy, *Crypto: Secrecy and Privacy in the New Cold War* (Penguin, 2002).

32   You can view the famous RSA munitions T-shirt (and even download original graphics to print your own) at "Munitions T-Shirt," Cypherspace, accessed June 10, 2019, http://www.cypherspace.org/adam/uk-shirt.html.

33   A good overview of some of the attitudes prevalent around this time toward cryptography and its ability to change society is Thomas Rid, *Rise of the Machines* (W. W. Norton, 2016). Another interesting perspective on this period is Arvind Narayanan, "What Happened to the Crypto Dream? Part 1," *IEEE Security & Privacy* 11, no. 2 (March–April 2013): 75–76.

34   Timothy C. May, "The Crypto Anarchist Manifesto," November 22, 1992, https://www.activism.net/cypherpunk/crypto-anarchy.html.

35   In 1991, Phil Zimmermann wrote the encryption software *Pretty Good Privacy* (*PGP*) and made it freely available. PGP was controversial in two ways: it used encryption strong enough to be subject to export controls in the US, and it deployed RSA, which was subject to commercial licensing restrictions. PGP soon made its way around the world and achieved broad acclaim. Zimmermann was the target of a US criminal investigation for the export control violation, which was eventually dropped.

36   In 1995, cryptographer Daniel Bernstein brought the first of a series of cases against the US government, challenging the export restrictions on cryptography. A similar case, *Junger v. Daley*, was launched in 1996.

37 An influential paper written by eleven cryptographic experts that critiques the idea of key escrow from a number of different angles is Hal Abelson et al., "The Risks of Key Recovery, Key Escrow, and Trusted Third-Party Encryption," *World Wide Web Journal* 2, no. 3 (1997): 241–57.

38 This slogan is generally associated with the crypto-anarchists of the 1990s (adapted from a similar slogan deployed by the US gun lobby) and can be found in a document prepared for the Cypherpunks mailing list: Timothy C. May, "The Cyphernomicon," September 10, 1994, https:// nakamotoinstitute.org/static/docs/cyphernomicon.txt.

39 The UK Regulation of Investigatory Powers Act 2000 Part III (RIPA 3) gives the state the power to compel, under warrant, the disclosure of encryption keys or decryption of encrypted data. There have been convictions in the UK under RIPA 3. Forgetting or losing a key is not strictly a defense, but it's possible to imagine situations where this could be a plausible defense argument.

40 Just try searching for this phrase on the internet. You'll be amazed by the number of articles taking (versions of) this phrase as their title.

41 Some of the information from the thousands of documents leaked by Snowden found its way into press articles in, for example, the *Guardian*, the *Washington Post*, the *New York Times*, *Le Monde*, and *Der Spiegel*. There are many resources concerning the Snowden revelations. The story behind the leaks is covered in Glenn Greenwald, *No Place to Hide* (Penguin, 2015); and *Citizenfour* (directed by Laura Poitras, HBO Films, 2014); and dramatized in *Snowden* (directed by Oliver Stone, Endgame Entertainment, 2016).

42 There are several repositories on the internet claiming to hold many of these documents, including "Snowden Archive," Canadian Journalists for Free Expression, accessed June 10, 2019, https://www.cjfe .org/snowden.

43 In May 2019 a weakness was reported in the WhatsApp messaging service that gave attackers access to smartphone data. Worryingly, the trigger required no user participation; the attack could be launched by a simple call to the phone: Lily Hay Newman, "How Hackers Broke Whats-App with Just a Phone Call," *Wired*, May 14, 2019, https://www.wired .com/story/whatsapp-hack-phone-call-voip-buffer-overflow.

44 Ed Pilkington, "'Edward Snowden Did This Country a Great Service. Let Him Come Home,'" *Guardian*, September 14, 2016, https://www .theguardian.com/us-news/2016/sep/14/edward-snowden-pardon-bernie -sanders-daniel-ellsberg.

45 The problems created by the complexity of cyberspace are exacerbated by the increased functionality of devices. Phil Zimmermann has proposed that "the natural flow of technology tends to move in the direction of making surveillance easier, and the ability of computers to track us doubles every eighteen months": Om Malik, "Zimmermann's Law: PGP Inventor and Silent Circle Co-founder Phil Zimmermann on the Surveillance Society," GigaOm, August 11, 2013, https://gigaom .com/2013/08/11/zimmermanns-law-pgp-inventor-and-silent-circle-co -founder-phil-zimmermann-on-the-surveillance-society.

46 Danny Yadron, Spencer Ackerman, and Sam Thielman, "Inside the FBI's Encryption Battle with Apple," Guardian, February 18, 2016, https://www.theguardian.com/technology/2016/feb/17/inside-the-fbis -encryption-battle-with-apple.

47 Danny Yadron, "Apple CEO Tim Cook: FBI Asked Us to Make Software 'Equivalent of Cancer,'" Guardian, February 25, 2016, https:// www.theguardian.com/technology/2016/feb/24/apple-ceo-tim-cook -government-fbi-iphone-encryption.

48 Rachel Roberts, "Prime Minister Claims Laws of Mathematics 'Do Not Apply' in Australia," Independent, July 15, 2017, https://www .independent.co.uk/news/malcolm-turnbull-prime-minister-laws-of -mathematics-do-not-apply-australia-encryption-l-a7842946.html.

49 Metrics concerning the size of the Tor network can be found at "Tor Metrics," Tor Project, accessed June 10, 2019, https://metrics.torproject.org/ networksize.html.

50 See, for example, Hannah Kuchler, "Tech Companies Step Up Encryption in Wake of Snowden," Financial Times, November 4, 2014, https:// www.ft.com/content/3c1553a6-6429-11e4-bac8-00144feabdc0.

51 The UK "National Cyber Security Strategy 2016–2021," HM Government, 2016, https://assets.publishing.service.gov.uk/government/ uploads/system/uploads/attachment_data/file/567242/national_cyber_ security_strategy_2016.pdf, explicitly identifies the importance of widespread use of encryption by noting that "cryptographic capability is fundamental to protecting our most sensitive information and to choosing how we deploy our Armed Forces and national security capabilities."

52 In 2015, a group of leading cryptographers outlined the security risks created by a range of approaches to facilitating law enforcement access to encrypted communications. See Hal Abelson et al., "Keys under Doormats," Communications of the ACM 58, no. 10 (2015): 24–26.

53 "Remarks by the President at South by Southwest Interactive," White House, Office of the Press Secretary, March 11, 2016, https:// obamawhitehouse.archives.gov/the-press-office/2016/03/14/remarks -president-south-southwest-interactive.

54 Some means of gaining legal access to data are probably more acceptable to society than others; hence, a holistic view of the issue is the best way of identifying the most acceptable trade-offs: Andrew Keane Woods, "Encryption Substitutes," Hoover Institution, Aegis Paper Series no. 1705, July 18, 2017, https://www.scribd.com/document/354096059/ Encryption-Substitutes#from_embed.

55 I say *traditionally* because mobile and fixed telephone networks are increasingly merging, with the encryption that used to protect only the first leg between mobile phone and base station now extending deeper into the networks than it used to.

56 To be clear, my point is that if we were to redesign the architecture of the internet and renegotiate security within that architecture, we should consider what level of security is needed for specific services. It is evident that, today, end-to-end encryption raises genuine concerns for law enforcement. A true negotiation to find an acceptable way forward requires all sides to come to the table willing to make compromises. The only likely alternative is ongoing conflict.

57 "Treaty between the United States of America and the Union of Soviet Socialist Republics on the Limitation of Strategic Offensive Arms (SALT II)," Bureau of Arms Control, Verification and Compliance, 1979, https://2009-2017.state.gov/t/isn/5195.htm.

58 Daniel Moore and Thomas Rid, "Cryptopolitik and the Darknet," *Survival* 58, no. 1 (2016): 7–38.

Chapter 9: Our Cryptographic Future

1 To be strictly correct, the analogy is that you place a copy of the letter in each of the new boxes and then give these to your enemies, each of whom now has one copy of the letter in a box that they can break into, and one copy in a box that they cannot break into.

2 This argument is particularly relevant to encryption. For other cryptographic services, such as data integrity, the situation might not be so serious. For example, if a digital-signature algorithm is broken and requires upgrading, it is possible to re-sign data using the new signature

algorithm. A problem would arise only if the digital-signature algorithm used at the time the data was first signed wasn't strong enough.

3 Because cryptographic algorithms are often computationally intensive, in many applications of cryptography they are implemented in hardware, rather than software. This means that a change of algorithm often requires replacement hardware. For example, when the WEP Wi-Fi security protocol was declared obsolete in 2003 because a series of cryptographic weaknesses had been discovered, not all Wi-Fi devices could be updated to new security protocols. Therefore, some Wi-Fi users were faced with the choice of purchasing a new device or continuing to use broken cryptography.

4 The perception of quantum as being mysterious, counterintuitive, and beyond the comprehension of most of us seems to be nurtured by the expert community. Nobel Prize–winning physicist Niels Bohr is often attributed as being the original source of the quote "Anyone who is not shocked by quantum theory has not understood it." Even popular explanations of quantum concepts tend to be framed from a position of the seemingly unknowable; examples include Jim Al-Khalili, *Quantum: A Guide for the Perplexed* (Weidenfeld & Nicolson, 2012); and Marcus Chown, *Quantum Theory Cannot Hurt You* (Faber & Faber, 2014).

5 Quantum random numbers have been commercially available since the turn of the century and are based on different types of quantum measurement. See, for example, "What Is the Q in QRNG?" ID Quantique, October 2017, https://www.idquantique.com/random-number-generation/overview; and "NIST's New Quantum Method Generates *Really* Random Numbers," National Institute of Standards and Technology, April 11, 2018, https://www.nist.gov/news-events/news/2018/04/nists-new-quantum-method-generates-really-random-numbers.

6 A relatively accessible insight into the development of quantum computers is John Gribbin, *Computing with Quantum Cats: From Colossus to Qubits* (Black Swan, 2015).

7 In the unlikely event that you have never hurled an angry bird at a pig, this is a reference to the core synopsis of Rovio Entertainment Corporation's phenomenally successful series of *Angry Birds* games.

8 Predictions about the future development timelines for quantum computing vary, as do views on what their eventual impact will be. The consensus appears to be that we will have powerful quantum computers . . . someday!

9 An algorithm published by mathematician Peter Shor in 1994, now known as *Shor's algorithm*, demonstrated that a quantum computer

could solve both the factorization and discrete logarithm problems. The original paper is Peter W. Shor, "Algorithms for Quantum Computation: Discrete Logarithms and Factoring," in *Proceedings, 35th Annual Symposium on Foundations of Computer Science* (IEEE Computer Society Press, 1994), 124–34. Shor's algorithm has subsequently been used to factor relatively small numbers on fledgling quantum computers.

10 In 2016, the US National Institute of Standards and Technology launched a program to design and evaluate postquantum asymmetric encryption algorithms that are believed to be secure against a quantum computer. This process is anticipated to take at least six years: "Post-quantum Cryptography Standardization," NIST Computer Security Resource Center, updated June 10, 2019, https://csrc.nist.gov/Projects/Post-Quantum-Cryptography/Post-Quantum-Cryptography-Standardization.

11 In 1996, computer scientist Lov Grover proposed an algorithm, now referred to as *Grover's algorithm*, that shows how a quantum computer can speed up an exhaustive search for a key by a square root factor. This means that an exhaustive search of, say, 2^{128} keys on a quantum computer will take "only" the time required for an exhaustive search of 2^{64} keys on a conventional computer. Hence, symmetric-key lengths need to double in order to maintain equivalent security levels against a quantum computer. However, it is worth noting that this algorithm requires vast amounts of quantum memory. The original paper is Lov K. Grover, "A Fast Quantum Mechanical Algorithm for Database Search," in *Proceedings of the Twenty-Eighth Annual ACM Symposium on the Theory of Computing* (ACM, 1996), 212–19.

12 An accessible explanation of quantum key distribution can be found in Simon Singh, *The Code Book* (Fourth Estate, 1999).

13 A review of some of the practical challenges facing the deployment of quantum key distribution can be found in Eleni Diamanti et al., "Practical Challenges in Quantum Key Distribution," *npj Quantum Information* 2, art. 16025 (2016).

14 The one-time pad is an extremely simple encryption algorithm whose modern form is sometimes called the *Vernam cipher*. It involves encrypting every plaintext bit into a ciphertext bit by adding a randomly generated key bit. In 1949, the one-time pad was shown by Claude Shannon to be the only "perfect" encryption algorithm, in the sense that an attacker cannot learn anything (new) about an unknown plaintext by observing a ciphertext. Unfortunately, the stringent requirement for truly random keys that are as long as the plaintext and must be freshly generated for

every single encryption makes the one-time pad impractical to use in most situations.

15 Internet-enabled versions of all these objects were available as commercial products in 2017: Matt Reynolds, "Six Internet of Things Devices That Really Shouldn't Exist," *Wired*, May 12, 2017, https://www.wired.co.uk/article/strangest-internet-of-things-devices.

16 Reliable projections for the extent of the future IoT environment are hard to compile, but organizations such as Gartner and GSMA Intelligence consistently predict numbers on the order of 25 billion global connected IoT devices by 2025. The precise figures don't matter; there are going to be loads of them!

17 Many internet-connected devices are sold with poor security protection or even none. A major future challenge is to persuade suppliers, retailers, and regulators to ensure that IoT technology is sufficiently secure. See, for example, "Secure by Design: Improving the Cyber Security of Consumer Internet of Things Report," Department for Digital, Culture, Media & Sport, UK Government, March 2018, https://www.gov.uk/government/publications/secure-by-design.

18 In August 2018, the National Institute of Standards and Technology launched an AES-style competition to develop new cryptographic algorithms suitable for deployment in constrained environments where conventional algorithms, such as the AES, are not suitable: "Lightweight Cryptography," NIST Computer Security Resource Center, updated June 11, 2019, https://csrc.nist.gov/Projects/Lightweight-Cryptography.

19 David Talbot, "Encrypted Heartbeats Keep Hackers from Medical Implants," *MIT Technology Review*, September 16, 2013, https://www.technologyreview.com/s/519266/encrypted-heartbeats-keep-hackers-from-medical-implants.

20 The most obvious risks are that the data is observed, corrupted, or lost. However, a more likely consequence is that the data is exploited. Indeed, for many (free) cloud storage services it is possible that the exploitation of users' data lies at the heart of the commercial proposition.

21 For an overview and additional references to cryptography designed for cloud storage environments, see, for example, James Alderman, Jason Crampton, and Keith M. Martin, "Cryptographic Tools for Cloud Environments," in *Guide to Security Assurance for Cloud Computing*, ed. Shao Ying Zhu, Richard Hill, and Marcello Trovati (Springer, 2016), 15–30.

22 The first *fully homomorphic encryption* (*FHE*) scheme was proposed by Craig Gentry in "A Fully Homomorphic Encryption Scheme" (PhD diss.,

Stanford University, 2009), https://crypto.stanford.edu/craig/craig-thesis
.pdf. Unfortunately, this scheme is completely impractical, being slow and
computationally heavy to use. David Archer of the research and development firm Galois acknowledged in 2017 that, although his mission was to
make FHE "practical and usable," while speeds were improving, "we're
still not near real-time processing": Bob Brown, "How to Make Fully
Homomorphic Encryption 'Practical and Usable,'" *Network World*, May
15, 2017, https://www.networkworld.com/article/3196121/security/how
-to-make-fully-homomorphic-encryption-practical-and-usable.html.

23 Peter Rejcek, "Can Futurists Predict the Year of the Singularity?" Singularity Hub, May 31, 2017, https://singularityhub.com
/2017/03/31/can-futurists-predict-the-year-of-the-singularity/#sm
.00001v8dyh0rpmee8xcj52fjo9w33.

24 For good introductions to artificial intelligence and how developments
might affect human society, see Max Tegmark, *Life 3.0: Being Human in
the Age of Artificial Intelligence* (Penguin, 2018); and Hanna Fry, *Hello
World* (Doubleday, 2018).

25 These figures come from "Data Never Sleeps 6.0," Domo, accessed June
10, 2019, https://www.domo.com/learn/data-never-sleeps-6.

26 The phenomenon of massive-scale data collection and processing is
sometimes referred to as *big data*. For good introductions to the possible implications of big data, see Viktor Mayer-Schonberger and Kenneth
Cukier, *Big Data: A Revolution That Will Transform How We Live, Work
and Think* (John Murray, 2013); and Bruce Schneier, *Data and Goliath:
The Hidden Battles to Collect Your Data and Control Your World* (W. W.
Norton, 2015).

27 An interesting report on the potential impact of developments in artificial
intelligence on cybersecurity is Miles Brundage et al., "The Malicious
Use of Artificial Intelligence: Forecasting, Prevention, and Mitigation,"
February 2018, https://maliciousaireport.com.

28 My observations concerning the intimate relationship between cryptography and trust are inspired by a talk given by Professor Liqun Chen
at the First London Crypto Day, Royal Holloway, University of London,
June 5, 2017.

29 Lexico, s.v. "Trust," accessed June 12, 2019, https://www.lexico.com/en/
definition/trust.

30 Although the Snowden revelations concerned ways in which governments were attempting to manage cryptography, these revelations inevitably led some people to mistrust cryptography itself.

31 An excellent read on the wider construction of trust in society, with a perspective on constructing trust in cyberspace, is Bruce Schneier, *Liars and Outliers: Enabling the Trust That Society Needs to Thrive* (Wiley, 2012).

32 For details of past and future Real World Crypto symposia, see "Real World Crypto Symposium," International Association for Cryptologic Research, accessed June 12, 2019, https://rwc.iacr.org.

Index